Rediscovering the Classics:
The Project Approach

Rediscovering the Classics: The Project Approach

Ruth Townsend
Marcia Lubell

Christopher-Gordon Publishers, Inc.
Norwood, Massachusetts

Credits

Christopher-Gordon Publishers, Inc.
1502 Providence Highway, Suite #12
Norwood, MA 02062
(800) 934-8322

Printed in the United States of America

10 9 8 7 6 5 4 3 2 1   04 03 02 01 00 99

Library of Congress Catalog Card Number: 98-073873
ISBN: 0-926842-89-7

To Dick and David, who make it worthwhile

Acknowledgments

We wish to thank our colleagues Leila Christenbury, Laura Walters, Joan Tansey, Kay Bushman Haas, Kelly Chandler, and Joseph Quattrini who read the manuscript in pieces and offered many helpful suggestions. We also thank Susanne Canavan for her patience and understanding during the time that we were writing this book. She knows that sometimes life does get in the way of even the most carefully planned scenarios. And most of all, we thank our students, who have been and continue to be our research partners. Their good-hearted commitment to our classroom explorations and experimentations are constant reminders of why we love teaching and what prompts us to share our work with other teachers.

Contents

Focuses on the development of a newspaper based on students' study of *Macbeth*. The instructions guide students in writing news articles, editorials, and feature stories as motivation to explore the conflicts of character and the effects of power on the personalities of the major characters.

Enables students to put Arthur Dimmesdale, a major character in *The Scarlet Letter*, on trial in a heavenly court. Instructions guide students in their research into the novel, in writing trial briefs, developing questions and responses for witnesses, and conducting the trial.

Guides students through the development of a literary talk show in which guests discuss *The Adventures of Huckleberry Finn* with its major characters and the author himself in the context of contemporary criticism of the novel. Students become involved in the project by creating monologues, dialogues, interviews, and dramatizations that reflect Mark Twain's humorous criticism of the vices and follies of humanity.

Directs students through a study of *The Lord of the Flies* as preparation for an election campaign. Instructions guide students as they prepare candidate promotions, speeches, debates, letters to the editor, news articles, editorials, and advertisements. The project culminates in a major campaign debate focusing on the complex issues of human nature explored in the novel.

Details procedures that enable students to compose a handbook to guide other students through their study of *A Tale of Two Cities*. Students design parallel time lines and plot puzzles, write character analyses and thematic discussions, raise unanswered questions and suggest possible answers, explain Dickens' complex use of language, and offer comprehension tips.

Provides students with activities that examine *The Great Gatsby* as the basis for a film script. The unit involves students in analyses of the literary elements and the plot details of the novel as they translate the story to the screen. The study culminates in student productions of their screenplays.

Enables student to create a modern version of *Hamlet*. Students explore the complexities of Hamlet's personality exacerbated by the circumstances confronting him by transferring the situation in which Hamlet finds himself to a modern context. In the process, students consider the universal topics of fear of death, the role of fate, betrayal, revenge, and moral corruption.

Preface

Most of the English teachers we know became teachers of English because of their love of literature. Like us, their fascination with language and story began early in their lives—you know the kind of children we were, the ones who read everything from comic books to literary classics, even when we were far too young to understand the passion that drove men and women to the desperate acts described in rich detail by writers who savor language. It didn't matter that we didn't understand everything we read; we were reading and in our imaginations sharing the lives of the heroic, the impulsive, the obsessed, and the gallant, wherever in the world and beyond their creators took us.

We admit to becoming teachers so that we could turn our passion into a profession and actually be paid to read and discuss great literature. We assumed that our enthusiasm, education, and commitment to teaching would transform us into academic Pied Pipers, leading legions of secondary students to share our love of literature and language. Alas, we discovered the reality of the contemporary, heterogeneously organized classroom in which students are generally indifferent to literature, even to reading. And even those who may be readers have difficulty seeing the significance of traditional literature and language instruction. The books assigned, the questions asked, the essays required, and the tests taken appear to have no importance to them beyond the immediate exigencies of the classroom. For them, English is a course required for graduation with little or no relevance to any other aspects of their lives, now or in the future. Faced with this reality, we knew we had to reconceive our approach to teaching if we were to pass the torch of the world's great literature on to our students.

Considering the pragmatic and academically diverse nature of our students, we decided to redesign our study of literature and language to mirror authentic experiences, to connect the classroom to the world, but to do so without sacrificing our students' literary heritage on the altar of relevance. From the inception of our efforts, we were committed to involving our students in the classics of literature, initially with the books that are part of our Anglo-American cultural heritage, because we believe that it is in these studies that students can begin to explore the universal questions that connect all humanity now and in the past. This is not to say that we ignore contemporary literature; quite the contrary, but books such as *Catcher in the Rye*, *The Day No Pigs Would Die*, and *The House on Mango Street*, by virtue of their subject matter and style, are much more likely to be accessible to our students. These are books that they can read and make meaning of without elaborate efforts by us to engage and hold onto them, which is often necessary with students who try to read a book as foreign to them in terms of setting and style as, for example, *A Tale of Two Cities*. However, with some help from us, students can discover that Dickens' story is not only relevant in terms of its narration of human struggle, but it is also rich with insight into the paradoxical nature of human beings who are caught up in a maelstrom of events over which they have no control except in their personal responses to circumstance.

The challenge for us is to teach the skills in a learner-centered environment that empowers students to take charge of their own learning and discover the relevance of literature in their lives. The purpose of this book is to share with our colleagues some of the ways we have found to create learner-centered classrooms for the study of literature. We have focused our attention on those classics of literature that are the most challenging for teachers and students but are also a part of the high school literary canon. For each title, we walk teachers through the teaching-learning process, beginning with engagement activities, step-by-step study strategies, ongoing assessments, the completion of projects, and the creation and use of evaluative rubrics.

It is essential to understand in our approach that the student-directed projects motivate the study of the literature, and not the other way around. That might sound iconoclastic to a pedagogical purist, but our purpose is to engage our students' interest and to hold their attention on challenging literature. Therefore, we involve them from the beginning of each study in a project that will appeal to them, such as a talk show, an election campaign, the production of a newspaper, a grand jury investigation, the creation of modern parallels, or a screenplay. Throughout these projects, students work collaboratively and independently on integrated English–language arts activities. And as they work, they become increasingly invested in their creations, discovering the authentic connections between their classroom activities and the world outside school. As teachers we facilitate the students' development of essential language arts concepts and competencies. As they create their screenplays, newspapers, and talk shows, they are developing their abilities to gather, organize, and interpret information. They learn to summarize, compare, and synthesize. They also develop competence in syntax, mechanics, and grammar as they use language in contexts of their own creation. And perhaps most important, they begin to reflect their understandings of the social and personal relevance of the major themes, characters, and literary styles of each great work through their own creations.

Introduction

"You know," a colleague of ours once quipped, "teaching is like being a stand-up comedian. You do your act; the audience either gets it or doesn't get it, and you are paid whether they applaud or not." There were chuckles and nods of agreement around the faculty room, then on to the business of school—bus schedules, hall duty, department budgets, and report cards. But the grain of truth in our colleague's statement resonated with us and made us feel uncomfortable. We wondered: Is what he said true, and if so, what is wrong with this picture of teaching as performance art? We knew the answer: everything.

Students are not in school to be an audience for someone else's show; the students are meant to *be* the "show," in the center of the spotlight, and the teachers are their coaches, prompters, and facilitators. That relationship seems obvious, but achieving it is a challenge for students and teachers alike. Traditionally, the teacher was the expert who dispensed knowledge by lecturing to students, who, like empty vessels, received the "word" and were then expected to memorize and demonstrate their knowledge in contexts defined entirely by the teacher. The more closely that the student adhered to the language and interpretation of the teacher, the ultimate authority, the more successful the student was deemed to be. In the same way, the texts were presented to students as revered documents to be dissected by the rules of critical analysis, as interpreted by the teacher. Each element of a literary piece was examined for itself, often without providing students with a sense of its relatedness to a literary whole. This made for an interesting exercise for the teacher and the few budding literary scholars in the class, but it left most students wondering why they couldn't just read the book for enjoyment or why the author couldn't have said what he or she meant in the first place so that the book wouldn't require days and days of analysis and interpretation.

For us and our students, this traditional approach to the study of literature, or a variation of it, was characteristic of high school classrooms of a generation ago. It was certainly the model with which we had grown up, and we continued it in our classrooms when we began teaching. The problem was that after a few years of teaching the great works common to the literary canon, we had to admit that this formal literary study was not working for increasing numbers of our students. The difficulties the classics presented to our students and to us seemed overwhelming. As a result, we began to abandon the classics of literature one after another. *The Scarlet Letter* was one of the first "great works" to be relegated to the back of the book room; then *A Tale of Two Cities* was deleted from our required reading list, followed by *The Great Gatsby*. Reluctantly we began to replace these classic works of literature with titles more accessible to our students.

At the same time, we began to experiment with different approaches to the teaching of literature, moving away from the traditional paradigm to the learner-centered classroom. We focused our students' initial experience with a text on reading it to enjoy the story; to live through a relationship with it, as Louise Rosenblatt (1978) has said. Of course we didn't want this aesthetic experience to be our students' only relationship with the text; we wanted them to make connections with events and characters, to discover ideas, and to define meaning for themselves from what they read. To that end we experimented with creating opportunities for students to act and do within a structured framework, rather than to listen and repeat, thus allowing them to construct meaning with teacher support but without teacher dictation (Applebee, 1993). We designed problem solving activities to enable students to make judgments, draw inferences, evaluate ideas, and make real-life connections between what they were reading and what they observed or experienced in the world (Mayher, 1990). We encouraged students to apply and synthesize their understandings in contexts of their own making and extend their learning beyond the text and our expectations. We structured collaborative group assignments that allowed students to demonstrate their strengths and capitalize on different intelligences. As we gained confidence in our redesigned literary studies, we involved students in assessing and evaluating their work. This opportunity provided students with far deeper understandings of the concepts and competencies on which their study had focused than did traditional testing. In effect, what we were creating was a "constructivist" approach to learning, one in which students and teachers work together to define problems and construct meaning (Applebee, 1993).

Student response to these constructivist learning experiences validated our belief that students' learning is best promoted by their active involvement in curriculum design. For example, one student, responding to her involvement with

Catcher in the Rye, *When the Legends Die*, *The Bean Trees*, and *Night*, said the following:

> I've learned to read differently now than I used to. Now I find myself making notes on everything I read to suck out all I can. I find myself noticing themes that are important, recurring symbols that I discover for myself or with my group; I write down lines that I especially like and connections that I make with my own experiences and sometimes with other books that I have read.

Another student described her evolution as a reader, writer, and thinker by saying, "Now I find myself observing little intricacies in character and plot that I might not otherwise have noticed. . . . I value my own thinking about what I am reading and my insights and connections to it."

Encouraged by the obvious success of our learner-centered approach as reflected in our students' comments about their involvement with contemporary literature, we decided to reintroduce some of the classics of literature into our curriculum and apply what we had learned about student involvement with more accessible contemporary literature to the study of challenging classic texts. Some of our colleagues questioned our decision to return such works as *The Scarlet Letter* and *A Tale of Two Cities* to the curriculum, claiming that these books have no relevance or value to students today. We argued that these timeless works of literature speak to the human condition in profound and unique ways. They address universal concerns that transcend limitations of time, culture, ethnicity, and history.

However, we do admit that to plan the study of these texts, which are so well-known and over-analyzed, presents all kinds of challenges, beginning with the recognition that we cannot teach everything we know about a piece and shouldn't even try. But then, that is a valid reminder for any text worth our students' study time. Therefore, we make choices about what in the work we will emphasize, and we allow our students to play a role in making those choices. The nature of the projects, the dynamics of the collaborative approach, the desire for active student involvement in all aspects of the study, including assessment and evaluation, determine the direction of the study. We recognize that the key to our students' success with these challenging literary works is determined by the extent to which we remain true to what we know. This enables students to take charge of their own learning through the following means:

- Active Involvement
- Student-Generated Contexts
- Real-World Collaboration
- Problem Solving
- Student-Empowering Assessment and Evaluation

ACTIVE INVOLVEMENT

Educator Jacqueline Grennon Brooks (1993, p. 4) reminds us, "Each of us makes sense of our world by synthesizing new experiences into what we have previously come to understand." For this to happen in students' study of any literary work, but especially the classics that relate to times and places that are unfamiliar to them, the learning activities must honor students' prior knowledge and encourage their participation in acquiring new knowledge. Part of what makes this active involvement so powerful is that it is based on learning that is described by John Mayher (1990, p. 104) as "the result of intentional or purposeful action . . . learning [that has] a sense of personal meaningfulness for the learner." Our task is to create opportunities for active involvement that provide this motivation. For example, before we even introduce *The Scarlet Letter*, we capture our students' attention by sharing a contemporary newspaper story with them about an honors student who was expelled from her high school for having a child out of wedlock. With *The Great Gatsby*, we introduce the concept of carelessness by asking our students to consider people they know or know about who are careless and make messes for others to clean up and to create scenarios about these people.

Active involvement continues as students read the text to enjoy it and to make meaning of it by responding in persona journals or letters, as they do with *Hamlet*. They write monologues and create pictorial caricatures and dialogues as inspired by *The Adventures of Huckleberry Finn*. Active involvement is most dramatically demonstrated in the collaborative projects, defined in part by the students. When the projects begin to take shape, as with the *Macbeth* newspaper, students become increasingly invested in their creations and committed to maintaining the integrity of Shakespeare's play as they have made meaning of it. In these and other creative ways, we help our students to sustain their involvement with classic and contemporary texts.

STUDENT–GENERATED CONTEXTS

Educational researcher Judith Langer (1994, p. 6) has defined the thought-provoking literature class as one in which students "negotiate their own meanings by exploring possibilities, consider understandings from multiple perspectives, sharpen their own interpretations from multiple perspectives, and learn about features of literary style and analysis through the insights of their own responses." These responses, Langer says, are more reflective of the readers' personal and cultural experiences than of a particular text. Perhaps the greatest challenge we have faced as we have constructed our classrooms has been in providing this kind of involvement for our students to explore and extend their experiences with literature. However, because of this challenge we focus considerable effort on creating student-generated contexts. We believe the results are worth the effort.

For example, as students read *The Lord of the Flies*, they consider the characteristics of an effective leader in preparation for an election campaign. The shape of the campaign is defined by the students who choose a candidate, create a party platform, write election speeches, and actually conduct an election campaign. Students studying *A Tale of Two Cities* compose a handbook for the benefit of other readers of the text. Based on their study of the novel, students create the components of the handbook, which might include parallel time lines, plot puzzles, or even possible answers to some of the unanswered issues Dickens leaves us to ponder. Based on their reading of *The Great Gatsby*, students plan, write, and produce screenplays. The productions reflect not only their creators' understanding of Fitzgerald's novel but also their inventive and often sophisticated ability to translate their ideas into a visual medium. We are always impressed with how much more our students know about visual technology than we do. Because of that, rather than try to direct their creating of video, CD, or computer products, we help them to structure their work, offer English–language arts support, and try to stay out of their way.

REAL-WORLD COLLABORATION

Ask business or professional leaders what they look for in employees, and they will tell you that the ability to work with others is high on the list of qualities necessary for success in the workplace. We know from our own experience the value of collaboration. Much of our best curriculum work has been and continues to be the result of shared effort. However, working with a like-minded, equally motivated peer is easy compared to organizing students into collaborative groups committed to exploring literature and demonstrating understanding in their own creations. To galvanize a class whose student profile might range from learning disabled to intellectually gifted, from academically motivated to educationally disengaged, and from school leader to potential school dropout can be impossible if we impose traditional structures and performance assessments on them. Collaboration in such heterogeneity requires the creation of groups that take advantage of diversity and multiple intelligences (Gardner, 1993).

For example, groups working on creating visual projects, such as a screenplay for *The Great Gatsby*, benefit from members who are spatially and musically intelligent. Groups creating dramatic interpretations, such as those included in the study of *The Adventures of Huckleberry Finn*, have an advantage with members who are bodily-kinesthetically intelligent. Groups that categorize, classify, infer, and test hypotheses as part of the study of *Hamlet* welcome members who have logical-mathematical intelligence. Of course, all groups rely on members who are linguistically intelligent, but the ability to use words effectively will not in itself enable a group to succeed in the multifaceted, collaborative activities that characterize the project-oriented classroom. Success in group activities in our heterogeneous classrooms also requires members' interpersonal and intrapersonal intelligences; different kinds of students must work together, which requires members to be sensitive to the feelings of others and to have the ability to influence a group. Group success also requires some self-knowledge and the capacity to develop self-discipline (Armstrong, 1994).

Because we recognize the power of different kinds of people working together, we study our students to try to get a sense of their dominant intelligences and then group them accordingly. The results have been academically and socially well worth our attention for the creation of groups of students who really can collaborate.

PROBLEM SOLVING

The need to solve a problem is another real-world experience that can engage our imaginations and our intellects. We present our students with specific and relevant dilemmas for which they must find solutions. For example, our study of *The Adventures of Huckleberry Finn* involves students in the contemporary controversy surrounding the novel, which some critics label as racist. Students are challenged to examine the book and decide for themselves the author's intent and the validity of the charges. Students explore *The Lord of the Flies* in the context of complex questions about human nature and the requirements of leadership—topics worth consideration by all responsible people. Our students' study of *The Scarlet Letter* involves them in fundamental questions about the nature of sin, guilt, justice, and forgiveness.

Vicariously, and thus safely, our students are able to consider these and many other universal problems that confront human beings. Not surprisingly to us, they discover that the basic issues of the human condition transcend time and culture and demand the best of our minds and hearts.

STUDENT-EMPOWERING ASSESSMENT AND EVALUATION

Grant Wiggins, president of the Center on Learning, Assessment, and School Structure, has influenced our beliefs about curriculum and instruction. Wiggins (1997) says, "Designing 'backwards' from assessment to curriculum . . . has a powerful logic" and "We need to think of assessment reform as central to instructional reform, not just as making better assessments."

So strongly do we embrace Wiggins' philosophy that it is embedded in all of our curriculum planning, to the extent that we design our lessons to enable our students to understand the concepts and develop the competencies that will prepare them to complete their projects successfully. The development of these projects requires ongoing assessment to provide students with necessary feedback. This kind of assessment also enables us to determine what our students know and are able to do and therefore informs our teaching and curriculum planning.

We see *evaluation*, a summative process, as different from *assessment*, a formative process. Evaluation provides an indication of each student's level of achievement. It is also a benchmark of student growth that reveals accomplishment and indicates a direction for future achievement.

We make this distinction between assessment and evaluation because we want to remove the stigma of a grade (evaluation) from an ongoing process (assessment) that manifests itself in a variety of student products and activities. We also want to create a learning environment in which students are invested in both the assessment and the evaluation of their work. Rick Siggons (1997), president of the Assessment Training Institute, claims that student-centered classroom assessment can help students to learn. We have discovered the truth of that assertion as we have increasingly involved our students in both the assessment and the evaluation of their work.

However, for that to happen we must be very clear with each activity about what we want our students to know and be able to do. Then together students and teachers can identify the dimensions and descriptions of expected performance for any task. For example, during their study of *Hamlet*, we periodically review their diary entries and paraphrases to assess their knowledge of the events of the play and their understanding of character conflict and dilemmas. This information guides our class discussions and suggests the direction of activities. During their study of *The Adventures of Huckleberry Finn*, we determine their knowledge of the novel with quick holistic assessments of their "entry tickets" (see chapter 3), and we assess the depth of their understanding of Twain's satiric characterizations, as reflected in their journals, using a simple criteria list generated in conjunction with the students.

To evaluate students' work, we engage them in the creation of rubrics. This process requires an investment of time because it involves the students in defining the elements to be considered and the criteria for performances that are to be considered excellent. We use a student- and teacher-generated rubric to evaluate our students' major projects—for example, their literary guidebooks to *A Tale of Two Cities*, their screenplays for *The Great Gatsby*, their *Macbeth* newspapers, and their analytical essays for *The Adventures of Huckleberry Finn*.

Task-specific assessments and evaluation instruments not only help students to understand the requirements of any task that they are assigned but also enable them to delineate the characteristics of excellence. This process takes the mystery out of grading by providing students with specifics of their strengths and their weaknesses. Of course, we could supply our students with all this information in teacher comments, and we often have. However, students seem to pay more attention to circled elements on a rubric than to written comments. Perhaps because the rubric is visual, they can see where they are on the grid: Where a 4 is circled, they are strong; where a 1 or a 2 is circled, they are weak and need to work harder. Moreover, the criteria for performance at the next level is right in front of them to follow so that they can work to achieve it.

In short, what we have learned about assessment and evaluation is that the more we involve our students in defining the parameters of excellence, the better able they are to stretch themselves beyond what they thought were their limits. But then, what is true about the power of student involvement in assessment and evaluation is true for all aspects of the constructivist classroom: It enables students to read, construct meaning, and make personal connections with great literature.

REFERENCES

Applebee, A. (1993). *Beyond the lesson: Reconstructing curriculum.* Albany, NY: National Research Center on Literature Teaching and Learning.

Armstrong, T. (1994). *Multiple intelligences in the classroom.* Alexandria, VA: Association for Supervision and Curriculum Development.

Brooks, J. G. (1993). *In Search of Understanding: The Case for Constructivist Classrooms.* Alexandria, VA: Association for Supervision and Curriculum Development.

Gardner, H. (1993). *Multiple intelligences: The theory in practice.* New York: Basic Books.

Langer, J. (1994). *A response-based approach to reading literature.* Albany, NY: National Research Center on Literature Teaching and Learning.

Mayher, John. (1990). *Uncommon sense.* Portsmouth, NH: Boynton/Cook.

Rosenblatt, L. (1978). *The reader, the text, the poem.* Carbondale, IL: Southern Illinois University Press.

Siggons, R. (1997, December). Using assessment to motivate students. *Education Update,* 1–6.

Wiggins, G. (1997, October). Understanding by design. Paper presented at the Association for Supervision and Curriculum Development Conference, Orlando, FL.

CHAPTER 1

Sex, Violence, and Just Desserts

"All the news that's fit to print," promises *The New York Times* in its banner. The question is: What is news, and what is fit to print? In this day and age, when we as readers are bombarded with "news," whether it's "fit" or not, we as English–language arts teachers are committed to enabling our students to become critical readers and knowledgeable consumers of the "news." For this purpose we involve our students in the creation of newspapers or news magazines. This requires our students to consider issues of newsworthiness, audience appeal, and appropriateness. Moreover, linking the creation of newspapers and news magazines to the study of literature affords rich opportunities for our students to make meaning of what they read in an authentic context.

In fact, the creation of a newspaper or news magazine provides a focus for our students' reading that enhances motivation as well as facilitates comprehension. The project engages students from the very beginning with the interesting task of reading the text for the express purpose of creating their own products, composed of stories and features generated by the text. To this end we organize students into small groups to allow them to design a newspaper or news magazine around the text. Their products may be in whatever editorial style best reflects their unique vision of the project. To help them define that vision, we require students to take the persona of inquiring reporters who review the events and characters of the text with an eye to finding material suitable for inclusion in their group's newspaper or news magazine.

The collaborative structure of the project is particularly effective with heterogeneous classes because of the many opportunities afforded students to make use of their varied strengths and intelligences. Students who are stronger verbally may be balanced by group members who have artistic strength. Students who are natural leaders have a legitimate opportunity to take charge in editorial roles, enabling students who work better on defined, specific tasks to succeed. Students who have technological expertise contribute their knowledge of desktop publishing, making it possible for students who have an eye for graphic design to translate those ideas into print.

Through the study and creation of newspapers and news magazines, students also gain expertise in a variety of essential English–language arts skills. They learn the difference between objectivity and subjectivity as they write factual news articles, opinion-generated editorials, and feature stories. They practice going from the general to the specific; they learn the practical importance of development, organization, voice, and audience.

Moreover, they extend their facility with technology as they put their products together. One strength of the newspaper project is the way in which it parallels real-life activity, mirroring workplace reality. For example, student teams must make decisions about authority, delegation of responsibility, and deadlines. They must decide who is in charge, what goes into the newspaper, which students will be responsible for specific components, and how the paper or magazine will be laid out. The variety of tasks associated with the creation of the newspaper or news magazine provides every student with an opportunity to excel at some aspect of the project.

Perhaps the most compelling advantage of the newspaper or news magazine format for the study of literature is the opportunity it affords for student-initiated investigation of a text. Students are not completing worksheets or answering teacher-generated questions. Nor are they limited to factual recall of events or the regurgitation in expository essays of the interpretations of literary authorities. Instead, they decide what events from the literature are newsworthy, or "fit to print," as well as what human interest angles to pursue and what issues from the literature prompt editorial comment. At the same time they increase their familiarity with the components of a newspaper. They learn to write feature stories, editorials, and news articles; they learn about advertising, layout, and graphic design. In addition, they learn the importance of engaging an audience, maintaining a consistent voice, reporting accurately, planning carefully, and editing for correctness of language mechanics.

The newspaper or news magazine project is an appropriate format for the study of many traditional as well as contemporary literary titles. Any book with a rich plot and sufficiently complex characters lends itself to such study. However, this approach helps our students most with making Shakespeare's plays accessible. This focus is intrinsically interesting for students and motivates them to read *Macbeth*, Shakespeare's complex text of violence, murder, and "vaulting ambition," with real enthusiasm.

GETTING STARTED

Students' enthusiasm begins with the prospect of creating their own newspaper or news magazine and taking charge of their own work. We assign our students to teams, taking advantage of the diversity of abilities and intelligences in our classroom. Ideally each team should have five students, at least one with obvious leadership ability and another with some facility in desktop publishing. After the teams have been selected, they are given an assignment designed to familiarize them with the contents of a newspaper. Student groups review at least two different popular newspapers and list the various kinds of stories and features in those papers. We ask them in their groups to identify the stories and visuals that engage them and to determine what it is about each piece that captures their attention. Each group summarizes its findings and reports to the class. Students will identify certain kinds of headlines, leads, photographs, and statistical data. The teacher might wish to label the appeals evinced in the examples students have contributed, such as identification with the audience, flattery, alarm, curiosity, or pity so that students can learn to make deliberate use of these appeals in their own newspapers and news magazines.

THE REPORTER'S NOTEBOOK

To involve students in the reading of the play, we begin with act 1, scenes 1 and 2, assigning parts for students to enact and allowing a brief time to prepare. At the end of the enactment, we model the process for keeping a detailed reporter's notebook of everything they witness that might prove newsworthy and provide material for stories for their newspapers or news magazines. We ask students to keep a double-entry journal. On the left side, they record the events that they think are significant. On the right side, they explore possible story topics associated with those events (Fig. 1-1).

Figure 1-1. *Double-Entry Journal Sample*

Notes (Scenes 1 and 2)	Possible Story Topics
A deserted place; three witches meet in thunder, lightning, and rain.	Witches real or imagined
They talk about a battle lost and a battle won and somebody named Macbeth.	The battle Macbeth
"Fair is foul and foul is fair, Hover through the fog and filthy air."	Weather conditions
A bleeding captain reports on the war.	Who's who in Scotland; their roles in the civil war.

The reporter's notebook provides an opportunity for students to get closer to the story by participating as witnesses to the events. It also provides a springboard for comparing their observations with those of their team members and an opportunity to deepen their comprehension by sharing, asking questions of each other and the teacher, and deciding which events are worth writing about (or that can be adapted for their particular audience).

We continue reading and acting out the rest of acts 1 and 2, with students compiling a reader's log for both acts. Periodically, we stop to meet in newspaper groups to share our observations and ideas about possible stories. Throughout this process we answer questions, clarify relationships, provide historical background, resolve linguistic difficulties, explain time intervals, and check reporters' notebooks. At the end of reading acts 1 and 2, students are ready to write their first news stories.

NEWS STORIES

When students convene in their newspaper groups, they review the collected data and story ideas to determine what news stories they need to report about the events of acts 1 and 2. At this point, we ask students to select someone from their group to be the editor, the person who will keep track of story assignments and be responsible for seeing that the work required to complete the newspaper is done. Each student takes on one story to develop and decides on the angle or approach to take with the story.

To prepare students for writing their stories, we share a sample story, with an approach obviously geared to an audience looking for the sensational or the bizarre. In spite of this, the reporter still had to reflect knowledge of the play.

Loyal Scots Triumph Over Attackers

by Jeff Lee

The Scottish army, under General Macbeth, successfully defended the kingdom from a surprise Norwegian attack yesterday afternoon at Fife. The invaders, heavily armed, came from the northeast. In the ensuing battle, the Scots were able to drive off the attack, but not without heavy casualties.

The Norwegians attacked the left flank of the Scottish army and nearly drove off the defenders. But Macbeth rallied his forces and carved out his passage in the middle of the attack, demoralizing and eventually breaking up the force. Macbeth showed remarkable courage and bravery, risking his life many times while fighting the foe. The Scots, following Macbeth's lead, all fought skillfully and bravely. The attackers were supplied with furbished arms and had hoped to win by their sheer size and strength. However, the battle lasted for only two hours, and the Norwegians were forced to retreat after suffering heavy losses.

> The King of Norway was unavailable for comment, apparently distraught from this news. A spokesperson for the king said, "Under no circumstances will his defeat discourage our present campaign against Scotland. We will eventually succeed in destroying them. It is only a matter of time."
>
> Duncan, King of Scotland, was ecstatic over the victory. "Macbeth is a valiant cousin! His actions on the field prove that he is a worthy kinsman. He will be greatly rewarded for his courage."
>
> There are reports that Macdonwald and the Thane of Cawdor acted against their fellow countrymen, supplying information to the invaders about the position of the Scots, which may explain the surprise attack that the Norwegians were able to launch.
>
> Another noteworthy soldier, General Banquo, led the charge under Macbeth. When asked about the battle, he said, "They surprised us at first, but we were able to overcome them because of our skill in battle. But we couldn't have won without the leadership of [General] Macbeth."
>
> A Scottish soldier said, "It is a pity that they [the Norwegians] retreated so fast. Otherwise we would have completely destroyed them."

We ask the students in their groups to analyze the structure of the sample story. We explain the characteristic news story pattern of the inverted triangle, presenting the most important details early in the story and the least important information last. We ask them to find in the sample lead the answers to the following questions:

- Who (Scottish army, Macbeth, the Norwegian invaders)
- What (victory over the Norwegians)
- Where (Scottish battlefield)
- When (yesterday afternoon)

In the rest of the story, the students notice that these basic questions are developed with interesting details that keep the reader engaged. They'll see that answers to *how* and *why* are also provided. (The *how* is Macbeth's fighting prowess and superior military strategy; the *why* is the bravery and courage of Macbeth and the Scottish army).

Analysis of this story provides us with the opportunity to show our students the value of putting the most important information in the lead and of following the lead with details given in descending order of importance. This organizational pattern enables the reader to get the facts quickly and the editor to cut the story from the last paragraph up to fit space requirements. We ask our students to examine the model story to identify the details from the later paragraphs of the story that expand on the six basic questions. We also ask them to notice the placement of the least important details at the end of the story—in this case, a quote from a Scottish soldier deploring the cowardice of the Norwegians.

This study of the model story lays the foundation for our students to write their own news stories, based on the following events in acts 1 and 2:

- Scotland's victory in the war
- Naming of Malcolm as Prince of Cumberland
- Macbeth as war hero
- Duncan's visit to Macbeth's castle
- Macbeth's elevation to Thane of Cawdor
- Duncan's visit to Macbeth's castle
- Assassination of the king
- Flight of Duncan's sons
- Elevation of Macbeth to king

Some students may want to write about events such as the witches' prophecies and Macbeth's response, the relationship between Macbeth and Lady Macbeth, or the plot to assassinate the king; however, we point out that knowledge of these topics is not public information and is not appropriate for a news story. But they may use this information in different kinds of articles that they will write in the future.

After students have written the drafts of their news articles, they meet in their teams to review them. Students focus on helping each member of the team write an effective news story, one that answers the six basic questions. They examine the drafts to help each other include the most important details of the story and organize them in the inverted triangle pattern.

News Story Review

What is the topic of the news story?
How does the headline engage the reader's attention?
What crucial information does the writer include in the lead
to answer the questions of *who, what, where,* and *when?*
What key facts does the writer include in the second and third
paragraphs to answer the questions of *how* and *why?*
What important details do you suggest
the writer add to those paragraphs?
What details do you suggest
the writer add to flesh
out the middle portion
of the news story?
(Background
information, quotes)

CREATING HEADLINES

Before creating headlines for their news stories, students bring in sample headlines from their local newspapers. They analyze the nature and content of those headlines, noting the way in which each succinctly targets the key part of the story to follow and at the same time uses language designed to attract reader attention. Then, still in their groups, students determine the best headlines for each news story they have written, keeping in mind the need to highlight the most exciting part of a story, grab the reader's attention, and yet fit the headline within the allotted space. For news stories describing the events in acts 1 and 2, some headlines our students have used include the following: "Scots Triumph Over Attackers," "Macbeth: New Thane of Cawdor," " Malcolm Named Prince of Cumberland," " King Murdered at Inverness," and "Princes Flee Country."

OBITUARIES

At this point it is appropriate for students to write an obituary for King Duncan, especially since the need for obituaries will increase as the play proceeds. We point out to the students that Duncan's assassination is a news story and not an obituary. However, his death warrants separate coverage as a news story of the actual murder *and* as an obituary to highlight key moments in his reign. We teach the obituary by bringing in extended sample obituaries of prominent people from major newspapers and news magazines. Our students examine them for content and format. They recognize that the lead paragraph includes the basic questions, the *who, what, when*, and *where* of the death of the subject. The lead also includes a summary statement of the key feature for which the person was known as well as the cause of death. The lead is followed by a summary of the highlights of the person's accomplishments and an overview of his or her life. The obituary concludes with information about the survivors and details of the funeral arrangements. To get the information they need to write Duncan's obituary, students will need to review what Duncan has done in acts 1 and 2, what has been said about him by Macbeth and others, the notes in their reporters' logs, and any information they can find about the real Duncan, perhaps from the introductory materials in their text.

Sample Obituary

Our beloved King Duncan, brutally murdered at Inverness late last night, served Scotland nobly and generously from 1034 to 1040 and will be remembered for his fair and just rule. His death comes at a particularly poignant time, as Scotland is finally celebrating victory after the recent civil wars. King Duncan had journeyed to Inverness, the home of his loyal general and cousin, Macbeth, Thane of Glamis and Cawdor, to celebrate the successful end of the wars. It was there that Duncan came to his untimely end by assailants as yet unknown.

Duncan came to the throne in 1034 following the death of his grandfather, Malcolm II. Remembered as a meek and virtuous monarch, Duncan thought well of all men. He was generous in rewarding those who served him loyally, but he was also capable of swift and firm justice when warranted.

His subjects and kinsmen have already begun to mourn his death. Macbeth, the newly named Thane of Cawdor, was overwhelmed by the loss of his revered king and kinsman. He said, "Duncan's virtues will plead like angels trumpet-tongued against the deep damnation of his taking off." Even heaven's cherubim "shall blow the horrid deed in every eye that tears shall drown the wind." Macduff, the thane of Fife, who discovered the body, grieved openly at the loss of his king, declaring that a "most sacrilegious murder hath broke ope the lord's anointed temple, and stole thence the life o' the building."

Duncan is survived by his older son, Malcolm, whom he recently named Prince of Cumberland, and his younger son, Donalbain. His wife, Sybil, predeceased him. His remains have been carried to Colmekill, the sacred storehouse of his predecessors and guardian of their bones.

FEATURE STORIES

We resume the reading and acting of the play with act 3 and continue to the end of it with students compiling their reporters' notebooks. This time they not only take notes on events that might prove newsworthy and keep track of possible news stories, they also collect details that could be turned into feature stories. To enable our students to take these notes, we introduce the feature story, which we define as an entertaining or informative story based on a current happening but providing interesting sidelights that might have been skipped in the news story. Periodically we stop to meet in the newspaper groups to share our observations and ideas about possible feature stories. Throughout this process we continue to be a resource for our students, answering questions, clarifying relationships, resolving linguistic difficulties, and explaining time intervals. We also continue to check their reporters' notebooks, occasionally suggesting possible feature story ideas they might have missed.

At the end of the reading of act 3, students convene in their groups to review collected data and story topics to determine what additional news stories they need to report on as well as to decide which feature story ideas would be of most interest to their readers. News story topics from this act include the murder of Banquo and the king's banquet. Feature stories could be about rumors surrounding the death of Banquo, a review of Macbeth's reign to date, an analysis of Macbeth's breakdown at the banquet, and gossip about the royal couple. Each group's editor records the feature story assignments and sets the deadline for completion of the drafts.

To help our students write their feature stories, we have them examine a news story and a feature story on the same event. By doing this, students can see that the feature story, in contrast to the news story, is more subjective in content and style. Feature stories appeal more to the emotions of the reader and are designed to offer a particular slant on a story. Students analyze the content and form of the feature story, noting that the feature writer adopts a narrative technique and saves a key point for the end of the story. We guide students to see that, even with this looser form, the feature writer must engage the interest of the readers in the opening statements and identify the central point of the story early in the piece. We also help them to see that the feature writer develops the story with details, illustrations, and examples in whatever order is best for telling the story, which may be chronological. Following is a sample feature story.

Macbeth, New Thane of Cawdor

by Mike Via

The reward of Macbeth with the thaneship of Cawdor for his victory against the rebels and his defeat of the Norwegians in the recent wars raises several questions in the minds of many loyal Scots. Chief among them is why Duncan named his son Malcolm Prince of Cumberland and therefore heir to the throne instead of honoring Macbeth with that title. Certainly Macbeth has as legitimate a claim to the throne as his cousin Duncan, since both are grandsons of the late King Malcolm II, for whom Duncan's son is named.

    The youth of Malcolm and his poor performance during the recent wars makes some Scots fearful of another attack by the Norwegians. Veterans of the war remember that Malcolm did let himself be captured and thus endanger the lives of many loyal Scots who had to rescue him.

    Another question has to do with the site of the Norwegian attack in Fife, territory of Macduff. How was it that Macbeth got to Fife so shortly after battling the rebel forces of Macdonwald, whom Macbeth unseamed from the nave to the chops, in the west of Scotland? By what extraordinary power was Macbeth able to inflict two resounding defeats on the enemies of Scotland in one day? And should not such a warrior as Macbeth be recognized as the appropriate leader of Scotland?

    Questions like these have led to rumors of witchcraft afoot in the land. Adding to these rumors are the several reported witch sightings in the battle areas. One report even has Macbeth and Banquo actually in the company of three weird sisters. Could it be that supernatural powers are at play in the fortunes of Macbeth—first helping him defeat Norway and then hindering his hopes for the throne?

    Only time will tell, but one thing is certain: Nothing is but what is not.

After students have written the drafts of their feature stories, they meet in teams to review their work. As they did in reviewing their news stories, they help each other to write an effective piece, one that attracts the attention of the reader and provides interesting sidelights and insights into the news events. They may use the following review sheet:

Feature Story Review Sheet

- What is the topic of the feature story?
- How do the opening remarks engage the reader?
- What crucial information responding to the *who, what, when* and *where* of the event does the writer include?
- What details does the writer present to expand upon or illustrate the sidelight on the event and thus provide a new insight into that event?
- What narrative elements does the writer include to distinguish the feature story from a news story of the same event?
- What suggestions can you offer the writer to enhance the story?
- What corrections does the writer need to make in spelling, grammar, and punctuation?

INTERVIEWS

Once students have reviewed their drafts of the feature stories and are revising them, we return to the reading and acting of the play in class with acts 4 and 5. Again students record notes on newsworthy events in their reporters' notebooks, listing possible feature story ideas as well. As before, we continue to be a resource for our students to resolve any questions they have about the reading. At the end of the reading, students reconvene in their groups to review new data and story topics. At this point, we introduce the idea of basing a feature on an interview. We ask students to list those events in acts 4 and 5 that are important for their readers to know and to list those people whose experiences or opinions would provide insight for readers of the events that have occurred. The events that students list include the following:

- Macbeth's meeting with the witches
- Murder of Macduff's family
- Meeting of Macduff and Malcolm
- Breakdown of Lady Macbeth
- Suicide of Lady Macbeth
- Siege of Dunsinane
- Defeat of Macbeth

Possible interview subjects include a witch, a survivor of the massacre at Fife, Lady Macbeth's doctor or gentlewoman, Macduff, and Malcolm. Students in each group select a person to interview, and the editor records the interview assignments, setting the deadline for completion of the drafts.

To help students conduct their interviews and write stories based on them, we ask the students to determine a tentative angle from which to pursue the story, pointing out to them that once they have gathered their information, the focus of the story may shift. We then guide them in the development of questions they will need to ask to elicit the information for their stories. The questions will vary, depending upon the event around which the interview is based. We model the kinds of questions they need to ask with questions for one of the witches, noting that the answers are found in act 4, scene 1. The purpose of our interview is to find out what happened when Macbeth sought the help of the witches in act 4:

- How long have you known Macbeth?
- What previous dealings have you had with him?
- What was it that Macbeth wanted from you?
- Why do you think he came to you?
- What did you tell him?
- How did you get this information for him?
- What was his reaction?
- What, if anything, did he say that he was going to do?

After we model the questions, students work in their groups to develop questions appropriate for each of the interviews they will conduct. To give authenticity to this activity, each student in a group adopts the persona of one of the characters to be interviewed, which means that the student has to prepare for the interview by going back to the text to study the role carefully. Again, the teacher should act as the resource. We model the process, assuming the role of one of the witches and allowing students to interview us with questions similar to the ones developed above. In framing our answers during the interview, we are careful to include as much of the language from the play as possible.

Once students have collected the answers from their own interviews, we show them how to turn the collected data into feature stories. We instruct them to look at the collected data and determine the central point or key idea for their story. We model this by looking at our data on the witch and decide that for our story we want to focus on Macbeth's reaction to the witches' prophecies about him. We remind students that not all of the information they collected will be relevant once we have limited our story to a particular angle. Following is a sample feature story from an interview:

Macbeth Rumored to Confer With Witches

"The firstlings of my heart shall be the firstlings of my hand," declared Macbeth as he left the cavern where he had met with the witches. According to Hecate, a prominent Highlands witch, what prompted Macbeth's declaration was the information given to him by the witches in response to his demand to know his destiny. This information was conveyed to him through visions in the witches' boiling cauldron.

Hecate noted that when Macbeth was warned by the first apparition to "Beware Macduff," he appeared not to be surprised. He said he already suspected that Macduff was his enemy.

However, when he was told that "none of woman born shall harm Macbeth," he seemed relieved to know that he had nothing to fear from Macduff. Nevertheless, he said he would kill Macduff anyway, "to make assurance double sure."

The witches called up another apparition, that of a child crowned with a tree in his hand, who told Macbeth that he had nothing to worry about because "he shall never vanquished be until Birnam wood to high Dunsinane hill shall come against him."

Hecate reported that Macbeth seemed delighted to hear this apparent good news but still wasn't satisfied and demanded to know whether or not Banquo's son, Fleance, would one day rule the kingdom. What he saw terrified him because he claimed the sight of so many kings resembling Banquo "seared his eyeballs."

"We tried to cheer him up," Hecate said, "offering to show the best of our delights, but he was not to be consoled. We vanished as he was cursing 'this pernicious hour,' but I heard him pronounce that he would execute the 'firstlings of his heart,' beginning with a surprise attack on the castle of Macduff. "

We examine the model with our students, noting that it follows the form of a feature story and incorporates the information from the interview without stating the questions asked nor including all of the answers. We also point out that the reporter does not include any references to him- or herself in the story. The focus is strictly on Hecate's recounting of Macbeth's reactions to the prophecies. Students are now ready to fulfill their assignments and interview the member of their group impersonating the character who can give them the information they need for their feature.

After the students have written the drafts of their interview features, they meet in their teams to review their work. We have them use the peer review sheet for the feature story. After students have reviewed each other's drafts, they revise their own work.

DISCOVERING THEMES

To guide students to consider the thematic threads that tie the events in the characters' lives together, we ask them to work in their editorial groups to review the major events of the play and connect those events to theme topics, such as power, fear and guilt, ambition, deception, and fate versus free will. Each group is responsible for researching one of the theme topics and reporting its findings to the class. In their groups, students list the events that seem related to their assigned theme topic, recognizing that many of the events will overlap. For example, Macbeth's consulting the witches to learn his fate fits all of the theme topics. When students look for examples of fear and guilt, they might cite the following:

- His visit to the witches
- His initial reluctance to kill the king
- His seeing the bloody dagger
- His terror at seeing the blood on his hands after the murder
- His inability to sleep
- His seeing the ghost of Banquo at the banquet
- Lady Macbeth's sleepwalking, insanity, and suicide

EDITORIALS

When the groups report to the class, we advise them to take careful notes for each of the theme topics and ask for explanations when they have questions because each newspaper or news magazine group will be responsible for creating editorials on these theme topics. When students reconvene in their groups, they study sample editorials from professional newspapers and news magazines. They notice that editorials cover a wide variety of issues on current topics of social and political concern to the community or the nation. They recognize that in the introduction the writer engages the reader immediately, then quickly moves to a position statement about the topic and the reasons for that position. They notice that the development section of the editorial includes facts and details that support those reasons and builds to a conclusion that reinforces the position by indicating its larger ramifications.

Students now look at the thematic threads of the play and develop thematic statements for each of them that are appropriate for editorial comment. To get them started, we share with them Lord Acton's statement about power: "Power corrupts; absolute power corrupts absolutely." Students come up with statements such as the following: Fear and guilt are inescapable; deception is an evil that defies trust and truth; excessive ambition leads to destruction; and each person holds one's fate in one's own hands. Students select a theme topic to develop into an editorial. Editors make sure that each theme topic is covered and assign deadlines for submission of drafts.

While students are drafting their editorials, we review with them the major images that reoccur throughout the play, such as blood, darkness, creatures of the night, the supernatural, sleeplessness, clothing, and false faces. One purpose of discussing the dominant imagery of the play is to provide students with some of the details they need to develop their editorials on the theme topics. For example, a discussion of fear and guilt must necessarily incorporate references to blood, darkness, and sleeplessness.

Students review the drafts of their editorials in their groups. To facilitate their review, students may use the following review sheet:

Editorial Review Sheet

- How does the writer engage the audience?
- What is the writer's position statement?
- What reasons does the writer offer in support of that statement?
- What evidence does the writer provide to explain the reasons?
- What does the writer conclude about the theme topic?
- What do you suggest that the writer add to enhance the effectiveness of the editorial? What do you suggest be omitted?
- What corrections does the writer need to make in spelling, grammar, and punctuation?

When students have completed their editorials, we ask them in their groups to list news stories from the play that still require coverage, such as the significant events in acts 3, 4, and 5, including the murder of Banquo, the banquet, the invasion of Scotland, the death of Lady Macbeth, and the defeat of Macbeth. Each member of the group assumes the responsibility for writing a news story on one of these events.

SPECIALS

While they are drafting these final news stories, we address another use for the information they had collected earlier about the play's imagery. Students examine sample newspapers, listing all of the special features found in most newspapers and news magazines, such as sports, advertising, horoscopes, weather reports, advice columns, recipes, fashion, gossip columns, puzzles, and movie reviews. We encourage students to parody these features, incorporating the imagery and the events in the play to create offbeat, engaging, and even humorous pieces for their newspapers or news magazines.

Following is a sample "weather report":

Felicia's Weather Corner

The death toll resulting from the recent earthquakes and aftershocks continues to rise, with the count now reaching eighty-six.

Some time near the witching hour last Thursday, the earth shook violently, and dreadful and strange things filled the night near the castle of the newly appointed Thane of Cawdor. According to a witness, falcons were hawked at and killed by mousing owls, and Duncan's horses turned wild in nature, broke their stalls, and ate each other. These strange eruptions preceded the discovery of the mutilated body of our beloved King Duncan. Since that time the sun has not shone; instead, dark night strangles heaven's traveling lamp.

These unnatural events have been experienced by terrified residents throughout Scotland. The wisest weather forecasters have said that these perturbations in nature might well continue until Duncan's murderer has been apprehended.

Witnesses have reported that there has been a multitude of strange and mystical creatures calling out at night, perhaps as an omen of evil yet to come. Some citizens have professed to hearing witches cackling and screaming obscenely.

Following is a sample "recipe":

Three Witches Stew

For those of you who love to serve a crowd with a great-tasting dish, here's a favorite from Three Witches Bar and Grill:

Grind 1 domestic cat.
Add 1 chilled fetal pig.
Stir together briskly, and set aside.
In a separate charmed pot add 1 toad (freshly selected from
    under a cold stone).
Add half a cup of sweltered venom, and set to boil for 20
    minutes.
Combine with the cat and pig mixture.
Add one fillet of feenny snake and bake for 45 minutes.
Pickle 1 eye of newt, 3 toes of frog, 1 lock of baby bat wool, and
    1 tongue of common house dog.
Mix all ingredients in an industrial-size, 50 lb. cauldron.
In a separate pot combine the scales of a dragon, the tooth of a
    wolf, a witch's mummy, salt sea shark steak, and root of a
    hemlock digged in the dark.
For a pleasant sauce, tenderize the nose of Turk and Tartar's
    lips.
Add all these ingredients plus a tiger's chaudron to the cauldron
    and cook until the gruel is thick and slab.
Finally, cool with baboon's blood and serve at room
    temperature to your hungry guests.

Each student selects one special feature to create, and the editors ensure variety and set a deadline for all articles.

LAYOUT

When the specials are completed, the teams review their collections of stories, features, and specials to determine the best layout for their newspapers and news magazines. They also examine the headlines they have already created, making revisions to fit the available space and the slant of the paper.

Ideally, students have worked with compatible computer programs, thereby enabling the editors and computer specialists in each group to put the newspaper or news magazine together easily. Again, students examine professional newspapers and news magazines to study layout and organization. They will see that the lead news story is the most dramatic or sensational one, and it is from that story that the main headline of the edition is determined. In this case, the defeat of Macbeth and/or the crowning of Malcolm would occupy the prominent position on page 1. Editorials may be in the middle or toward the end of the newspaper or magazine. Other features may be placed strategically to balance coverage and heighten reader interest. However, games, weather, recipes, advice columns, comics, and horoscopes tend to be at the end. Aside from a few directives, such as putting the major stories at the beginning, we leave the layout to the discretion of the students.

ASSESSMENT AND EVALUATION

Before students make their final revisions on their newspapers or news magazines, we take time as a class to develop a rubric for assessment and evaluation of these publications (Fig. 1-2). To guide students in the creation of the rubric, we provide the categories, which include content, development, organization, style, and presentation. For each category, we ask students to identify the characteristics of an exemplary product. For content, students identify the need for full coverage of the critical events and ideas in the play; they also identify the need for accuracy of facts as well as evidence of creativity. For development, students identify the need for specific details to flesh out their pieces. For organization, students identify the need for logical and appropriate sequencing of the layout of the newspaper as well as of individual pieces. For style, students identify the need for variety of sentence structure, accuracy of language usage, and a recognizable and consistent tone for the newspaper's intended audience. For presentation, students identify the level of the newspaper's visual appeal, using adequate and appropriate graphics.

We formalize the rubric, making additions and clarifying categories as needed; then we distribute the rubric to each editorial group to guide final revisions and self-assessments.

Once students produce their newspapers or news magazines, we evaluate their performances in two ways: a grade for group work and a grade for individual work. Throughout our study of *Macbeth* and our preparation of the *Macbeth Newspaper*, students produce components of the paper that we assess and/or evaluate. For example, each student keeps a reporter's notebook that we periodically collect and assess to determine how thoroughly the students understand the events of the particular scenes that we are considering at that point in our study. Students also assess each other's comprehension of events and characters by sharing their entries and story ideas and getting feedback from their peers. At the end of our study of the play, we collect the reporters' notebooks and evaluate the quality

Figure 1-2. *Rubric for Assessment and Evaluation of Newspapers*

	Excellent	Good	Competent
CONTENT	_____	_____	_____
Full coverage, accuracy of facts, appropriate details, creativity			
DEVELOPMENT	_____	_____	_____
Sufficient discussion and number of details			
ORGANIZATION	_____	_____	_____
Logical and appropriate sequencing of layout and individual pieces			
STYLE	_____	_____	_____
Variety of sentence structure, accuracy of language usage, recognizable and consistent tone			
PRESENTATION	_____	_____	_____
Visually appealing, adequate and appropriate graphics, accuracy of copyediting			

COMMENDATIONS

RECOMMENDATIONS

and depth of perception of student entries. This score counts as 10% of the student's individual grade for work on this unit. As students write their stories, we determine which products to grade. For example, the first news story involves students in a significant study of the elements of news story writing. Students assess each other's work in peer reviews (see page 14) and then we use the following criteria to evaluate student products:

Criteria Sheet for News Articles

- Accuracy and significance of information
- Degree to which the lead paragraph contains the crucial information to answer *who, what, where,* and *when*
- Degree to which the article progresses from the most important details to the least important and develops key facts from an incident
- Degree to which the article maintains a consistent and credible point of view and includes only facts that a reporter could have known
- Degree to which the article remains objective and avoids subjectivity
- Degree to which the article makes use of quotes from characters to react to the events of the scene

Much of the assessment work is accomplished by peers in the groups. For example, when students write their feature stories, they review each other's, as previously explained. Students then rewrite their stories making use of the feedback they have been given by members of their groups. A portion of a student's individual grade for the newspaper is based on the quality of the feature story. The same precedures are followed for the stories created from interviews. We have found that the desire of the group to produce the very best newspaper possible makes this student peer assessment work especially well. Students are particularly critical of the work that will go into a common product, because they know they will be judged for this as well as for their individual pieces. Thus they take the peer review process very seriously.

When we come to look at the editorials, we believe that, in addition to the peer review described earlier, we need to evaluate students' work with a formal rubric. Students' performance on this task reveals the depth and breadth of their understanding of the ideas in the play to such an extent that it merits separate consideration at the time the editorials are written, rather than waiting to incorporate this grade into an overall individual grade for the newspaper. Figure 1-3 shows the rubric we have used with the *Macbeth* editorials. Although the editorials have received close scrutiny and have been awarded a grade with the aid of this rubric, the most important grade is, of course, the result of our evaluation of the newspaper itself.

Figure 1-3. *Rubric for Assessment and Evaluation of Editorials*

QUALITY	5 The paper	4 The paper	3 The paper	2 The paper	1 The paper
Content: the extent to which the paper exhibits sound understanding, interpretation, and analysis of the task	Conveys a substantial and insightful understanding of a key theme from *Macbeth*, takes an editorial position and defends it perceptively and comprehensively; demonstrates an in-depth comprehension of the complexities of ideas and characters in the play as well as the ways in which Shakespeare's imagery contribute to those ideas.	Conveys a clear understanding of a theme from *Macbeth*; takes an editorial position and defends it convincingly; demonstrates an understanding of significant ideas surrounding the theme, the motivations and personalities of the characters, and the use of imagery.	Provides an accurate, but not necessarily complete, understanding of an idea from the play; takes a position and defends it adequately; demonstrates an understanding of the issues surrounding the theme, the motivations and personalities of the characters but not necessarily the contribution of the imagery.	Provides a brief understanding of an idea from the play; takes a position but tends to summarize story rather than provide reasons for that position; gives a sketchy and sometimes inaccurate idea of the point of the theme, the personalities of the characters; ignores imagery.	Exhibits limited understanding of the implications of the theme on which the essay is based; may not take a position nor do anything but summarize. May contain inaccurate information about the play.
Development: the extent to which ideas are elaborated through the use of specific, accurate, and relevant evidence from the sources	Supports position with convincing, cogent reasons, key facts, details, images, and relevant direct quotes to prove the truth of the position; acknowledges opposition and discredits opposing arguments.	Supports position with appropriate reasons, facts, details, images, and direct quotes to prove the truth of the position; acknowledges opposing arguments.	Supports position with reasons, facts, and details; contains some reference to imagery; a few quotes.	Supports position with at least one reason, limited specific facts or details; some may be irrelevant or inaccurate.	Conveys vague or unsupported ideas, or presents random list of details. Includes inaccurate and/or irrelevant references from the text.
Organization: the extent to which the paper exhibits direction, shape, and coherence	Introduction has a sophisticated discussion of issue in general statement, provable thesis; body pages develop aspect of thesis in a logical clear way; appropriate topic sentence for each body page; conclusion infers larger connection to real world.	Introduction has a relevant general statement, provable thesis; body pages develop appropriate topic sentence for each body page; conclusion infers larger connection to the real world.	Introduction has a general statement and provable thesis; body organized logically; conclusion summarizes content.	Some attention to thesis in introduction and attempt to organize discussion, but organization is simplistic or formulaic; conclusion vague and may be misleading or not follow from discussion.	No provable thesis. Shows little evidence of organization and is difficult to follow; weak conclusion.
Style: the extent to which the paper exhibits effective use of words, sentence structure, and sentence variety to convey ideas and information to a given audience	Conveys ideas and information in original and precise language, with a noticeable sense of voice. Makes effective use of sentence structure and length to convey ideas; uses transitions effectively.	Conveys ideas and information in original and precise language. Shows consistent use of sentences that are varied in length and structure; consistent use of transitions for coherence.	Uses ordinary language or language from the text to convey ideas and information. Some sentence variety but little variety in sentence beginnings; some attention to transition.	Uses ordinary, often imprecise, language to convey ideas and information; sentence flow choppy, illogical. Relies on sentences that lack variety in structure and length and may be constructed incorrectly.	Includes vague, inappropriate, and/or incorrect language. Contains mostly simple sentence structures, marred by run-ons and/or sentence fragments that interfere with meaning.
Mechanics: the extent to which the paper exhibits use of conventions of standard written English	Exhibits correct spelling, grammar, punctuation, paragraphing, and usage.	Exhibits generally correct spelling, punctuation, paragraphing, grammar, and usage.	Exhibits minor errors in spelling, punctuation, paragraphing, grammar, or usage that do not interfere with communication.	Exhibits errors in spelling, punctuation, paragraphing, grammar, or usage that may interfere with communication.	Exhibits errors in spelling, punctuation, paragraphing, grammar, or usage that often interfere with communication.

Students receive both a group grade and an individual grade for this project (Fig. 1-4). The group grade, based on the criteria created with students in Figure 1-2, counts 50%.

For the individual grade, 10% is based on the reporter's notebook, and 40% is based on a holistic assessment of the following criteria:

- Quality of articles contributed to the newspaper
- Extent of individual contribution to completion of the final product—typing, layout, specials, etc.
- Degree of constructive participation in peer review sessions
- Extent of acceptance of responsibility for prompt completion of all articles
- Degree of fulfillment of assigned role (as illustrator, editor, etc.)

Figure 1-4. *Evaluation Summary of* Macbeth *Project*

Evaluation of newspaper (group)	50%
Reporter's notebook (individual)	10%
Contribution to group (Individual)	40%
	100%

By awarding two grades to each student, one for the individual contribution to the *Macbeth* project and one for the group product, we acknowledge and reward individual efforts and also recognize the value of collaboration and cooperation, both in the process and the product.

RECOGNIZING ACHIEVEMENT

After students refine their articles and put their newspapers or news magazines together, they share them with the class during an awards ceremony at which we celebrate students' accomplishments and present awards, winners, and honorable mentions in the following categories:

- Best newspaper, overall
- Best news story
- Best feature story
- Best editorial
- Most creative "specials"

We expand the categories and the types of awards within each category to respond to the quality of the products and the needs of the students to have their efforts recognized in some tangible way. Frequently, we invite the principal or, if possible, the editor of a local newspaper to present awards as if presenting Pulitzer Prizes for journalism. Finally, we showcase the newspapers and news magazines in the school library.

The creation of newspapers and news magazines has done much more than provide motivation and a vehicle through which students study the literature. It has provided our students with an opportunity to connect their schoolwork with a real-world activity. They have had to read, write, speak, and listen effectively, be self-directed, think creatively, make decisions, solve problems, assume responsibility for their work, work effectively in collaborative groups, and use technology to facilitate the creation of a professional product.

The newspaper and news magazine project format works well with the classroom study of *Macbeth,* but it works equally well in teaching many other challenging texts whose complexities of plot, language, and theme might otherwise intimidate students and deter us from including these works in our curricula. Rather than abandon these texts, especially those that make up our Anglo-American literary heritage and contain significant insights into universal truths about the human condition, we present them in the context of the newspaper or news magazine. This format helps to make complex and sophisticated literature accessible to all our students.

ADDITIONAL TEXTS

Additional texts for which the newspaper project is effective include the following:

Julius Caesar by William Shakespears: The assassination of Julius Caesar, the ensuing civil war, the personal conflict among the principals, and its dramatic resolution invite rich and varied treatments in news stories. The issue of what makes a good leader, the degree to which power can or should be invested in one person, and the implication of mob behavior invite reflective editorials and feature stories. The historical setting stimulates students to create entertainment reviews, advertisements, sports reports, and weather reports.

House of the Spirits by Isabel Allendei: The revolution, the political upheavals, and extraordinary events in the lives of the major characters lend themselves to interesting news stories. The conflict of political beliefs and the complex, multitextured characters traced over several generations provide rich materials for editorials and feature stories from many different perspectives. The setting and the span of the text prompt students to create a variety of special features, advertisements, and cartoons.

Their Eyes Were Watching God by Zora Neal Hurston: This book lends itself to the creation of a themed news magazine, focused on the gradual emancipation of women. Because the plight of African American women featured in the book is characteristic of all women in the early 1900s, students can examine the issues addressed in the text from a historical perspective and compare the attitudes toward women today with those of the past. Editorials and feature stories as well as specials provide students with opportunities to come to grips with their own attitudes toward women, marriage, and unconventional behavior.

Inherit the Wind by Jerome Lawrence: This controversial play, based on the actual trial of a school teacher accused of teaching evolutionary theory in a biology classroom rather than creation theory, as required by the school board, resonates with students today. The same conflict between those who insist on a literal interpretation of the creation story and those who advocate an evolutionary explanation of creation still rages. This controversy lends itself to the development of newspaper editorials supporting one view or another.

To Kill a Mockingbird by Harper Lee: The trial of Tom Robinson, a Black man falsely accused of rape in a small Southern town, offers students an opportunity to examine the history of racial discrimination within the context of their study of this novel. The events surrounding the trial and the personalities of Robinson and Atticus Finch, the defense attorney fighting for an unpopular cause, provide students with ample material for writing news stories and editorials. The subplot involving Finch's children and Boo Radley prompts feature stories and specials.

CHAPTER 2

Sin and Guilt, the American Way

Humanity's obsession with sin and guilt—crime and punishment—is reflected in our myths and legends since the beginning of recorded time. Indeed, it is at the very core of the world's religious and philosophical constructs. Nowhere is this obsession more apparent than in Western civilization's historical fascination with the moral behavior of public figures, especially our political and religious leaders. Small wonder then that Americans have long been intrigued by the sinner, the evil one, or the criminal, especially when the alleged wrongdoer is one whom we admire or hold in some esteem.

Perhaps that predilection explains our contemporary fascination with criminal trials, especially now that the most infamous of cases are being tried in public on television. We "enlightened" folks of the 20th century are as entertained by the spectacle of evildoers on display as our ancestors were by public hangings, floggings, and pillorying of miscreants in centuries past. In fact, our response to the public examination of sin may be even more reprehensible than that of our predecessors in that instantaneous media exposure invites us all to become prosecutor, defense attorney, judge, and jury, all emotionally and intellectually involved in the most minute details of the proceedings. No details of the life and heart of the accused go unexamined, untried, and unjudged.

Our students are familiar with such public examinations and are as intrigued by the issues of sin and guilt as they are by the proceedings of the courtroom. Never ones to miss an opportunity to build on what in the world engages our students, we capitalize on their interest in trial by jury to involve them in Nathaniel

Hawthorne's classic tale of sin and guilt in Puritan Boston. However, we don't begin our discussion with the events of a June day in 1640; instead, we share with our students a contemporary story (1990). We offer the following details:

- A high school senior is expelled from the honor society because she had a child.
- The school's faculty council says the girl failed to uphold the requirements of character and leadership.
- A federal district judge refuses to reinstate the girl into the honors society because she had premarital sex, not because she had a child out of wedlock.

We invite our students to discuss the actions of the girl, the faculty council, and the judge, and to imagine themselves as members of that student body and their parents as residents in the town. "What do you think about the girl's action? Does it matter that she had premarital sex and became pregnant? What do you think about the judge's action and that of the faculty council? What if this situation happened in your school? Would it make a difference if the girl were popular or unpopular; if she were your friend or someone you dislike? How would the students react? How would the community react?"

The discussion gets impassioned, often continuing in the hallway after class. Everyone has an opinion, but, not surprisingly, students express no sympathy for the faculty council or the judge. This leaves the teacher to play the role of advocate for the heavies in the scenario, defending the unpopular decisions on the basis of the need to maintain standards of moral behavior and personal responsibility. In response, students demand to know who has a "right" to set standards and determine "morality" for students—or for anyone, for that matter? The cry goes up: "What we do in our own time is our business!"

INTRODUCING *THE SCARLET LETTER*

With that the stage is set for us to introduce *The Scarlet Letter* as a story about a similar private act that has public consequences. Because our students are involved emotionally in a real-life case, they are better able to understand the passions and reactions of the Puritans of Boston in the 1640s. They are also primed to consider the implications of a private act of passion for public response. This response raises questions about fairness and equity, implication and fact, judgment and compassion, and punishment and forgiveness—issues we will explore as investigative reporters on the scene in Boston that warm June day to follow "a tale of human frailty and sorrow."

To engage students in this 350-year-old tale, we ask them to imagine themselves as the descendants of Hester Prynne, a woman who they believe has been unfairly condemned by history. To help them redeem her reputation, they hire a law firm that specializes in historical restitution. Not surprisingly, we assume the personae of their legal advisors. However, only they, as the relatives, have the necessary access to the evidence that must be gathered to institute a case that will clear her name and theirs of the mark of infamy that has tainted it. To that end they are to journey back to the Puritan Boston of 1640 to uncover the truth of Hester's plight and bring to justice those responsible for her unwarranted suffering.

In preparation for their journeys, our students must do some preliminary research on the Puritans and their culture, politics, and religion. In addition, they are to gain enough information to understand the Puritans' response to the private act of passion involving Hester. For this purpose the "descendants" go to the library and the Internet with some specific questions.

- What were the major tenets of the Puritan religion?
- What was the nature of Puritan government?
- To what extent did the leaders become involved in an individual's private life?
- What punishments were imposed on wrongdoers, and for what purpose?

The students report that Puritanism is a Protestant doctrine that developed in the 16th century within the Church of England. The Puritans demanded greater strictness in religious discipline, even insisting that this strictness extend to civic government. It surprises the students that the Puritans recognized no distinction between religious and civil law, which led the Puritans, we note, to have authority over all aspects of an individual's life. Students report that the Puritans were influenced by the teachings of John Calvin, who taught that human beings are inherently evil and are saved from a fiery hell only by the grace of God. The Puritans also believed that humanity was in danger of damning itself to hell for any variety of misdeeds. Therefore, it was the responsibility of the community to save individuals from eternal damnation through strict adherence to rules and severe public punishments.

Once the students have shared their information on the Puritans, we ask them to begin their investigations and to record their findings in a log. The first entry is to reflect on their reactions to the challenging task of being thrust into 17th-century Puritan Boston. One student, Josh, wrote the following:

> I embarked on my journey with a sense of dread and apprehension. I worried about how these people would react to my presence and if they would accept me into their confidence. I also worried about my negative preconceptions about their way of life and how that might interfere with my fairness in reporting the events I witnessed. How tolerant would I be of a government that had a right to pass moral judgment on a person's private behavior? Would I be able to cope with the

kinds of public punishment I had heard about, such as branding, flogging, disfiguring, stoning, hanging—the kinds of punishment that make standing in the stocks as the object of public ridicule seem less terrible than it probably was?

ENCOUNTERING THE TEXT

We read chapter 1 aloud to the students, encouraging them to envision the scene and record the details with which Hawthorne depicts the nature of the Puritan community. Once we discuss these details and the mood that is established through them, we ask our students to resume writing in their reporters' logs and record their first impressions of Puritan Boston. Jessica wrote the following:

> . . . the people were dressed in dark clothes, mostly black and gray, and gathered around the prison, obviously waiting eagerly for some prisoner to emerge. I discovered that the Puritans built the prison shortly after they laid out the burial ground. I was surprised that such a religious colony wouldn't build a church first. The prison, covered with rust and iron spikes, looked old and forbidding. In front of it was a weedy grass plot full of pigweed and burdock. I was intrigued, though, by the presence of a beautiful wild rose in the middle of such ugliness.

Students must read chapters 2–4 to discover why all those people were waiting outside the prison door and what transpired that might be of interest to them. To focus students' log entries, we, as their legal advisors from the modern world, send them periodic directives to guide their investigation. Their first directive is to witness the public shaming of Hester Prynne and her subsequent reunion with her long-lost husband (chapters 2–4).

> To: Investigators on location
> From: Hawthorne Associates
> Re: Investigation of events in Puritan Boston, June 1640
>   Get detailed information about the following:
>
> • Hester Prynne and the townspeople
>
> • Interrogation of Hester on the scaffold
>
> • Hester in prison after she leaves the scaffold
>
> We suggest that you organize yourselves into groups of three and assign yourselves different topics to investigate. This will make your work go much more quickly.

An excerpt from Amy's investigator's log included the following:

> A striking young woman, holding a baby, stepped from the prison. On her dress was fastened an elaborately embroidered *A*. The *A* was perhaps the most interesting and colorful object

in the entire gray town, and the woman the most beautiful person. I felt an immediate sympathy for this poor woman. She walked proudly across the grassy patch to the scaffold and ascended its steps clutching her child. The governor, a judge, and the ministers looked down on her from a nearby balcony. Her sentence, as I overheard it from several people around me, was to stand on the scaffold till noon. As she stood, a wistfulness appeared on her face that contrasted sharply with the stern expressions of the townspeople. I thought that she might be the only human in this crowd who was free, despite her imprisonment, to dream. I found myself admiring her courage in facing up to that crowd without flinching. I hadn't been prepared for how beautiful she would be. She alone, among all those women who watched, carried herself with dignity and grace.

Chris wrote the following:

> The magistrates kept badgering poor Hester to name the father of her baby, but she wouldn't tell. Reverend Wilson said, "Speak, woman! Speak, and give your child a father!" Another minister, Mr. Dimmesdale, also tried to convince her to tell the name of her child's father, but it sounded half-hearted to me. What bothered me was that some man in that crowd had to be the child's father. There he was, letting Hester take all the punishment by herself. What kind of man would do that? And why would Hester protect a guy like that?

Sara dealt with the confrontation in the prison between Hester and her husband and wrote the following:

> I followed Hester back into the prison and hid in the shadows to learn what I could about her. Soon after, she and the baby became hysterical, and the jailer, fearing for her life and that of her child, called for a physician. To my surprise, the physician turned out to be the stranger who had appeared in the crowd with an Indian earlier in the day. He said his name was Roger Chillingworth. Strangely, Hester clutched her baby protectively and seemed afraid of the physician. Then I discovered that this Roger Chillingworth was actually Hester's long-lost husband. No wonder she was afraid of him! She seemed to think that he might want some kind of revenge on her or her child, but he didn't. He made her swear not to reveal his identity. She agreed to this because he threatened to harm the baby's father if she didn't.

ORCHESTRATING THE STUDY

We move quickly through the initial reading of the book, following the same pattern, giving each student group memos from Hawthorne Associates to direct their investigations. We assign research in groupings as follows: chapters 5–8, 9–13, 14–19, and 20–24.

Chapters 5–8: The Scarlet Woman

> To: Investigators on location
> From: Hawthorne Associates
> Re: Hester's life as a scarlet woman
>   Get detailed information about the following:

- Hester's life as an outcast

- Nature of Pearl

- Attempt to take Pearl from Hester

Following their reading of chapters 5–8, we guide our students through the staging of a psychodrama. This is a powerful technique, not only for helping students to make meaning of what they have read but also for engaging them in the emotional drama of these chapters. This engagement will be necessary for them later when they have to assume the personae of the various characters in order to create a trial at the conclusion of their reading. To stage a literary psychodrama requires some practice for students to get into the spirit of it, and it takes no small amount of courage on the part of the teacher to guide them through it. However, take heart, because this approach is an effective technique for encouraging the students to assume the responsibility for their own learning. The teacher is the facilitator, sometimes asking questions, sometimes rewording students' responses to add depth to the comments. When necessary, the teacher has the students review specific passages that underscore the emotions they have been re-creating in the psychodrama.

Before class we ask a willing student to assume the role of Hester and stand in the center of the classroom wearing a scarlet *A*. Her role is to be the visual center of the drama. The class members become the townspeople. We then ask them to say whatever they want to about Hester, taking their cues from chapter 5. To get them going, we ask them what they think of Hester and what kinds of things they have said to her before. Of course we model the process with appropriate comments, such as, "You brazen hussy, to the devil with you and your wicked child." We have them jot down a few such appropriate epithets to use in the psychodrama. It doesn't take long for them to get into the activity.

After a few minutes we turn to Hester and ask her why she would stay in Boston and endure such treatment. Then we ask the entire class to help our "Hester" by assuming the role with her. We ask, "You hear how the people are treating you; what do you think and feel? Why do you endure such treatment?" If students can't answer the questions, we direct them to the text, having them focus on specific sections—for example, chapter 5, page 67, lines 9–34 (Amsco edition, 1970). We conclude by summarizing what's been revealed in the first psychodrama. Even students who have had difficulty with the reading or have given it short shrift can review key passages and keep up with the progress of the story.

We repeat the process with Hester reflecting on Pearl. Again, we ask the class, as Hester, what their feelings and fears are about Pearl. To help students respond we direct them to chapter 6 (page 81, lines 9–17), where Hester expresses her anguish. We conclude this minidrama by having a "Hester" and a "Pearl" enact the conversation between them (page 82, line 33, to page 83, line 29).

We summarize what's been learned here about Pearl, deliberately using Hawthorne's language to characterize her—for example, "imp," "not amenable," "defiant," "airy sprite," "capricious," "perverse," and "inscrutable"—explaining the meanings of the words as necessary. We expect students to begin incorporating some of the language of the novel into their scenarios.

Finally, we imagine Hester and Pearl at the governor's palace. Our "Hester" must again endure the interrogation of Governor Bellingham and Mr. Wilson, roles we ask the class to assume. We expect them to ask, "What kind of mother are you?" and other questions that threaten Hester with the loss of her child. To help our students, we direct them to chapters 7 and 8 (particularly page 93, line 13, to page 95, line 25), where Governor Bellingham begins his questioning of Pearl. Once our students reveal their understanding of what's happening here, we ask them to shift their role-playing to Hester, expressing what they think is going on her head—for example, "What will happen to me if I lose my child?" We direct them to page 96 (lines 9–35), where Hester vehemently defends her right to her child and demands that Dimmesdale speak for her.

Our students' investigative reports reflect the understanding and insight that result from a directed reading within the context of a psychodrama. Jennifer wrote the following:

> Hester's having to wear the scarlet letter on her bosom was intended to remind her that her sin is not only public but private and must be atoned for in her heart, or she would suffer forever in the afterlife. Apparently the Puritans had a much greater faith in the afterlife than I do, because I consider my grave to be my final statement to the world. The thought, much less the fear, of eternal punishment would be the most dreadful part of a sentence for sin.
>
> Something more than her submission to Puritan law must have kept Hester in the colony, living in her thatched cottage alone with her child. She supported herself by creating beautiful needlework, which was seen on the greatest men of the town but never on the veil of a bride. She also sewed rough garments to give to the poor, who often mocked her despite her kindness to them. Children also mocked her in the streets, and clergymen would give sermons about her. I can't imagine how she could stand such horrible humiliation, especially from pastors who are supposed to be comforting and merciful. I guess Puritan clergymen didn't believe in compassion for sinners.

Beth, who initially had difficulty with the reading, wrote the following:

> Pearl, who wears gorgeous dresses made by her mother, seems to be a very lively child with a vivid imagination, even though she has no friends except for the ones she creates. Pearl is always with her mother and must suffer from the ridicule they receive. I wonder why Hester and Pearl don't just leave.

Later Beth added the following thoughts:

> When Hester went to the Governor's Hall with Pearl to deliver gloves, Pearl seemed especially dressed up for the visit. It seems that the governor, Reverend Wilson, and Reverend Dimmesdale had all teamed up against Hester to try to take Pearl away from her. Hester had no intention of allowing anyone to take her child from her. She turned to Mr. Dimmesdale, the pastor in charge of her soul, to argue for her. He finally persuaded the governor and Mr. Wilson that Pearl should stay with Hester, arguing that she was not only Hester's joy but also her torture, as a constant reminder of her sin. As if the scarlet letter weren't enough! Why did Mr. Dimmesdale argue so much for Hester? I also notice that throughout this entire ordeal, Chillingworth, who was also there, was silent, but soaking in everything with as much if not more attention than I did. What's he up to?

Chapters 9–13: Living With Sin and Guilt

To: Investigators on location
From: Hawthorne Associates
Re: Living with sin and guilt
Get detailed information about the following:
- Suffering of Dimmesdale
- Malevolence of Chillingworth
- Ambiguity of the scaffold and the *A*
- Changing perception of Hester

To help our students with the study of these chapters, we plan for them to create a visual representation of what they learn about the characters and symbols. This visual representation requires students to translate their understandings of the psychology of the characters and the significance of the symbols into concrete images that they can glean from contemporary publications. This process forces them to think abstractly as they make connections between people and events in 17th-century Boston and images from late 20th-century America. To do this well, students must study the text; they have to recognize the abstractions and determine how they will represent them visually. Obviously, this activity demands higher level thinking skills.

We ask students to create a collage centered around the scaffold scene described in chapter 12. Through their depiction of Dimmesdale, Chillingworth,

Hester, and Pearl, they will reveal their understanding of the torment of these characters as a result of sin and guilt. We divide our students into groups of three, deliberately taking advantage of the multiple intelligences of our heterogeneously grouped students. Each group has at least one student who has exhibited some facility with translating ideas into visual images. Each group reviews chapters 9–13 to determine what it wants to reveal in the collage about each character and how it wants to convey the ambiguity of the scaffold and the *A* that dominate this midnight encounter. Then they comb through an assortment of popular magazines that we have supplied, such as *Time, Life, Newsweek,* and *People.* To help clarify the significance of the visual images, members of each group select appropriate quotes that they superimpose on the collage. They also write a detailed explanation of the ideas reflected in their visual creation.

Students present their collages, explaining their thinking. We conclude the assignment by summarizing what they have revealed about each of the characters and the symbols. For example, we learn about the torment of Dimmesdale's hidden sin and the vain hope for redemption that has brought him to the scaffold in the middle of the night. We learn about the depth of Chillingworth's hatred and the destructive effects of his desire for revenge not only on Dimmesdale but on himself. Student visualizations of Hester reveal her growing strength in the face of her suffering. The most successful collages represent the scaffold and the strange *A* in the sky as casting shadows over everything that the characters think and do.

The research for the collages and the thinking reflected in them inform the students' investigative journals. Adrienne wrote the following:

> Mr. Dimmesdale, now weak and pale, overwhelmed by guilt, shame, and sadness, goes to the scaffold at night and tries to find relief from his sin but doesn't succeed. Chillingworth, his figure increasingly misshapen, dark, and cruel, rejoices in Dimmesdale's suffering. Chillingworth immerses himself totally in his revenge. There is no other point to his life. Hester has gone through a major transformation. The *A* on her bosom now stands for *Able* as she helps the sick and needy. However, "the scarlet letter has not done its office." It was supposed to bring her shame and humility and change her for the better. Instead, she changes from a passionate being to a thinker whose thoughts, if known, would have been considered blasphemous. She even thought about committing suicide and killing her baby. She envisioned changing the relationship between men and women. Hester was probably the first American feminist . . .

Another student, Carlos, wrote the following:

> . . . the *A* that lit up the sky revealed Chillingworth looking at Dimmesdale on the scaffold. He seemed to be enjoying the evidence of the poor minister's torment that had brought him to the scaffold. Chillingsworth's devilish look frightened me. He did not seem demented or deranged, just evil. I worried about what he would do to the minister when he got him alone again.

Chapters 14–19: Hester Takes Action

To:	Investigators on location
From:	Hawthorne Associates
Re:	Hester's efforts to save Dimmesdale

Get detailed information about the following:

- Hester's confrontation with Chillingworth
- Hester's plan for escape with Dimmesdale
- Hester's problems with Pearl

To help our students with these chapters, we put them in small groups and assign a different section to each group. Their task is to enhance the class's understanding of their chapter(s) by scripting key ideas and feelings of the characters and then performing their script for the class.

For chapter 14, the confrontation between Hester and Chillingworth, we instruct students to include Hester's ambivalent feelings for Chillingworth, the fears for Dimmesdale that cause her to confront Chillingworth, the essence of their conversation, and the evidence of Chillingworth's vengefulness that results in his saying, ". . . it has all been a dark necessity. . . . It is our fate. Let the black flower blossom as it may!" (page 152, lines 19–24).

For chapter 15, the section devoted to Hester and Pearl, we instruct students to include Pearl's capricious character, her obsession with the scarlet letter, and Hester's ambivalent feelings toward her daughter that cause her to give a false explanation for the source of the *A*, about which Hawthorne comments, "In all these seven bygone years, Hester had never before been false to the symbol on her bosom" (page 158, lines 17–18).

For chapters 16–17, the meeting between Hester and Dimmesdale, we instruct students to focus on what they reveal about their feelings for each other and the extent of Dimmesdale's suffering. Dimmesdale confesses his despair when he tells Hester, "Of penance I have had enough! Of penitence there has been none" (page 168, line 22). We encourage them to script this entire section to show just how hypocritical he feels for remaining a respected pastor in the eyes of his people. We also direct students' attention to Dimmesdale's anger at Hester when he learns the truth about Chillingworth and his judgment of the old man's sin as being blacker than his. "He has violated in cold blood the sanctity of a human heart . . ." (page 171, line 16).

For chapters 18–19, about Hester, Dimmesdale, and Pearl, we instruct students to focus first on Hester's short-lived freedom from the scarlet letter and her desire to unite the two people whom she loves the most. However, Pearl rejects Hester without the scarlet letter and Dimmesdale when he will not walk with them in town. In reaction to Dimmesdale's kiss, she "broke away from her mother and, running to the brook, stooped over it and bathed her forehead, until the unwelcome kiss was quite washed off . . ." (page 187, line 9).

Students enact their dialogues, initiating a discussion of the relevant section. We assess their learning by examining the investigative logs of each student for these chapters. Jon, for example, wrote the following:

> After her midnight meeting with Dimmesdale on the scaffold, Hester knows that something more vile than his guilt is gnawing at him; she suspects Chillingworth of using his penetrating powers to probe Dimmesdale's soul and torture it. She feels that her sin has caused the downfall of both men—it has tormented the Reverend and turned him into a ghost, and it has turned Chillingworth into a vindictive fiend. She feels that it is her responsibility to inform Dimmesdale of the identity of his housemate and asks her husband to release her from her promise of secrecy. . . . Grudgingly, Chillingworth allows her to tell. I don't think it matters to him because he can still hurt Dimmesdale even with his knowing the truth. All he needs is to make him live longer and make him feel guiltier. Obviously, Chillingworth's whole life is revolving around getting revenge; he's not human any more. All he wants to do is plot, probe, and harm Dimmesdale and to "let the black flower blossom as it may."

In another part of his journal, Jon wrote about Hester's walk into the forest with Pearl to await the minister:

> The forest, though wide open, is ironically a private place . . . the forest is believed to be where the devil has his meetings. There is a mysterious and magical quality about it. Here the sun shines on Hester. In town, she lives in the shadows. To satisfy Pearl's pleas for an explanation of the scarlet letter, Hester tells her daughter that she once met the "Black Man" and signed his book, and the scarlet letter is his mark. When she sees the minister, they don't know what to say to each other at first. Then Dimmesdale tells her that he has not found happiness; although he has done penance, he is not penitent. He feels that he is a hypocrite for not publicly confessing, but he cannot bring himself to do it. He feels extremely guilty preaching to his worshiping congregation when he knows that he is a sinner. When Hester tells him the true identity of Roger Chillingworth, Dimmesdale is shocked and at first unforgiving. She had known all along and had let him suffer. She had betrayed him. However, he forgives her and says that Chillingworth has sinned a darker, blacker sin than theirs because he "violated the sanctity of the human heart." Hester then convinces Dimmesdale to leave Boston with her and Pearl, but when she calls Pearl to join her and Dimmesdale, Pearl demands that her mother put back on the scarlet letter, which she had taken off earlier.

Chapter 20–24: Dimmesdale's Temptation and Redemption

>   To: Investigators on location
>   From: Hawthorne Associates
>   Re: Dimmesdale's temptation and redemption (chapters 20–24)
>   Get detailed information about the following:
>   • Dimmesdale's reaction to the plan to leave Boston
>
>   • Events on election day
>
>   • Aftermath

Because of the psychological implications of Dimmesdale's action, we guide our students through another psychodrama, this time with Dimmesdale in the center of the class. In groups of three, students review the temptations and the minister's responses to them, described in chapter 20. Then we divide the class in half, assigning one half to call out the temptations to Dimmesdale. For example, when he encounters an elderly widow who is looking for a comforting word of scripture from her pastor, his dark side, represented by this half of the class, shouts out such thoughts as, "Tell her she's an old witch, that there is no such thing as a mortal soul, that she is a fool." The other half of the class urges him to be kind and reprimands him for even thinking such thoughts: "Remember who you are. This old woman trusts you; an unkind word from you would kill her." If students can't come up with these kinds of responses, we have to ask leading questions, such as, "What would happen if he did speak unkindly to her? Look on page 192 to discover what he thinks might have happened had he succumbed to his dark side."

In this manner we play through the rest of the temptations: his encounter with the deacon, the young girl, the children, and the sailors. When students have difficulty recognizing an incident, we ask more questions and refer them again to the text.

Quickly we summarize what happens between Dimmesdale and Chillingworth when the minister arrives home. To prepare for a review of chapter 23, we select four students to assume the roles of Dimmesdale, Chillingworth, Hester, and Pearl, and we ask them to script the final scaffold scene (pages 222–227). This is easy for them to do because this section is rich in dialogue. In the meantime, the rest of the class is preparing for its role as the townspeople, who will be observing these dramatic events and reacting in various ways. We ask each of them to decide what he or she will say about what will happen on the scaffold that day. During the enactment of the scene, we prompt students portraying the townspeople to react in character to what they hear and see, reminding them that Hawthorne says that not everyone heard and saw the same things. Students imagine the townspeople making the following comments:

> I simply do not believe a word of this so-called confession. It is
> complete and utter nonsense. The poor man is about to die,

and there are actually people who believe that he knows what
he is saying. I know Reverend Dimmesdale. He would never
have committed any kind of sin, much less one as terrible as
Hester Prynne's.

Just look at the disgrace that Hester Prynne has brought upon
Mr. Dimmesdale. He knew that he was going to die, so he took
it upon himself to try to clear Hester even though he had no
obligation to her. I hope Chillingworth pays for speaking badly
about Reverend Dimmesdale, such a saint he was, even marked
with a holy A for *angel,* you know.

People always believe what they want to believe. It's just
ignorance not to believe that Dimmesdale is telling the truth. I
know what happened; I know he's Pearl's father. That's why he
wanted Hester and Pearl up there with him. He's disgraced us
all. Very convenient of him to die right after he confessed.

After we stage this final scaffold confession, we have our students summarize
in their investigative logs what Dimmesdale's confession means to each of the
four major characters in the novel. We direct them to chapters 23 and 24 for help.
Amy wrote the following:

To set himself right in the eyes of God so as not to burn in hell,
Dimmesdale decided to ascend the scaffold with Hester and
Pearl. Although it took some courage for him to do this, he did
it mostly out of fear, just as he had hidden his sin out of fear.

Evan wrote these comments:

Pearl "forgives" him and kisses him. She is no longer an elf-
child; after her mother and father had atoned for their wrongs,
the spell was broken.
    Chillingworth is angry because Dimmesdale has escaped
him; Chillingworth has nothing left to live for now that the
minister has escaped him by confessing and then dying. In the
end, Chillingworth shrivels up and dies; he is a leech without a
host and cannot survive.

Sarah made this observation:

When Dimmesdale died, Hester was left without the comfort of
the hope of being with the man she loves in Eternity; nor had
he comforted Hester with vows of eternal love. There is nothing
left for Hester in Boston, so she leaves to raise Pearl in Europe.
However, in later years Hester returns to live out her life in
Boston, the scene of her great passion and her penance.

As a final log entry, students are invited to give a personal reaction to
Dimmesdale's confession and to decide whether he is redeemed by it, thus aton-
ing for his failure to stand by Hester and share her punishment.
Sonia made this decision:

I have absolutely no sympathy for the minister, whose final words were praising God and telling Hester that their sin would probably prevent them from meeting in their immortal lives. What a selfish man! He might at least have given Hester the comfort of believing that she would have an eternal life with the man she had suffered for, or he could at least have told her that he loved her. After all, she had endured seven years of humiliation to protect him. Obviously, his position came first, even before love. He didn't deserve Hester; he was undeserving of her devotion. The scarlet *A* that was supposed to have been on his chest represents his sin as a hypocrite, not his atonement.

DIMMESDALE ON TRIAL

Having completed their investigation of the events surrounding Hester's humiliation, the investigators receive the following memo:

> To: Investigators on location
> From: Hawthorne Associates
> Re: Hester Prynne's vindication

> Your reports have given us grounds to believe that we can restore your ancestor's good name by bringing the facts of your research to light in a civil trial of Arthur Dimmesdale, whose cowardice and failure to honor his responsibilities as a clergyman and a man are responsible for the defamation of Hester's good name, which has forever labeled her as the "scarlet woman." The result of this action will be the removal of the shame associated with your name.

> To this end we advise you to file the following charges against Arthur Dimmesdale:

> - Violation of his religious vows
> - Dereliction of his responsibilities to Hester Prynne, his parishioner; Pearl, his daughter; and the people of Boston
> - Responsibility for the defamation of Hester Prynne's name and consequently that of her descendants

> We have prepared detailed directives for you to conduct this trial in the Court of Universal Justice. We will supply you with the very best legal counsel available.

This memo provides our students with a link between their investigative study of the novel and a context for considering the universal issues that Hawthorne explores in *The Scarlet Letter.* We use the framework of a trial for this exploration because the format itself engages our students' interest and keeps them responsible for their own learning. To provide the necessary freedom to explore these issues in depth, we don't feel compelled to follow all prescribed trial procedures, and we convince our students to suspend their disbelief long enough to allow characters long dead to participate in the trial and create a court of Universal Justice bound neither by time nor place.

In preparation for the trial, we work with the class to identify the various roles that have to be assumed. Typically, students suggest that there be two lawyers on a side and no more than five witnesses per side. The rest of the class will function either as reporters or jurors. Of course, some students are interested in being the judge, but to help ensure serious procedure and decorum and to move the case along in a timely fashion, we reserve that role for ourselves. There are other roles that could be assigned, but we discourage this because it will only complicate the proceedings. As a ground rule for the trial, we insist that students decide on a specific set of witnesses for the defense and a different specific set of witnesses for the plaintiffs. Witnesses from either side may be cross-examined, giving both sides access to all the witnesses.

Before roles are assigned, each student writes us a letter indicating what role he or she would like to play, why, and what pretrial beliefs each has regarding the guilt or innocence of Arthur Dimmesdale. We encourage students to elaborate upon these beliefs in order for us to determine the best casting for the trial, taking into consideration the different abilities and talents of our students. Obviously, we need serious students and good speakers to be the lawyers, as they must be able to think on their feet and devise pointed, probing questions. For our witnesses, we need students who enjoy pretending to be another character and who are also willing to go back to the book for the information that will enable them to portray their characters accurately. For students who want a less conspicuous role and who need more time to understand what happened in the book, we assign them to the jury, explaining that they will review the text together to draft a list of stipulated facts from which the trial participants, however loosely they discuss the events, may not deviate. Depending upon the size and talents of the class, at least two students take on the role of reporters. They meet together to decide on the kinds of articles they will include in their reports on the trial. At least one article will cover the background of what has led up to the trial, and another will be based on an interview with one or more of the "descendants." After the students are assigned their roles, we give them detailed instructions to guide their preparation.

Trial Preparation

Lawyers
Step 1: Complete a one-page brief outlining your case. The *plaintiffs* should include what the charges are and why you believe them to be true; what you will argue and how you will convince us of Dimmesdale's guilt on each charge. In-

clude a list of your witnesses and what each will contribute to your argument. The *defense* should include what the charges are and why you believe Dimmesdale to be innocent of them; what you will argue and how you will convince us of his innocence. Include a list of your witnesses and what each one will contribute to Dimmesdale's defense.

Step 2: Decide who does what—opening, direct for which witness, cross-examination for which witness, redirect, closing.

Step 3: Devise questions for your witnesses and work with them to determine what kinds of answers you need to help you make your case.

Step 4: Work with your witnesses to help prepare them for the questions that the opposition will ask.

Step 5: Prepare the questions that you would like to ask in cross-examination to break down the testimony that you expect from other side's witnesses.

Step 6: Reconcile your presentation of the case with the facts in the book, which will be presented by the students who play the jurors.

Step 7: Revise your brief and write your opening statement.

Step 8: Add witness affidavits to your brief.

In one trial, the plaintiffs decided to call Juliet Prynne Jones, a descendant of Hester; Roger Chillingworth; Pearl; Mistress Hibbins; and the Reverend Mr. Wilson. The defense called the Reverend Arthur Dimmesdale; Hester Prynne; Eliza Gunting, a townsperson; and Governor Bellingham. Obviously, we allowed students to create fictional townspeople from Boston of the 1640s as well as fictional descendants of Hester Prynne.

Day 1

On day 1 of trial preparation, we distributed the following directives and allowed students time to work on the assignments:

> To: Defense team and plaintiff team
> From: Hawthorne Associates
> Re: Day 1 of trial preparation
>
> Meet to map out a strategy for attacking or proving the charges against Dimmesdale. Prepare a one-page scenario of how you will deal with each charge and how you will use the testimonies of each witness. Refer to your investigative logs and the text throughout your preparation.

To: Witnesses
From: Hawthorne Associates
Re: Day 1 of trial preparation

Develop a brief affidavit in which you state your name, your
role in the events leading up to Dimmesdale's confession on
the scaffold, and your thoughts about the charges based on
your understanding of what occurred. Make sure you review
your investigative logs and the pertinent sections of the book
so that you can better recall what you did and what you said
at key moments in the narrative.

To: Reporters
From: Hawthorne Associates
Re: Day 1 of trial preparation

Meet together to develop your thoughts on the articles that
you will include in your report on the trial and on the events
that led to the trial. One article should be written on the background of the trial and the community's response to the indictment of the Reverend Mr. Dimmesdale. Another article
should be based on your interview of one of Hester Prynne's
descendants.

To: Jury members
From: Hawthorne Associates
Re: Day 1 of trial preparation

Meet with Governor Bellingham to develop a list of stipulated facts from which the trial participants, however loosely
they discuss the events, may not deviate. For example, the
defense cannot deny that Dimmesdale and Hester committed
adultery. That is simply a fact. Draw up a list of no fewer than
10 such facts. Present this list to the plaintiffs and to the defense. They have the right to challenge any facts you present.
Final facts must be agreed upon in a conference by lawyers
from both sides, with the judge presiding, before the trial can
begin. Refer to your investigative logs to refresh your memo-
ries and to confirm your statements of fact.

Students get a good start on their assignments in class and complete them as
homework.

Day 2

Day 2 of trial preparation gives us an opportunity to check our students' work and gives them time to continue preparing for the trial.

On day 2 of trial preparation, we distributed the following assignments:

> To: Defense team and plaintiff team
> From: Hawthorne Associates
> Re: Day 2 of trial preparation
>
> 1. Complete your one-page argument (called a *brief*) outlining your case. Your brief should say what the charges are, why you believe them to be true or false, and how you hope to convince the jury of your view.
> 2. Decide who on your legal team does what: opening, direct questioning of witnesses, cross-examination of witnesses, and closing
> 3. Devise questions for your witnesses and review the questions they have created. Work with them to determine the kinds of answers that are needed to help you make your case.
> 4. Work with your witnesses to help prepare them for the questions the opposition will probably ask.
> 5. Prepare questions that you would like to ask in cross-examination to break down the testimony you expect from the other side's witnesses.
> 6. Reconcile your presentation of the case with the facts as presented to you by the judge.

> To: Witnesses
> From: Hawthorne Associates
> Re: Day 2 of trial preparation
>
> 1. Complete your affidavits. Be sure to include who you are, your role in the events leading up to Dimmesdale's death, and your thoughts about the charges based on your knowledge of what happened. Submit copies of your affidavits to the judge and to the lawyers for both sides.
> 2. Work with your lawyers to determine the questions you should be asked. Discuss how to answer those questions. What sections in the book can help you? Have them handy for use during your testimony. You may use your notes during your testimony, but you don't want to seem to be reading your answers.
> 3. Work with your lawyers to try to anticipate answers for probable cross-examination questions.

To: Jury
From: Hawthorne Associates
Re: Day 2 of trial preparation

1. Agree on the list of facts that you will present to the lawyers from both sides. You should have a list of no fewer
   than 10 facts.
2. Present your list of facts to the lawyers. If challenged by
   the lawyers, be sure you can support your list with direct
   evidence from the text.
3. Confer with lawyers from both sides as well as with the
   judge to finalize the list of stipulated facts.
4. Take notes during the trial on the testimony of each witness and the arguments presented by the lawyers. These
   notes will be useful later in presenting your final report.

To: Reporters
From: Hawthorne Associates
Re: Day 2 of trial preparation

Interview the witnesses to get their views on the events and
what they expect will happen at the trial. Divide the task between (or among) you; review notes on what each of you
learned and compare what the witnesses told you with what
you know of the events. Here's where your investigative logs
will help you. Then decide who will write what and get started
on your stories. Hawthorne Associates expects you to submit
your reports tomorrow.

Sample Documents and Statements

In one trial, the list of facts agreed upon by the lawyers, the jury, and the
judge were as follows:

- Hester Prynne committed adultery with Arthur Dimmesdale.
- Dimmesdale hid his part in the sin.
- Dimmesdale is medically treated by Roger Chillingworth.
- Chillingworth's physical appearance deteriorates during the seven
  years that he lives with Dimmesdale.
- Dimmesdale sickens gradually but steadily.
- Dimmesdale tortures himself out of guilt.
- Dimmesdale confesses his sin on the scaffold and then dies.
- Chillingworth dies within a year of Dimmesdale's death.
- Chillingworth leaves his fortune to Pearl.

The following is a sample from the brief filed by the defense:

> Enclosed please find copies of our legal brief for the upcoming trial. You will note that we plan to call four witnesses to the stand: Hester Prynne, citizen, city of Boston; Pearl Prynne, minor, city of Boston; Eliza Gunting, citizen and saint, city of Boston; the Reverend Arthur Dimmesdale, former spiritual leader of the city of Boston.
>
> At this time we wish to repeat our protest of this trial as an absurd miscarriage of justice. The charges levied against our client are totally unfounded. However, in an attempt to defend our client, we are prepared to propose the following defense:
>
> To answer the charge that he violated his religious vows, we will prove beyond a shadow of a doubt that the Reverend Dimmesdale was directed in all of his behavior, both public and private, by his commitment to his religious vows.
>
> To answer the charge that Dimmesdale was derelict in his responsibilities to Hester Prynne, Pearl, and the people of Boston, we will prove that the Reverend Dimmesdale encouraged Hester Prynne in her efforts to atone for her sin, supported her efforts to retain custody of her child against those who claimed that she was unfit, and in so doing prevented her from succumbing to the temptations of the witch, Mistress Hibbins, to give herself to the devil. We will also show that he provided exemplary spiritual leadership to the people of Boston.
>
> To answer the charge that Dimmesdale is responsible for the defamation of Hester Prynne's good name and that of her descendants, we will show that this charge is absurd, that in no way was the Reverend Dimmesdale involved in the defamation of Hester's good name; moreover, her descendants have not suffered loss of respect or opportunity because of negative associations with the name Prynne. The truth is that they have actually *benefited* from carrying the name Prynne, since it is instantly recognized, and thus they have reaped fame and fortune, thanks to Nathaniel Hawthorne.
>
> Furthermore, we will discredit each of the plaintiffs' witnesses and prove their bias and malice in attempting to malign the saintliness of the Reverend Dimmesdale's name.

The plaintiffs presented the following as their opening statement:

> Good morning Your Honor and ladies and gentlemen of the jury.
>
> We are here to bring to light the truth surrounding the tragic events that have resulted in the defamation of Hester Prynne's character and the association of her name with sin and guilt that has subjected her descendants to great pain and suffering. The truth is that the Reverend Dimmesdale is responsible for the events that resulted in Hester's condemnation. We will prove that the Reverend Mr. Dimmesdale did violate his religious vows by becoming

involved in an illicit affair with Hester Prynne, by failing to publicly acknowledge his part in that sin, by failing to honor his professed commitment to public confession of sin, and by failing to accept the punishment he deserved at the hands of the Puritan fathers.

We will also prove that the Reverend Dimmesdale was derelict in his responsibilities to Hester Prynne, who looked to him for strength and guidance; to Pearl, whom he denied as his daughter and neglected for seven long years despite her requests for his public acceptance. He allowed Hester to suffer public condemnation and rejection, and his daughter to be shunned and tormented, rather than reveal his part in the sin. Not only is he guilty of this dereliction of duty to Hester and his own child, but he misled his trusting parishioners for seven years into believing that his personal torment was a result of his concern for their spiritual well-being. His hypocrisy knew no bounds.

We will also prove that Reverend Dimmesdale bears sole responsibility for the defamation of Hester Prynne's good name and that of her descendants. For more than 350 years, the name *Hester Prynne* has been inextricably associated with sin and shame. She has been dubbed the "scarlet woman" and has been the object of ridicule throughout history. Even people who have never read Nathaniel Hawthorne's book know Hester Prynne as "the whore of Boston." Imagine the humiliation of her descendants in carrying a name forever associated with adultery. For all of this shame and suffering, the Reverend Dimmesdale must finally be held accountable.

The defense will claim that the Reverend Dimmesdale has suffered enough, both at his own hands and from the evil Roger Chillingworth. They will also claim that his final confession on the scaffold exonerated him, but his confession came too late to spare Hester and her descendants the stigma of the scarlet letter.

After you have examined the facts, heard the witnesses, and weighed the evidence, you will have no choice but to condemn the Reverend Mr. Dimmesdale on all charges, thereby vindicating at long last the honor of the Prynne name.

The following is a sample of the questions prepared in advance for the direct examination of one of the defense witnesses, Ms. Eliza Gunting:

1. Could you please state your name and occupation for this court?
2. Where do you live?
3. Where do you worship?
4. How long have you worshiped there?
5. Are you familiar with the sermons of the Reverend Mr. Arthur Dimmesdale?
6. How have they helped you in your everyday life?
7. Now that you know that Reverend Dimmesdale is the father of Pearl Prynne, do you view his sermons differently?
8. How so?

9. How did the Reverend recommend that sinners repent?
10. Have you heard what he has done to himself?
11. Do you feel that he would demand this punishment, or anything surpassing this, from any member of his congregation?

One reporter filed the following news story from his interview with a descendant of Hester Prynne:

Shocking Revelation in Minister's Trial

"No matter how this trial turns out," declared Juliet Prynne Jones, a descendant of Hester Prynne and a plaintiff in the case against the Reverend Arthur Dimmesdale, "at least the world will know the truth about Hester Prynne."

The "truth" to Jones is that her ancestor, Hester Prynne, was a victim of circumstance and the irresponsible behavior of Arthur Dimmesdale. Certainly that is the theme of the plaintiffs' case against the defendant. The chief lawyer for the plaintiffs, Marie Criticos, charged Dimmesdale with violation of his religious vows; dereliction of his responsibilities to Hester Prynne, their daughter Pearl, and the people of Boston; and responsibility for the defamation of Hester Prynne's good name and that of her descendants.

The testimony of Mr. Dimmesdale's parishioner, Eliza Gunting, focused on what she labeled as the Reverend's hypocrisy in carrying out his responsibilities to herself, Hester, and her neighbors. However, the most damaging testimony was that of Hester Prynne when she told the court that Mr. Dimmesdale assured her that their relationship was consecrated in heaven; that in the eyes of God, the ultimate judge and jury, they were as good as married.

Under cross-examination, Hester Prynne said—in response to a question about her marriage to Mr. Prynne, better known as Roger Chillingworth—that she had last seen her husband in Amsterdam when he had sent her to Boston, promising to follow her within a very short time. When, after two years, Mr. Prynne had failed to communicate with her and failed to arrive in Boston, Hester believed that her husband was dead.

The plaintiffs argued that her belief in her husband's death made her even more vulnerable to the unseemly overtures of her minister.

Jones is convinced that the compelling testimony of Eliza Gunting and Hester Prynne will convince the jury of Dimmesdale's responsibility for the adulterous act that has blackened the family name.

The trial lasts, on average, three days. The jury deliberates, presents its verdict, and explains the rationale for its decision.

We like to videotape the proceedings so that we have an accurate record to review and so that students can watch themselves in action—they love that. They may take a copy home to watch with friends and family or come after school one day for a special viewing. It's always fun to hear what they have to say, especially about what they "should have said," or the inaccuracy of some testimony, or the lack of logic of an opening or closing statement. We always like to point out to them what they did well—for example, the lawyers' ability to think quickly or the passion and perceptiveness of witnesses' responses to unexpected questions. This tape is particularly useful to the jury as its members review the testimony from the trial and seek to come to a decision that fulfill their mandate from the judge.

PUTTING IT ALL TOGETHER

To give students an opportunity to assess the trial as a whole and their own performances in it, we give each group a culminating assignment.

The lawyers are asked to do the following:

- Refine and submit their briefs. These include their opening and closing statements, their questions for each witness, their cross-examination questions, and any rebuttal statements they made during the trial.

- Write a reflective piece in which they assess their individual performances and the effectiveness of their team's strategy. They are given the opportunity to include questions that they wish they had asked and to comment on the trial as a whole.

The witnesses are asked to do the following:

- Resubmit written affidavits as well as their answers to the questions they were asked by their lawyers.

- Write a reflective piece in which they assess their individual performances and the effectiveness of their testimony in establishing the guilt or innocence of Reverend Dimmesdale. They are given the opportunity to include testimony that they wish they had given and to comment on the trial as a whole.

Each member of the jury (which has rendered a verdict) is asked to do the following:

- Submit a summary of the deliberations, including the rationale for the verdict, explaining the findings on each charge and the recommendations to the Universal Court of Justice regarding the claim of the descendants that their good name has been unfairly maligned as a result of events that occurred in Puritan Boston.

- Explain how the testimony of each witness and the arguments of the lawyers informed his or her personal opinion about Dimmesdale's guilt or innocence. Textual references to support the decision on the guilt or innocence of Dimmesdale should be used. Here the jurors may take issue with the lawyers' presentations and argue for a different verdict based on their own understanding of the text.

The reporters are asked to do the following:

- Submit the stories they have written.
- Write a reflective piece in which they assess the effectiveness of the testimony in establishing the guilt or innocence of the Reverend Dimmesdale and the arguments of the attorneys for the defendant and for the plaintiffs. They too must use textual references to justify their assessments.

EVALUATING STUDENT PERFORMANCE

Because of the complexity of the study of this novel, we need to establish in advance for our students the criteria for evaluation of each aspect of their work. All students are evaluated on their investigative logs (Fig. 2-1), trial preparation (Fig. 2-2), and trial performance or reporting (Figs. 2-2 and 2-3).

Because there are different roles to play in the trial, each of which makes different kinds of demands on the students, we have to match the scoring rubrics to the specifics of the tasks. Even though we generally subscribe to the practice of engaging the students in the creation of evaluative instruments, we have not done so in this case because it would divert too much time and attention from the trial. But we do make these scoring guides available to students as they prepare for the various tasks on which they will be evaluated.

Figure 2-1. *Rubric for Assessment and Evaluation of Investigative Logs*

4

Content
Significant personal interaction with the text
Abundant accurate facts
Excellent insight
Depth of perception
Consistent point of view of the descendant

Development
Focus on assigned task for each entry, not plot summary
Abundant details to support observations
Direct quotes where appropriate

Form
Clearly addresses topic
Strong personal voice
Variety in sentence structure
Correct use of punctuation, vocabulary, grammar, and spelling

3
Content
Personal interaction with text
Accurate facts
Some insight
Point of view of descendant

Development
Attention to assigned task, goes beyond plot summary
Details generally support observation
Some use of quotes

Form
Addresses topic
Personal voice
Few errors in punctuation, vocabulary, grammar, and spelling; do not
interfere with meaning

2
Content
Limited personal response
Mostly accurate facts
Some attention to point of view

Development
Limited details
Support largely a summary of story

Form
May only touch on topic
Limited attention to voice
Errors in punctuation, vocabulary, grammar, and spelling; may interfere
with meaning

1
Content
No personal response
Few facts
May contain errors of fact
Sketchy summary

Development
Limited details
Support largely a summary of story

Form
Does not address topic
No attention to voice
Serious errors in punctuation, vocabulary, grammar, and spelling;
interfere with meaning

Figure 2-2. *Rubric for Assessment and Evaluation of Trial Preparation and Participation*

4.   Complete accurate fulfillment of each aspect of their tasks
     Abundant accurate details to support their positions
     Depth of insight
     Faithfulness to original text
     Relevant use of textual references
     Convincing, clear, articulate presentation of their positions
     Effective maintenance of persona
     Coherent, rehearsed performance
     Sophisticated use of language
     Correct language mechanics

3.   Fulfillment of each aspect of their tasks
     Accurate details to support their positions
     Some insight
     Some attention to original text
     Use of textual references
     Clear presentation of their positions
     General maintenance of persona
     Evidence of rehearsed performance
     Appropriate use of language
     Few errors in mechanics that do not interfere with meaning

2.   Some attention to most aspects of their tasks, but failure to
          develop one or more aspects fully enough
     Some accurate details, but failure to select the most relevant to
          support their positions
     Little attention to original text
     Hesitant or rambling presentation
     Failure to stay in persona
     Generally appropriate use of language
     Some errors in mechanics that may interfere with meaning

1.   Failure to complete one or more aspects of their tasks
     Few details and some inaccuracies
     No attention to original text
     Presentation that lacks focus, contains irrelevancies, and conflicts
          with facts from the text
     Little or no attention to persona
     Some inappropriate use of language
     Errors in mechanics that consistently interfere with meaning

Figure 2-3. *Rubric for Assessment and Evaluation of Reporters' Articles*

	Excellent	Good	Competent
CONTENT	_____	_____	_____
Scope of articles, accuracy of facts, creativity, clearly focused point			
DEVELOPMENT	_____	_____	_____
Fully realized individual pieces, effective use of quote			
ORGANIZATION	_____	_____	_____
Logical, engaging			
STYLE	_____	_____	_____
Mature, accurate use of mechanics, attention to voice and audience			

COMMENDATIONS

RECOMMENDATIONS

CONCLUSION

Studying *The Scarlet Letter* within the context of a trial provides an authentic and contemporary framework that will not only engage students in the text but also facilitate their ability to make meaning of the classic tale of sin and guilt. The trial with its diverse requirements enables students to hone the following essential English–language arts skills:

Research: Assuming the persona of a descendant of Hester Prynne provides a personal lens through which they read the text and record their observations and reactions in investigative logs.

Analysis: Depending on the role that students assume in the trial, they must analyze their research to select the data that is relevant to the position they want to support.

Organization: Students then organize that data into a coherent, effective argument and/or report.

Oral Presentation: All students are required to practice oral communication skills, ranging from sophisticated legal presentations to group debate in which they must convince others of their beliefs.

Listening: The trial demands that lawyers, witnesses, jurors, and reporters must be active listeners who are able to articulate what they hear, interpret its significance, and evaluate its relevance and validity.

Writing: In addition to creating their written investigative logs, all students have the opportunity to practice and develop writing skills in different modes of writing, including arguments, summaries, analyses, and reflections.

We recognize the demands that the trial context makes on the teacher and classroom time. But when we consider the opportunities provided by this rich, integrated, and real-life experience for our students, particularly those of diverse abilities and intelligences, we know that the investment of time and energy is worth our and our students' commitment to this complex project.

ADDITIONAL TEXTS

Additional texts for which the trial is effective include the following:

Song of Solomon by Toni Morrison: This is clearly a book in which criminal action, including murder, occurs. The complexity of the crimes, the characters, and the racial motivations prompting them lend themselves to the exploration of the novel through a trial. This focus helps to make this very challenging novel accessible to students and provides a vehicle for them to examine the struggles of one man attempting to find his heritage and thus his identity.

Wuthering Heights by Emily Bronte: This story raises questions about the nature of child abuse, its effects on the abused throughout their lives, and the implications of revenge. In the framework of a trial (students can decide who goes on trial, as there are several worthy candidates), students examine the intricacies of the plot, the shifts of perspective, the complexities of the characters, and the nature of passion.

Ethan Frome by Edith Wharton: This book examines husband-wife responsibilities, attitudes toward marriage and divorce in the early 1900s compared to today, and human longings. These issues can be explored by a trial in which Ethan is charged with adultery, neglect, and attempted suicide. This format enables students to examine the other characters and their roles in the tragedy.

Death of a Salesman by Arthur Miller: The format of a trial is an especially suitable vehicle for studying the character of Willy Loman and the effects of his failures as a husband and a father. In putting Willy on trial, students are also investigating the 20th-century distortions of the American Dream in which manual labor is denigrated, impressions are valued over personal integrity, and the belief prevails that the end justifies the means.

Fences by August Wilson: This play also explores the issues of marriage and parenthood, this time in the context of a working-class African American family in Pittsburgh. Troy Manson is guilty of adultery, abandoning his wife, and refusing to let his son live his own life without authoritarian interference. An interesting variant of the trial here might be to have a court custody case over the care of Troy's illegitimate daughter after the mother dies in childbirth.

CHAPTER 3

Kind Hearts and Rapscallions

"Haint we got all the fools in town on our side? And ain't that a big enough majority in any town?" asks the king, one of Huckleberry Finn's notorious "rapscallions," as he and the duke plot to swindle the orphaned Wilks sisters out of their inheritance. Certainly the "fools" in Mark Twain's Pikesville of 1850 were alive and well in their contemporary counterparts, just as their kind are today. The universality of Twain's satirical targets makes it possible, even easy, for our students to recognize people they know, including themselves, in the caricatures that populate the episodes of *The Adventures of Huckleberry Finn*. With these caricatures, Twain entertains us, but at the same time he forces us to look at human beings consumed by greed, bigotry, hypocrisy, self-righteousness, and pretentiousness, along with those ordinary people who regularly take advantage of the misplaced goodwill and kindness of the innocent and naive.

Twain had the courage to expose the perverse side of human beings and to raise major social issues of his time, issues that are still to be resolved in our time. Among the more controversial is that of racial injustice and its impact on both perpetrator and victim. Rather than write a social treatise on injustice, Twain reveals the destructive consequences of one human being demeaning another, of enslaving one person and empowering another because of color. As teachers we can appreciate Twain's intent; however, our students may not share our appreciation. The challenge, then, in the reinvented classroom is for us to enable our students to get beyond a literal reading of the text, which might lead to a misunderstanding of the novel's intent, to an understanding of Twain's satire.

But let's be realistic. We have to help our students recognize satire when they see it. To that end, we show our students some cartoons that reveal one or more human weaknesses that they would easily recognize in an amusing context.

Because these cartoons are not particularly abstract, our students have no trouble understanding their satirical intent. In Figure 3-1, illustrator David Nayor shows a child pointing to a location on a map of the world that we recognize as South America. He says he is pointing at New York and proudly asserts that "Of

Figure 3-1. *Geography Lesson*

"Of course, I learned all about geography right here in the great state of New York."

course, I learned all about geography right here in the great state of New York." Nayor suggests that youngsters have no idea of geography but have a lot of false confidence in their presumed accomplishments. This cartoon is as much an attack on the American educational system as it is on student arrogance and ignorance. In Figure 3-2, Nayor depicts youngsters lounging at the mall, making little productive use of their time, but complaining about how unreasonable their teachers are in expecting them to have enough time to do all the homework they assign. In so doing, Nayor is criticizing student laziness and false priorities.

Our students enjoy seeing the cartoons; they get into the spirit of the satire. At this point, we ask each of them to find two more satirical cartoons from a collection of current political and social cartoons that we have culled from newspapers and magazines. Working with partners, they select appropriate pieces, identify the target of the satire, and speculate abut the motivation of the cartoonists.

The class review is lively as students share their cartoons and their analyses. From this collection we brainstorm for the characteristics of satire as demonstrated in the cartoons: (a) exaggeration and oversimplification, (b) understatement and overstatement, (c) distortion, and (d) contrast. These techniques, evident in modern satire, are also recognizable in *The Adventures of Huckleberry Finn.*

Figure 3-2. *Overheard at the Mall*

INTRODUCING THE NOVEL

To take our students into the text, we read the author's notice:

> Persons attempting to find a motive in this narrative will be prosecuted; persons attempting to find a moral in it will be banished; persons attempting to find a plot in it will be shot.
> —By order of the author   *Per G.G., Chief of Ordinance*

"What," we ask them, "do you make of this?"

The responses vary from "I guess the writer doesn't really want us to analyze the book" and "You better watch out, it's illegal to make us answer questions and write papers about this book" to "Yes! There's *no* hidden meaning in this book."

"Well," we ask, "do you really believe that Twain will banish or shoot us if we do what he says not to do?"

Students laugh at this and acknowledge that it's unlikely that he means exactly what he says; he is exaggerating to make fun of teachers and other people who think they have to analyze everything they read.

Of course we agree with them, and then we ask them to consider what people usually do when they are warned against a certain action. Our students admit that when they are prohibited from doing something, that is exactly what they want to do. So, we suggest, by forbidding us to look for a motive, moral, or plot in *Huckleberry Finn*, Twain is actually urging us to do just that. In fact, saying one thing but meaning another is a pattern of the book. Twain's story is told by a naive backwoods boy who takes everything he sees and hears literally, but Twain doesn't expect us, the more sophisticated readers, to accept Huck's perception of reality. Twain wants his readers to look beyond the literal for the deeper intent of his narrative.

THE DOUBLE-ENTRY JOURNAL

We explain to our students that as we read the book we are going to look for a deeper purpose of the novel, recognizing that the interpretation of what Huck Finn, the narrator, sees and experiences is not necessarily that of the author. To enable our students to keep track of this difference we ask them to keep a double-entry journal; on the left side, students record Huck's perceptions of significant events and people and his observations about himself and society. On the right side, students indicate what they think are Twain's views of those same events and people.

To model the process, we take another look at the two social cartoons (Figs. 3-1 and 3-2). This time we show a blank double-entry journal form on an overhead transparency. We walk students through the process by creating a journal entry for Figure 3-2 that looks like this:

A young boy, pointing to a spot in South America, says confidently that he knows all about geography "right here in the great state of New York."	By showing the boy thinking that he knows all about geography pointing to someplace in South America and calling it New York, the cartoonist is laughing at the contradiction between what the boy thinks he knows and his obvious ignorance. The humor lies in that contradiction.

The technique of the cartoonist mirrors Twain's technique in writing *Huckleberry Finn*. Helping our students to understand the difference between Huck's narration and Twain's intent enables us to tackle the most controversial aspect of this book: Huck's use of the vernacular, which includes the word *nigger*. This word, which offends all fair-minded people, has led to condemnations of the novel and a misunderstanding of Twain's attitude toward Blacks. The truth is that Twain was outraged by the treatment of Black people so much so that in December 1885, the same year that *The Adventures of Huckleberry Finn* was published, he wrote a letter to the dean of Yale Law School on behalf of one of its first Black students. In it he says, "We have ground the manhood out of them [Black men] and the shame is ours, not theirs, and we should pay for it." Twain's actions were honest to his words; he offered to pay room and board for a Black law student.

Just as we are not to confuse Huck's reference to Black people as "niggers" with Twain's consideration of Blacks as dignified human beings, so we must not confuse Huck's understanding of events and people with Twain's perception of the human condition.

THE LITERARY TALK SHOW

To provide a context in which our students explore Twain's intent in exposing the vices and foibles of human beings, we introduce the idea of the literary talk show. Of course they are very familiar with the talk show format, but the "literary" designation puts a whole other spin on the popular media genre. Preparation of the show will consist of their study of the novel; the creation of interviews, dramatizations, monologues, and dialogues; and original literary responses to their reading, which will provide the resources for them to script their shows. The format of a literary talk show consists of a host interviewing the author—in this case Mark Twain, perhaps—and selected guests, including characters from the book and even real or imagined literary critics. The purpose of all these characters is to capture the content and flavor of the novel in order to explore the author's view of humanity and arrive at a statement that reflects our students' understanding of Twain's "moral and motive."

Obviously, the preparation of such a show requires collaboration. To that end we invite students to organize themselves into groups of five or six. For this project we do not assign students to groups unless we have some students who are not automatically included in a group. The only restriction we impose is that each group contains both males and females. Because this project requires students to do much of the work together outside class, we have found it more effective for students to work with others of their choosing. Even though this may result in homogeneous groups, in this particular project, the productivity of all students is enhanced as a result of working with their friends or at least with people with whom they are comfortable. To promote students' commitment to their groups, we ask them to eventually give themselves a name that is inspired from their reading of the text. Some imaginative names begin to emerge early in their readings—for example, "the Bullrushers," "Borrowed Chickens," and "Dog My Cats."

CONFRONTING THE TEXT

Once the groups have been formed, we explain to our students that in order to collect the information that they will need to create the elements of their productions—particularly the interviews with the author—they should develop their journals as they read the book, noting the contrast between Huck's voice and interpretations and Twain's satiric intent. To get them started, we read chapter 1 aloud. Of course, we prepare a dramatic reading so that we simulate Huck's "back-woods southwestern dialect" to convey his view of the world; his literalness, his pragmatism, and his naivete.

After the reading, we ask our students to inquire about anything they don't understand. For example, someone might question what "stretchers" are or what is meant by the widow "tuck[ing] down her head and grumbl[ing] a little over the victuals." We answer the questions literally. Then we work together with the class, identifying the perspectives of Huck and Twain on the specific topics in each of the first four paragraphs of chapter 1. To prevent students from simply summarizing the plot, we cue them with directed questions that get at the essence of each paragraph. For example, for paragraph 1 we ask what Huck says about lying; for paragraph 2 we ask them what Huck believes about his money; and so on through the first six paragraphs, until our students demonstrate their ability to articulate Huck's perception of a topic. In the same way, we ask students guiding questions about the responses they think Twain wants his readers to have to Huck's perceptions. The result might be as shown in Figure 3-3.

To write the journal entries for the rest of the chapter, students work in their groups. They do not have to work paragraph by paragraph as we did in the opening section, but they should work systematically through the chapters, touching on what they consider to be the highlights, such as attitudes toward smoking, heaven and hell, and the killing of the spider. Obviously, not all students focus on the same "highlights," which makes the discussion of individual journals helpful to the group.

ORGANIZING THE STUDY

We organize the reading of the book into episodes, beginning with "Tom Sawyer's Gang," chapters 2–3 (Fig. 3-4). We tell our students that after reading these chapters, each group will create a dialogue between Tom and Huck in which their personalities are revealed.

To help focus their reading, we tell them that Huck joins Tom's robber gang. We ask them to predict what Huck will expect to do as a member of the gang. Then we assign the reading of chapters 2 and 3.

At the beginning of the next class session, we ask each student to write at least one question or observation, based on the reading, as an *entry ticket*. We allow only 5 minutes for this activity. We use the entry ticket as a strategy throughout the reading of the novel to check our students' understanding of what they have read. We find the entry ticket to be an effective, quick assessment of student comprehension. More significant, the questions and observations generated by

Figure 3-3. *Sample Journal for Huck Finn, Chapter 1*

Huck thinks it's okay to lie because everybody does it.	It's doubtful that Twain believes it's okay to lie or that everybody lies. Certainly he wouldn't want his readers to think he is lying in this book.
Huck has $6,000 that earns him $1 interest a day, "more than a body could tell what to do with."	Twain seems to be laughing at Huck, thinking that he has more money than he could possibly spend. He could also be laughing at Huck for not knowing what to do with his money.
Huck doesn't appreciate the efforts of the Widow Douglas and Miss Watson to try to civilize him.	Twain could be making fun of Huck for not appreciating the comforts of civilized life; and/or he could be poking fun at civilized life for being boring.
Huck says he would rather be a robber with Tom Sawyer than live with the widow; however, Tom tells him he can't be a robber unless he has a respectable life.	Obviously, Twain does not want us to believe that Tom is literally a robber. Twain points out the absurdity of being a "respectable" robber.
Huck can't stand the orderliness of civilized life, including "grumbling over your victuals."	Twain seems to be having fun with Huck's naivete.
Huck loses all interest in the story of Moses as soon as he discovers that Moses is dead because Huck "takes no stock in dead people."	Twain wants us to see that Huck has no interest in history and lives in the present. He cares about what is of practical value to him.

Figure 3-4. *Organization of* Huck Finn

1. "Tom Sawyer's Gang," chapters 2–3
2. "Pap's Return," chapters 4–7
3. "Protecting Jim," chapters 8–16
4. "The Grangerfords," chapters 17–18
5. "The Duke and the King," chapters 19–23
6. "The Wilks Sisters," chapters 24–30
7. "The Freeing of Jim," chapters 31– 43

the students determine the shape of the conversation during class time. In this way, students have considerable control over the learning that takes place in the classroom.

Entry Ticket

Huck's Pap seems unbelievable to me, which makes me wonder why Twain put somebody like that in a book that's supposed to be realistic. I can't believe any kind of father would actually be mad at his son because he could read. So what are we supposed to think about Pap?

Observation

The new judge and his wife deserve what Pap does to their house. How gullible can you be to think Pap Finn was going to change overnight. Twain must not have any respect for judges if he creates a caricature as foolish as this judge.

We quickly review the entry tickets, return them to the students, and then ask them to share their questions and observations with the entire class. If students are at first reluctant to voice their questions, we interject some of the more relevant questions that we have gleaned from the entry tickets. However, we encourage students to feel free to ask their questions themselves, even if we have to ask specific students to comment. We don't try to address every question or observation, only those most crucial to an understanding of the novel. We assure the students that most of their questions will be answered in the course of our activities, beginning with the completion of the double-entry journal for chapters 2 and 3.

Because the creation of the double-entry journal is still new to the students, we spend some class time modeling the first couple of entries for chapter 2 (Fig. 3-5).

Figure 3-5. *Sample Journal for* Huck Finn, *Chapter 2*

Huck agrees with Tom to play an elaborate trick on Jim, but he is worried that Jim might wake up and ruin his escape from the widow.	Huck does want to do whatever Tom wants to do, even if he thinks better of it. Twain tells us that Tom and Huck don't have any respect for Jim and seem to believe that it's perfectly okay to make a fool of Jim.
Huck joins the robber gang, swearing to a bloodthirsty oath that Tom got from pirate books. Huck offers Miss Watson to be killed if he violates the oath.	Shows the absurdity of these children planning to rob and murder anybody. Obviously, they are young and innocent.

From then on, students work on completing the entries for the rest of chapter 2 and for chapter 3. We offer guidance as needed, suggesting topics that could be included in the journal, such as demanding and taking female prisoners, robbing on Sunday, praying, attacking the Sunday School picnic, and rubbing the lamp for a genie. The point is to direct students to the chapter highlights and steer them away from plot summary. In effect, we are teaching some *critical reading skills* through the creation of the double-entry journal, particularly those skills that enable our students to read for *main ideas,* from which they make logical, supportable *inferences*. The entry tickets encourage *questioning* and *connecting*. Other activities will promote *visualizing, predicting*, and *connecting*. In this way our students are learning the skills of sophisticated readers, those strategies that empower them to look beyond the literal meanings of the words to find the more abstract meanings. Investing this much time in guided practice with the initial journal entries helps to prepare the students to work independently on subsequent readings. The students who most appreciate this systematic approach to understanding the difference between Huck's perception of events and people and Twain's intent are those who might otherwise have the most difficulty in making this distinction.

CREATING MONOLOGUES

To begin to create material for their literary talk shows, students work together in their groups to review the episode involving the robber gang. Their task is to compose a 1-minute monologue for Huck and the other boys complaining about some aspect of their experiences with the gang. Yakov created the following piece for his group's show, illustrated with Figure 3-6:

> Robber gang, my big toe. We haint taken no more 'n turnips and other stuff. Boy, Tom Sawyer is such a liar. I thought this thing here was for real, and he does talk like it is. Well, what was I supposed to do, humor him as he made a saphead outta me? I quit, plain and simple. He could go on and read his silly ol' books and make up stories of elephants and stuff; I ain't having it. I tried to hang around and be a faithful robber, but we ain't done no murderin' and no robbin' and haint ransomed nobody neither. Heck, all we did was steal ol' vegetables, and Tom called them "ingots" and "julery." Well, I think he is just making the whole thing up just to make all of us look innocent or somethin' like that. Anyway, as I said, I quit; it ain't no fun just jumping around and calling a Sunday School picnic a bunch of A-rabs. The idea was great though, goin' aroun' and killin' and robbin', but Tom made the whole thing boring, 'cause all we did was chase a Sunday school.

The students enjoy this activity; it's fun to experiment with the dialect, take advantage of classmates' different abilities, and also discover some answers to the first set of entry ticket questions.

Figure 3-6. *Student Computer-Generated Drawing of Huck*

CREATING CARICATURES

To prepare our students for reading chapters 4–7, we tell them that they are going to meet Huck's father, Pap, reminding them that what Twain the writer has a character say is not necessarily what Twain the man would say or believe, as he often makes fun of his characters. For their entry tickets following the reading, students write their impressions of Pap and state one action that contributes to those impressions. In their groups they share their views of Pap in order to decide what Twain is criticizing in presenting Pap in this exaggerated manner. We direct students to look particularly at Pap's behavior in the judge's house, his treatment of Huck, and his tirade against the government. To take advantage of the group's thinking, we suggest that students conclude their group time together by writing their journal entries for sections in chapters 4–7 dealing with Pap.

The journal entries relating to Pap provide the verbal material for creating a cartoon representation of Pap, one that reveals the human weaknesses that the students have identified as targets of Twain's satire. Students who don't have the artistic ability to create caricatures of Pap may piece together their cartoon in collage fashion with cutouts from magazines brought to class for that purpose. Each group presents its cartoon to the class, explaining what is being attacked and referring to the section of the novel that inspired the creation. Students read the appropriate passages aloud, dramatizing the dialect as well as they can. The purpose here is to enable students to recognize Twain's deliberate exaggeration of Pap so that we not only laugh at him but also see his embodiment of bigotry, greed, and hypocrisy. These vices are ugly; they deform us and defile our humanity.

Joe focused his cartoon (Fig. 3-7) on Pap's contempt of education and his foolish pride in his illiteracy. As the "balloon" states: "I don't want no son o' mine gettin' a ejucation. I didn't get none and look how great I turned out!"

Figure 3-7. *Caricature of Pap*

Joe focused his cartoon on Pap's contempt of education and his foolish pride in his illiteracy. As the "balloon" states: "I dont want non son o' mine gettin' a ejucation. I didn't get none and look how great I turned out!"

CREATING DIALOGUE

After students have read chapter 8, they have some questions, particularly about what Jim is saying. To help them find the answers to their questions, we read aloud the dialogue between Huck and Jim, beginning with Jim's explanation of why he has run away. Reading aloud to our students enables them to grasp much more of Jim's meaning than they did from their silent reading of this unfamiliar dialect.

Because character is revealed best in dialogue, we ask our students to create a dialogue in which Huck explains the faking of his murder and his arrival on Jackson Island. We encourage students to incorporate as much of the dialect in their dramatizations as they can in order to maintain the tone of the novel.

The following sample reveals Huck's cleverness during his escape as well as Jim's desire for freedom:

The Jackson Island Two

by Sugar Hogshead

Huck: Whatcha doin', Jim?

Jim: I been a wonderin'. How'd ya come ta be on here island when folks in town all think yo died?

Huck: I run off, Jim. I had to on account of Pap woulda killed me fer sure if 'n I stayed.

Jim: Den you's right, Huck. You had to go. Just don' see why ever'o thinkin' yer dead.

Huck: Well, Jim, it's like this. I had to cover my tracks so Pap wouldn't look fer me no more, ever.

Jim: How'd ya come to be here?

Huck:	First I had to plan an escape. It warn't too hard 'cause Pap was gone drinkin' every night an' I had time.
Jim:	So what'd ya do?
Huck:	After huntin' round Pap's cabin fer a time, I found an old saw an' I started working a hole in the wall. Pap come afore I's finished though. He was his usual self (which wasn't good for me). That was the night he tried to kill me. He was drunk outta his head and screamin' he's seein' snakes. Then he gets to screamin' at me 'bout how I'm the death angel. He gets to chase'n me, but I was quick an' he couldn't touch me, and he got tired 'ventually 'n stopped.
Jim:	He didn't lay a finger on yo, did he, Huck?
Huck:	Not a one.
Jim:	Well, dog my cats, Huck, if'n yo Pap didn' kill yo, who did?
Huck:	I ain't dead! All they seen was blood, an' it weren't my blood, neither. It was pig blood.
Jim:	How'd they come ta take a pig's blood for yern?
Huck:	Hush up, Jim. I's gettin' there. See, I knew I could catch me a boat, on account that the river was risin' 'n all, 'n I got luck an catched myself a right fine canoe. Later I caught a raft fer Pap to sell fer drinkin' money, an' he off an' went to town. Well, I finished sawing the hole in that log, an' then I loaded up my canoe. Last, I shot myself a hog.
Jim:	Oh, that's the way of it!
Huck:	Yup. I cut that hog's throat 'n let it bleed right there in the cabin. While she was bleedin' I wrecked up the rest of the place like there'd been a fight. I dragged a bag of rocks to the river (to leave tracks like a body) an' threw them in. An' as the finishin' touches, I bloodied up an ax an' stuck my own hair to it. I got rid of the pig aways down from the cabin, shoved off in my canoe, an' never looked back.
Jim:	Well, I'll be. That's all mighty fancy, Huck. Wish I had brains like that.
Huck:	Well, there's a fine thing. I spill everythin' to you an' you sit and won't tell me nothin'. Come on, I won't tell. I can't, I'm dead, 'member.
Jim:	Yeah, I reckon yo is. Well, if yo won't tell, I run off, Huck.
Huck:	Jim! Now why'd ya go do a crazy thing like that?
Jim:	I had to, same as you. I hear Miss Watson the widow talkin'. Miss Watson said a man offered her a whole lot of money to sell me down to Orleans, an' she was considerin' it purty hard. I couldn't let myself get sold down South, so I took off, right then. I hadn't got no

> fancyness like you, Huck. I jus' had to go, an' go I did. I lit o'er to the sho' an' hid dere all night an' all de next day. Dey didn't miss me none, though, 'cause I'm always gone afore sunrise, an' de servants would take a holiday soon as the Missus left. After dark I ran down dat river, fixin' ta get myself a raft. I jump right in and swim near half across an' get myself in among the driftwood. I didn't make no track. Well, dat raft come along an' I climb up on it, but only fer a rest, 'cause I had to go off when I seen a man on the sho'. I swam in an' I've been livin' on berries 'n truck ever since.

Huck: Jim, you're in a heap o' trouble.

Jim: I know it.

EXPLORING IDEAS

Students read the rest of the episode involving Jim and Huck's growing relationship through chapter 16. To reinforce their understanding and synthesize their learning, we ask each group to explore the characters of Jim and Huck by considering the roles that each plays. For example, they consider *Jim as a protector of Huck; Huck as a protector of Jim; Huck as a liar;* and *Huck as a practical joker.* Students look for evidence of these roles as they read, and in each case they identify any evidence of Twain's attacks on human vices and follies. They record all their findings in their journals. In class, students work in their groups to develop presentations of one of the character roles revealed in these chapters.

For example, a group dealing with Jim's instinctive protectiveness of Huck concentrated on chapter 9, in which Jim finds shelter from the storm for himself and for Huck and protects Huck from seeing the dead body in the floating house. Students also looked at the chapters related to the incident on the *Walter Scott* in which Jim tries to dissuade Huck from taking the risk of boarding the sinking wreck. In addition, they examined chapter 15, in which Jim worries about Huck and tries to find him when they are separated in the fog. In each instance, Jim's good heart is revealed, but so is his naivete and superstition, on which Twain bases much of his humor.

A group considering Huck as protector of Jim studied chapter 8, when Huck agrees for his own selfish reasons not to tell on Jim; chapter 11, when Huck gets information in St. Petersburg about the townspeople's plans to search for Jim; and chapter 16, when Huck protects Jim from the slave hunters. In addition to understanding the conflict that Huck experiences between his good heart and his sense of civic duty, students saw that Twain is attacking the vices of bigotry and cowardice.

A group exploring Huck as the practical joker focused on chapter 10, in which Huck plays an almost fatal trick on Jim with the snakeskin, and chapter 15, when Huck tries to convince Jim that he had imagined the fog and their separation. Once again Jim's gullibility allows him to be fooled, at least initially.

A group exploring Huck's increasing facility with lying looks first at chapter 11, when Huck is caught pretending to be a girl; chapter 13, when Huck convinces the ferryboat man to save the "family" on the *Walter Scott;* and chapter 16, when Huck fends off the slave hunters by telling them that his father has smallpox. In each instance, students discovered Twain's satiric attacks on the hypocrisy and greed of supposedly upstanding folks.

Some groups are quickly inspired with an idea, whereas others need suggestions from the teacher. When groups ask for ideas, we suggest that they might create a rap, a song, a poem, a monologue, a dramatization, a collage, or a series of limericks. While we encourage variety among the groups, we do not insist that each group's presentation be unique. Even so, the results of our students' efforts are usually varied, always interesting, and sometimes even inspired.

The group responsible for tracing Huck's increasing ability to lie dramatized the time that Huck disguised himself as a girl, finagled the ferryboat man to save the "family" on the *Walter Scott*, and convinced the slave hunters that his Pap was suffering from "the pox." Students created poster-board, audience-reaction signs with words or phrases on them that expressed Huck's success or failure in lying. For example, in chapter 11, when Huck forgets that he previously told Judith Loftus that his name is *Sarah* Williams and tells her it's *Mary* Williams, one member of the group held up the OOPS sign and invited the class to join in the verbal response to Huck's slip. Later, when Mrs. Loftus tosses "Sarah Mary Williams" a lump of lead, and Huck instinctively clasps his legs together as any boy would—instead of spreading his legs, as a girl would, to allow her skirt to catch the lead—a group member held up a sign that said SNAGGED and, of course, expected the class to chime in with "snagged." When Huck is more proficient with his lying, as with the ferryboat man and the slave hunters, students held up a sign that said WAY TO GO!

To further involve their audience in the presentation, students distributed response sheets for their classmates to complete after viewing the dramatizations.

Practice Makes Perfect

Rate Huck's performance as a liar. Give him **** if he's terrific, *** if he's okay, ** if he's got a lot to learn, and * if he's a total washout.

___ Huck pretends to be a girl.

___ Huck tries to save the robbers.

___ Huck tries to save Jim from the slave hunters.

___ Huck tells Jim that he only dreamed about the storm.

A group focusing on Jim's protectiveness of Huck created a collage, using pictures from magazines to reflect Jim's finding the cave, covering the dead body, trying to dissuade Huck from boarding the *Walter Scott*, and searching for Huck in the fog. Students selected an appropriate quote from the text to accompany each visual representation. The significance of each part of the collage was explained by a different member of the group.

> Chapter 9: *"Well, you wouldn't a' ben here 'f it hand't a' ben for Jim. You'd a' ben down dah in de woods widout any dinner, en gittin' mo' downded, too; dat you would, honey."*
> Huck, the White boy, is supposedly superior to the Black slave and therefore the one to take care of Jim, but actually it's Jim who takes care of Huck.

> Chapter 9: *"Come in, Huck, but doan' look at his face—it's too gashly."*
> Jim doesn't want Huck to see the horror of a dead body; he wants to protect him from emotional pain, the way you would expect a caring father to protect his son.

> Chapter 12: *"I doan' want to go follin' 'long er no wrack. We's doin' blame well, en we better let blame well alone, as de good book says. Like as not dey's a watchman on dat wrack."*
> Jim sees danger for both himself and Huck if they go on the wrecked ship, but Huck's curiosity doesn't let him listen to Jim. When Huck boards the wreck, Jim follows to protect him.

> Chapter 15: *"When I got all wore out wid work, en wid de callin' for you, en went to sleep, my heart wuz mos' broke bekase you was los', en I didn't k'yer no mo' what become er me en de raf.' . . . Dat struck dah is trash, en trash is what people is dat puts dirt on de head er dey fren's en makes 'em ashamed."*
> Jim has been worried to death about Huck, afraid he has been lost in the storm. Jim seems to care more for Huck than even for himself, and here all Huck has been doing is trying to play another trick on Jim.

The group exploring Huck as a practical joker wrote a song to be sung to the tune of the theme song from *Gilligan's Island.* The class joined in on the chorus.

Huckleberry Finn and a Slave Named Jim

by The Screech Owls

There once was a boy named Huckleberry Finn
Who ran away with a slave named Jim.
With him Huck made some big mistakes,
Like tricking Jim with rattlesnakes.

Chorus: Huckleberry Finn and a slave named Jim

Then one day a rain storm came,
And washed down a house frame by frame,
Huck insisted they look inside,
Where they found a man had died.

Chorus: Huckleberry Finn and a slave named Jim

> Then Huck saw a great big wreck,
> He just had to explore the deck.
> "Huck," Jim said, "jes' let it be,
> Them crooks are killers, believe you me."

Chorus: Huckleberry Finn and a slave named Jim

> A good excuse was what Huck sought,
> So those killers would be caught.
> To make that happen he had to lie
> But leastways no one had to die.

Chorus: Huckleberry Finn and a slave named Jim

> A soup-thick fog split Huck from Jim
> Who feared the boy was lost to him.
> Huck claimed the fog was all a dream
> And made poor Jim feel real mean.

Chorus: Huckleberry Finn and a slave named Jim

> But ole Jim was no one's fool,
> And saw that Huck was just bein' cruel.
> Huck's lie 'mos' broke his heart to bits
> So Huckleberry promised no more mean tricks.

The group exploring Huck as protector of Jim created a dramatization of Huck's divided conscience. Students placed two chairs back to back; sitting in each chair was a Huck. One Huck was the "good" boy who obeys the law and the rules of his society. The other Huck was the "bad" boy who follows his heart and violates the law and the rules. The visuals were signs held over each Huck to identify who was which. As each Huck articulated his thinking—first in chapter 8, then in chapter 11, and especially in chapter 16—a student displayed a sign identifying the chapter from which this scene came. Students filled out a chart showing Huck's reasons to tell, on one side, and Huck's reasons not to tell, on the other. The final section of the chart asked students to explain which Huck Twain prefers and why.

SYNTHESIZING THE LEARNING

To synthesize the learning represented by their presentations, we may, depending on the makeup of the class and the nature of the group projects, assign a composition in which we ask the students to trace the changes in Huck as reflected in the adjustments in his relations with Jim and his growing awareness of human weaknesses. To facilitate the writing of this assignment, we advise students to review their journals, the work they did on their own presentations, and the other students' presentations from chapters 8–16. To help students organize the composition, we remind them that the introduction should explain what they intend to prove about Huck's development; the body of the composition should include detailed examples of those changes in Huck; and the conclusion should include a statement of what they believe Twain wishes to say about the relationship between Huck and Jim. Sonia revealed her insight in the following composition:

The Changing Attitude of Huck Toward Jim

Huck's attitude toward the runaway slave Jim changes dramatically throughout their river journey. At first, Huck treats Jim in a manner that was very characteristic of most Southerners of the 1850s. Huck refers to Jim with the derogatory term *nigger,* and he takes advantage of him merely to gain a good laugh. Jim is simply not a real person to Huck, and because of this Huck does not offer him much respect. In fact, he plays a variety of tricks on Jim.

Huck's first and most harmful trick is placing a dead snake in Jim's blanket. Huck doesn't want to hurt Jim; he just wants to have some fun. But the dead snake's mate enters the camp and bites Jim on the heel. The result of this is disastrous, as Jim is laid up for almost 3 days. The prank could have proven fatal if poor Jim had not managed to get out all of the snake's "pison." Still, despite the severity of Huck's "harmless joke," Huck does not seem to learn any lesson from it except that the trick confirms Jim's previous superstition about the unluckiness of snakes. Huck doesn't see that it was actually wrong for him to play the joke on Jim in the first place, and because of this Huck does not hesitate to play a second joke on poor Jim.

His second prank seems to provide the basis for a major turning point in the relationship between Jim and Huck. When Jim thinks that Huck had gotten lost within the thick fog the previous night, Huck decides to make Jim believe that he imagined the whole thing. However, when Jim finally discovers that he is again a victim of one of Huck's jokes, he is deeply hurt.

Jim says, "my heart wuz mos' broke bekase you wuz los', en I didn't k'yer no mo' what become er me en de raf'. En when I wake up en find you back ag'in an' all safe en soun', de tears come, en I could a got down on my knees en kiss yo' foot. I's so thankful. En all you wuz thinkin' 'bout wud how you could make a fool uv old Jim wid a lie. Dat truck dah is trash, en trash is what people is dat puts dirt on de head er dey fren's en makes 'em ashamed" (p. 129).

This statement seems to tell us that Jim's entire role has changed. Instead of humbling himself to Huck or ignoring the joke altogether, Jim defends himself with a pride and an authority that Black people would not think of showing a White person at that time. Evidently it is not Jim who is ashamed of his behavior but Huck who feels guilty for hurting Jim's feelings. As Huck says, "It was 15 minutes before I could work myself up to go and humble myself to a nigger; but I done it and I warn't ever sorry for it either." Huck says he'll never play another mean trick on Jim.

Huck needs Jim because he needs a friend, and whether he admits it or not, he also needs somebody to care for him. Jim is that somebody. He refers to Huck as "honey," and he takes over Huck's shifts on the raft just to let Huck sleep. Huck gradually begins to understand that Jim has feelings like everybody else and that he cares for Huck. However, Huck still cannot see Jim as being entirely human, least of all equal to him and entitled to equal treatment. Because of this, Huck begins to have second thoughts about carrying Jim aboard the raft with him. Huck still wants to act lawfully. He decides that he will tell on Jim the moment they reach Cairo. Yet, as soon as Huck has made his decision, Jim begins to praise him, saying such things as "Jim won't ever forget, Huck. You's de bes' fren' Jim's ever had en you's de on'y fren' old Jim's got now. Dah you goes, de ole true Huck, de on'y white gentleman dat ever kept his promise to ole Jim." Because of this, when Huck is approached by two slave hunters, he simply cannot tell on Jim. Instead, Huck finds himself telling the two men that it is his poor sick father on the raft instead of a runaway slave. It is at this crucial juncture that Huck's feelings for Jim are solidified. Whether the action is unconscious or not, Jim has become the father that Huck has never had.

RIDICULE AND RAPSCALLIONS

After our students have completed reading chapters 17 and 18, they return to their groups to identify the human weaknesses that Twain ridicules here. They usually recognize the hypocrisy of the Grangerfords and the Shepherdsons going to church to hear a sermon on brotherly love and then resuming their deadly feud. They also see the absurdity of a feud, the reasons for which no one seems to remember. Students are less likely to recognize Twain's ridicule of the romanticism of death and of cultural and social pretentiousness. Our students' degree of involvement with these more sophisticated satirical attacks determines the attention we give these concepts.

The cultural pretentiousness of the aristocratic Grangerfords may be apparent to our students as Huck describes the paintings on their walls: "Mainly Washington and Lafayettes, and battles, and Highland Marys . . . and crayons by Emmeline Grangerford." If our students comment on the entry tickets about Emmeline's pictures—"blacker, mostly, than is common"—or on her obsession with suffering and death as evidenced by her scrapbook and poetry, then we discuss the satiric intent there and encourage students to find contemporary parallels.

We emphasize the contrast Twain makes between the two young boys, Huck and Buck. Even their names suggest the many parallels; however, we want our students to recognize the major differences between them. To this end we ask each to create a chart detailing the similarities on one side and the differences on the other.

How Huck and Buck Are Alike	How Huck and Buck Are Different
They are the same age, have similar names, like to play practical jokes, react according to the rules of their society, don't like to be "sivilized," and don't like school.	Only Buck thinks it is right to kill the Shepherdsons; only Huck helps a runaway slave; only Buck tries to shoot someone; only Huck is sickened by the feud.

The most significant difference is revealed in chapter 18 when Huck is disgusted with the actual killing of human beings, even though he had been disappointed earlier in the story when Tom Sawyer's gang didn't shoot anyone. These aristocratic people are just as cruel and despicable in their behavior as Pap, and with even less cause; they should know better, but, as Huck says, their behavior "made me sick."

Students continue reading chapters 19–23. We ask them to write an entry ticket expressing their reaction to the duke and the king and to cite some specific words or deeds that generated that reaction. We use the entry tickets as the basis of a class discussion of the duke and the king as the "rapscallions" whose greed is the focus of the satire in this section of the novel. Students easily recognize their eagerness to take advantage of the naivete and generosity of others as well as their indifference to the pain and suffering they cause in others. The discussion prepares students to resume work in their journals, stating Huck's observations, which are a little less naive now than earlier in the book, on one side and Twain's satirical intent on the other.

INSIGHT INTO HUMAN NATURE

We focus special attention on the last section of chapter 23. Here Huck discovers Jim as a human being, a father who can grieve over the pain of his child. This focus makes a poignant contrast to the senseless slaughter of children by the Grangerfords and the Shepherdsons and the selfish indifference of the duke and the king to the orphaned Wilks sisters. Students review what Huck has learned about Jim to this point in the story to determine if Huck has any new understanding of Jim. To that end, we read aloud the section beginning with "I went to sleep and Jim didn't call me when it was my turn . . ." through the end of the chapter. They recognize immediately the depth of guilt that Jim feels for having unfairly punished his poor deaf daughter. For the first time, Huck understands the devotion Jim has for his family. We ask students to list their insights and compare them with those of other members of their group. Students note these new understandings of Jim in their journals and make inferences about Twain's intent in creating this incident. "What," we ask them, "do you think Twain wanted us to recognize that Huck would not be capable of understanding because of his acceptance of the rightness of his 'betters' in society?" Their responses reflect their understanding of Jim as a sensitive human being, certainly one much more devoted to his children than Pap is to Huck or the aristocratic Colonel Grangerford is to his children.

When students have completed reading through chapter 30 and making their journal entries, we ask them to identify the two human weaknesses satirized in chapters 19–30 and to provide a brief explanation of how they know. These explanations, based on evidence from the text, become the basis for our students to find examples in contemporary life that these human vices still exist—in different guises, but as cruel and destructive as anything that Twain describes in *Huckleberry Finn*. Current newspapers and news magazines provide more than enough examples of hypocrisy, greed, gullibility, bigotry, cowardice, pretentiousness, and deliberate cruelty for our students to draw parallels between the fictional depictions in *Huckleberry Finn* and the real-life reports. Depending on the nature of the class, students may work in their groups to complete their research. The reports of their findings and the parallels with evidence from the novel may take different forms, again depending on the class. An oral report from each group, presented with a chart depicting the parallels, may be appropriate. In another class we might ask each student to compose a composition. Here Jennifer compares examples of greed and gullibility in the novel with the behavior of today's hucksters and their victims:

The More Things Change, the More They Stay the Same

People aren't perfect. They never have been and never will be. Throughout history, greedy people have taken advantage of gullible and often willing victims. The truth of that condition is evident in Mark Twain's novel *Huckleberry Finn*, written in the late 1800s, and in the actions of people today.

One example of greed and gullibility in *Huckleberry Finn* involves the king at a camp (revival) meeting. The king and Huck wander into a small town and come across at least 1,000 people crowding under sheds and listening to preaching. The preachers are shouting, "Oh, come to the mourners' bench! Come, back with sin! Come, sick and sore! Come, lame and halt and blind! Come, poor and needy, sunk in shame! Come, all that's worn and soiled and suffering! Come with a broken spirit! Come with a contrite heart! Come in your rags and sin and dirt! The waters that cleanse is free, and the door of heaven stands open—oh, enter in and be at rest!" All the listeners are reacting enthusiastically, yelling and then crying.

The king, realizing an opportunity to make some quick money off these people who seem to be buying everything they hear, jumps up to the platform and begins his "sad story." He tells everyone that he has been a pirate for 30 years in the Indian Ocean but that last night his whole outlook on life changed. He was robbed and put ashore with no money, but now he is mighty glad that this happened. He is a changed man and wants to go back to the Indian Ocean to try to reform all the pirates. The king makes sure to mention that he doesn't even have 1 cent to his name, but nevertheless he will return to the ocean. When he reforms a pirate, he promises he will say, "Don't you thank me, don't you give me no credit; it all belongs to them dear people in the Pokeville camp-meeting, natural brothers and benefactors of the race, and that dear preacher there, the truest friend a pirate ever had!" Just as the king expected, the people yell to take up a collection, and the king collects $87.75, thanks to the gullibility of the townspeople. Obviously, they all want to believe the pirate story, so they give money without even thinking.

Another instance of greed and gullibility also involves the king and the duke, this time playing with the emotions of the Wilks girls. When Huck and the king are paddling toward a steamboat, they come across a young man who mistakenly believes that the king is Mr. Wilks from England. The king tells him that he isn't, but he is able to learn all about the Wilks family. Mr. Wilks' brother, Peter, has just died, so the king inquires about the people in the town and the financial situation of Peter Wilks. There are two brothers, it seems, who live in England and were informed about a month ago that Peter was sick. One of the brothers, named William, is deaf and dumb and the other is Harvey. Peter left Harvey a letter that tells where he hid his money. Peter had hoped to see his brothers before he died, although his nieces, Mary Jane, Susan, and Joanna, took care of him. The king sees another chance to make some big money, so he and the duke, posing as the Wilks brothers, arrive in town.

The king and the duke are greeted in town and act grief-stricken when they hear that their dear brother has died before they had a chance to see him. They put on a great act of sobbing over the coffin, and Mary Jane and her sisters believe the king and the duke without question. Even when a longtime friend of Peter Wilks, Dr. Robinson, insists that this is a trick (he recognizes the English accent of the king and the duke as fake), the girls will not listen. They are in an emotional state and are completely gullible. They are easily manipulated because they want so badly to believe in the king and the duke that they even turn over their own money to them for investment. Huck, though, can't stand to see these girls being taken advantage of, and he tells Mary Jane the truth about the king and the duke. In the meantime, another set of "Wilks brothers" arrive, claiming to be William and Harvey. In the end, when the money that Huck hid in the coffin to keep it away from the king and the duke is discovered, Huck, the duke, and the king all escape to the raft, but this time the king and the duke don't get away with any money. They get too greedy, so they lose everything. But without Huck and the timely arrival of the real Wilks brothers, the king and the duke might have succeeded.

An article on David McTaggart, a former executive of Greenpeace, an international wildlife protection agency, reveals the weaknesses of greed and gullibility. In most cases, people believe the claims of that organization without a second thought because of its reputation for protecting the environment. Then David McTaggart, greedy for money and power, joined the organization. Even though he said that he had been a "successful real estate executive who saw the light at age 39 and decided to save the planet," the truth is actually quite different. McTaggart was actually a failed real estate promoter who left investors and relatives in debt and who would disappear right before his projects completely failed. McTaggart saw the environmental group as a way to get money and power. He began by siphoning money from Greenpeace savings accounts, money to protect the Earth, into his own accounts. McTaggart even produced a propaganda film called *Goodbye Joey* in which some scenes were staged by paid kangaroo shooters who were eventually fined for torturing kangaroos for the film. Even after the fraud was reported, thousands of people still believed the film was an honest depiction of what was occurring, and they continued to donate $20, $30, or even $100 to save kangaroos.

More recent is the case of Ellen Cooke, former treasurer of the National Episcopal Church, who has been found guilty of embezzling $2.2 million in church money from 1990–1995. Cooke stole the money to support her lavish lifestyle, which included two opulent homes, limousines, private schools for her sons, travel, and expensive gifts for herself and her friends. She had been able to embezzle the money by controlling the church accounts and assuring the church leaders that she was carefully investing the money—donated to support the work of the church, specifically in its work for the needy. The judge who sentenced Cooke to 5 years in jail called her a "common thief" who looted church funds "to live the lifestyle of someone she was not."

Sadly, human weaknesses such as greed and gullibility are passed down from generation to generation, which makes *Huckleberry Finn* a novel as relevant today as it was 100 years ago. Children learn values from their parents and from the society around them. Unfortunately, too many children are learning that greed is okay as long as you don't get caught. This cycle of corruption will have no end unless we expose and punish the greedy people who prey on the gullibility of others.

Chapter 31 requires special attention because it is the turning point in Huck's emotional odyssey. To appreciate the significance of Huck's dilemma, we have our students review their notes on "Huck as Protector of Jim" from chapters 8–16. We want them to consider the moral conflict that Huck has wrestled with throughout the river journey, trying to decide whether to protect Jim or turn him in. Now Huck faces a crisis. He must decide once and for all to follow his good heart and protect Jim or to follow his social conscience and report on Jim's whereabouts.

THE FINAL EPISODE

Not only do some literary critics have difficulty with the last section of *Huckleberry Finn*, chapters 32–43, but so do our students. They don't understand why Huck agrees to Tom's elaborate hoax, especially after what Huck has learned about Jim. Our goal as teachers is to give our students the opportunity to draw their own conclusions, however. By examining the book through the lens of social satire, our students can see that Twain is using the final episode of his novel to make yet another attack on the vices and follies of human beings.

In their groups, students list the things that bother them about the last episode of the novel. They may also list what they like about it. What seems to bother most students is the apparent contradiction between Huck's earlier growth in understanding Jim's humanity and his willingness now to play games with Tom that prolong Jim's captivity. Nor do students readily comprehend Jim's willingness to tolerate the indignity of his treatment at the hands of Tom and Huck, considering his growing assertion of himself as a person worthy of respect. We remind students that throughout the novel, Twain regularly has Huck say one thing or perceive reality one way while Twain suggests a very different perception for the reader.

Keeping the requirements of the literary talk show in mind, students explore possible reasons for Twain's creating such an ending for his novel. Each group is to arrive at an explanation of the targets of Twain's satire—that is, what human weaknesses or vices he is attacking in this section. The work that our students have invested in drawing parallels between Twain's satiric attacks on human weaknesses and contemporary examples of those same weaknesses helps our students to recognize the satire in this final episode. Once we complete our consideration of the ending of the book, we allow time for students to complete their journals.

CREATING THE LITERARY TALK SHOW

The groups are now ready to begin planning their talk shows. To help them, we give the following directions:

The Literary Talk Show

You are the writers of the literary talk show. The producer tells you that on [a specific date] Samuel Clemens, better known as Mark Twain, is to be the guest on an upcoming show. You are to consider the questions that the talk show host will ask the author of *Huckleberry Finn.* You may decide to have the questions revolve around one major issue or concern, such as the moral and motive of the book, recent charges of racism, the purpose of the ending, or the contemporary relevance of satiric attacks on human weaknesses.

Once you have determined the focus of the discussion, your script (allow 20 minutes for a show, including the host's questions and Mark Twain's answers), you may let Twain bring with him characters from *Huckleberry Finn* who express their own points of view about their behavior. Here the journals, monologues, dialogues, and dramatizations will be helpful.

The show can be presented live or pretaped on video. The obvious benefits of video include the opportunity (a) to revise, (b) to create a professional format with music and credits, and (c) to enhance the production with computer graphics and thus present a more polished product.

Although we encourage the use of video for the project, sometimes we find that time constraints, limited access to appropriate equipment, or lack of technical support can preclude a video presentation. Nevertheless, the planning and scripting is done within the context of a television talk show, a format with which are students are very familiar.

In their groups, students brainstorm for ideas on the format of their shows and begin to draft their proposals. They then fill out the following proposal form:

Proposal for Talk Show

A good literary talk show tries to re-create the content and flavor of a book in order to make some significant comment on it or arrive at some insight into it. The purpose of your show is to demonstrate your understanding of Twain's intent and the continuing impact of the book on each generation of readers.

Describe the focus and content of your literary talk show.

Describe the roles of each member of your group, both in planning and performing your presentation. Each member must contribute to planning, writing, and performing.

One student group, "Borrowed Chickens," outlined the focus and format of its literary talk show as follows:

For our literary talk show, we will focus on the satire by asking Mark Twain to comment on hypocrisy and greed after we reenact the following scenes:

1. The church, where the Grangerfords and the Shepherdsons semingly appreciate a sermon on brotherly love while they sit there with rifles between their legs, and plan how to kill each other after the service is over.
2. The revival meeting at which the duke pretends to be a reformed pirate.
3. The ferryboat, where the captain agrees to save the robbers from drowning only after Huck convinces him that they are relatives of rich, old Mr. Hooker.

There will also be a debate between Mark Twain and the talk show host, who will criticize the ending of the novel as flawed and racist. Mark Twain will maintain that the ending is a logical conclusion to the narrative, the intent of which is satirical.

After students have had some class time to plan their talk shows, develop proposals, and begin drafting scripts, we check their progress by having them fill out the chart in Figure 3-8.

Figure 3-8. *Talk Show Project Progress Chart*

Date:

Group members: _____

_____

_____

Work we accomplished this period (clarify contributions of each group member): _____

_____

_____

_____

Work we need or plan to do outside class (specify who will do what):

_____

_____

_____

Work we plan to do in class next time we meet in groups:_____

_____

_____

After we have approved the design for the production, making revisions where necessary, students work on their scripts. This takes two or three class periods. Students with access to video cameras complete their projects at home. For students without their own camcorders, we schedule after-school time for them to use the video equipment from our media center. In some cases, students present their talk shows live, and we videotape them. Whether the productions are professional in quality or clearly amateurish, they always demonstrate our students' insight into Twain's satiric intent in *Huckleberry Finn*. The script created by the "Dog My Cats" group exemplifies the students' investment in the novel. All the parts were performed by group members, some of them having to assume more than one persona.

Script for "Dog My Cats" Production

Announcer: Welcome to *Talk Television* with Michelle Perino. Here she is now. Let's greet Michelle! [Display APPLAUSE sign.]

Michelle: Today on *Talk Television* we're talking about Mark Twain's *The Adventures of Huckleberry Finn*, its satiric intent, and the controversy over the novel in some schools. Sitting with me now is a professor at Columbia University, Dr. Brunhilde Key. Dr. Key, you have written many articles and essays about why certain novels, including *Huck Finn*, should be banned from schools. What are your reasons for censoring this novel?

Key: I think it's obvious. It is one of the most racist novels ever written. All of the characters are racist—some more than others, but all of them are racist.

Michelle: Why do you say that? I agree with you that some are racist, but *all* of the characters?

Key: Throughout the novel everyone treats Jim as inferior because of his race and tries to make a fool of him. At the end of the novel, even Jim feels that he isn't as good as the other characters because of his race. He goes along with Tom and Huck's crazy plan to help get his freedom because he thought they were smarter than he just because of their race. He allows himself to suffer because of his color. A later guest will elaborate on this point.

Michelle: Are there any other reasons that you feel this novel should be banned from schools?

Key: Absolutely. Not only is this novel racist, but the hypocrisy, greed, and lack of concern for human life that the characters show should not be allowed in schools, either. The characters in this book are terrible role models for our children. It will teach them those qualities, and the effect will be devastating to our community. If we allow our children to read this novel, someone might want to act like one of these characters. This was the case with *The Catcher in the Rye:* Mark Chapman killed John Lennon because of the influence of Holden Caulfield. Do we want another tragedy to result from children reading *Huckleberry Finn*?

Michelle: Holden Caulfield didn't try to kill anyone. I don't see how it is the fault of the novel in cases like Chapman's. People realize the difference between right and wrong, and if they choose to do wrong it is not because of the actions of a character. Teachers today help children to understand the novels they read if they are not able to understand them by themselves.

Key: I agree with your last statement, but I do not believe there is anything worth understanding in *Huckleberry Finn.*

Michelle: That's a debatable statement and one I'm sure Samuel Clemens, better known as Mark Twain, would like to respond to. Here, now, is Samuel Clemens to do just that. Welcome, Mr. Clemens! [Enter Clemens. Display APPLAUSE sign.] Thank you for joining us, Professor Clemens. What is your response to Dr. Key's assertion that there is nothing worth learning in *Huckleberry Finn*?

Clemens: The novel does not promote racism, greed, or anything else that Dr. Key has accused it of doing. I satirized these aspects of 19th-century society by creating caricatures, exaggerating and distorting behavior, and understating and overstating ideas to reveal human weaknesses. For example, in the preface of the novel I asked the readers not to look for any real meaning in the book. This obviously means the opposite of what it says. Do you really think an author would not want you to get anything out of his work?

Key: The trouble with this is that you, or should I say Mark Twain, want readers to get your twisted opinions and morals from the book. Just look at the obvious racism shown in the enslavement of Jim, the greed reflected in Pap, the hypocrisy of Miss Watson, and the lack of concern for human life exhibited by the Grangerfords and the Shepherdsons.

Michelle: Before you respond to that, Professor Clemens, we have to break for a commercial, but when return we will have a special visitor from the novel itself. Don't go away.

Commercial

Young Man: Why are you looking so down in the dumps?

Young Woman: I'm supposed to take a test on *Huckleberry Finn* and I haven't had a chance to read the book.

Young Man: *(chuckling)* That's no problem! Just go into the student book store and get yourself some *Pit Notes.*

Young Woman: *Pit Notes?* What are they?

Young Man: They tell you in one easy-to-understand paragraph what the book is about, and then there's a line describing the main characters.

Young Woman: Yeah, but what about the plot?

Young Man: The story is covered in another short paragraph. I just read the one on *Huckleberry Finn,* and it's really neat.

Young Woman: Sounds like what I need, all right. But does it bring up the analytical questions that teachers are always asking?

Young Man: *Pit Notes* will never let you down. It's all there: the satiric attacks on human weaknesses, the symbolism of the river and the shore, the relationship between Huck and Jim—everything you ever need to know.

Young Woman: Wow. Thanks for the tip. It's the *Pits* for me!

Michelle: If you are just joining us, we are talking about *Huckleberry Finn* with our special guests: Dr. Brunhilde Key, a professor at Columbia University, and Samuel Clemens, better known as Mark Twain, the author of *Huckleberry Finn*. Mr. Clemens, you have three special guests here today, is that right?

Clemens: No, unfortunately Jim wasn't able to come. The show was in conflict with his daughter's wedding.

Michelle: Why don't you bring the first guest out and introduce him to us?

Clemens: This is Huckleberry Finn's father, Pap Finn. [Pap Finn enters. Display BOO sign.]

Michelle: Hello, Pap, welcome to the show.

Pap: What's all these folks gawkin' at? Seems as if they ain't never seed no rich man 'afore. That's what I am too, 'n don't be forgitin' it. Soon as I gits me my rights I'll be 'bout the wealthiest man you ever seed.

Key: You see, Michelle, Pap is a prime example of all the horrible role models in this book. Almost every character speaks as incorrectly as he does, not to mention the greed he displays. This man tried to steal money from his own son.

Pap: Don't you go callin' me a "role model," an' don't you say nothin' 'bout my boy, nuther. I ain't never done nothin' wrong by him. The widow, she's the one who done it, sendin' him to school so he can put on all those frills.

Key: Listen to that. This man is antieducation. How can such material be suitable to read in our classrooms?

Michelle: Clemens, you've been very quiet. Do you have any response?

Clemens: I can't believe this. Just look at Pap. He's a caricature. How can you possibly think that I, as Mark Twain, intended the reader to take seriously a word he said?

Pap: Mark Twain? Is he who you all are talkin' 'bout? Why, I heared of him. He letta slave go free in his book, that's what I heared. The minute I hear such trash, I made up my mind I'd never read nothin' Mark Twain ever wrote, even if I could read.

Key: Mr. Clemens, you just heard that statement. Are you denying that Pap exemplifies immoral and racist behavior?

Clemens: I'm not denying that at all. Pap is a bigot and a racist. I made him that way so that I could satirize people like him.

Key: What about all the characters who think like Pap? Why would you want to make fun of every character in the book?

Michelle: Professor, what do you mean by that?

Key: Every character in the book is a despicable role model.

Pap: Hold on now, lady. Don't you go callin' me no "role model."

Key: Oh yes, excuse me.

Michelle: Professor, can you elaborate on what you mean by "role model"?

Key: Actually, your other guest, Huckleberry Finn, could explain it better than I.

Michelle: Okay. Let's bring him out. Please welcome Huckleberry Finn. [Huck enters. Display APPLAUSE sign.] How are you, Huck?

Huck: I'm fine, ma'am.

Key: Huck, would you please tell us about some of the friends you met on the river, specifically Buck Grangerford?

Huck: I don't right like talkin' 'bout Buck, considerin'.

Key: Please, Huck, could you just tell us what happened?

Huck: Well, Buck's family had this feud goin' with some other folks, an' one day their boy and the Grangerford's girl run off together. Neither family took too kindly to that an' they ended up killin' each other off. It was somethin' terrible. The mos' terrible part was that I knowed they was runnin' off—well, I sorta knowed— and I didn't say nothin'. I wish I had, though.

Key: There you have it. This novel contains violence and promotes cowardice. Huck admitted that he would rather have had the feud continue than risk his own neck to stop such senseless killing.

Clemens: Give the kid a break! He witnessed the slaughter of two families. The fact that he wished he could have prevented it shows how much he values human life.

Key: But what about Buck? He didn't value human life.

Clemens: Exactly; that's what I was satirizing. Buck and his privileged family didn't value human life in the least because they were part of this savage feud, which was accepted in their society.

Michelle: All right, now I understand how the other characters have faults, but what about Huck and Jim? They're the heroes, right? So they don't have any faults.

Key: On the contrary. Huck and Jim have the most harmful faults of all. They fail to accept their equality as human beings. Huck, why don't you explain how you freed Jim?

Huck: Well, all me and Tom done was try to free him. Miss Watson's will was what really done it. But we dug him out 'n all. Tom had a real nice plan. He knows everything 'bout prisoners. Some of Tom's plans didn't make much sense, but Jim allowed we was White and so he was satisfied.

Key: And why were you satisfied with Tom's plan?

Huck: I dunno. I guess I figured Tom knowed what he was doin', bein' a reader of books and stuff. Besides, it would get Jim just as free as my plan would, an' it was more fun.

Key: Do you see? The entire end of the book ruins Huck and Jim! Twain builds up their characters throughout the novel until they practically see each other as equals. Then at the end of the story, Huck and Jim act as if they learned nothing. This is obviously gross inequality. Twain is basically saying that equality for Blacks and Whites is not possible.

Michelle: Clemens, you look upset. Do you have anything to say?

Clemens: I don't know where to begin. Professor Key, you have completely misunderstood the book's intent.

Michelle: Why do you say that?

Clemens: The book wasn't about the characters—it was about their society. That's why the characters had so many faults; they were in a flawed society.

Key: So why did Huck and Jim go through their transformations in the middle of the book if they were supposed to be so faulty?

Clemens: In the middle of the book they weren't in society! They were traveling on the river. In the end they become unequal again because they are back in society. And remember; Jim, a slave all his life, and Huck, an ignorant 12-year-old boy, are both products of that society.

Key: Listen to yourself. You can't admit that—Mark Twain was racist, and so you're making elaborate excuses when the truth is so simple.

Michelle: Please calm down.

Clemens: Don't call me a racist, and don't tell me what the truth is. It took me 8 years to figure out all I wanted to say. I think I know what I mean.

Michelle: I think we need a commercial break so we can sort all of this out.

Commercial

Young Woman: I see you're writing an essay on *Huckleberry Finn*; that's what I have to do by tomorrow. Gosh, you've really written a lot—like five pages. Excuse me for asking, but how long did it take you to write five pages on this book?

Young Man: It's easy when you've got *Pit Notes.*

Young Woman: *Pit Notes?* Did they help you write all that?

Young Man: You bet. They give only the bare bones facts of a book—you know, the main characters, a plot summary, and the main idea of the book. Besides, this is the only study guide that will give you the background history of the Mississippi River and the Louisiana Purchase.

Young Woman: Wow. No wonder you wrote so much, and all from *Pit Notes.*

Young Man: Like I always say, "Before I write an essay, I make a *Pit* stop!"

Michelle: Welcome back. We've been talking to Samuel Clemens, better known as Mark Twain, and Dr. Brunhilde Key about the controversial novel, *Huckleberry Finn.* To conclude today's program, let me ask if either of you has anything to add to what you have already said?

Clemens: Yes, I want to emphasize that I wrote this book because I was disgusted by the people in society. The novel is satirical. I don't understand how Dr. Key can sit here and call me a racist.

Key: Easily—I didn't see the novel as satirical in the least.

Clemens: Then you need to learn how to read.

Key: I'll ignore the insult.

Michelle: Dr. Key, hearing Mr. Clemens speak of his intent in writing *Huckleberry Finn,* have you changed your mind about the book?

Key: Absolutely not. It should be censored. Twain and his novels are racist.

Clemens: I don't care if my novel is banned from schools, because I don't want my opinions forced on children. I'm not much for booklearning in classrooms, anyway. But my book is not racist, nor am I. I helped some Black children go to college. Don't ever call me a racist.

Michelle: That's all the time we have for today. I would like to thank all of our guests for joining me today. Tune in tomorrow when we visit Holden Caulfield in the mental hospital and talk to the author of *The Catcher in the Rye*, J.D. Sallinger, in his first-ever public appearance. [Display APPLAUSE sign.]

ASSESSMENT AND EVALUATION

Assessment and evaluation are ongoing throughout our study of *Huckleberry Finn*. As students read the novel, we determine their familiarity with the text through periodic entry tickets. Students' comprehension of the nuances of their reading is assessed through their double-entry journals. To assess these journals, we apply the following criteria:

- Accuracy of references to the text
- Completeness of significant details
- Understanding of satiric intent
- Insight into differences between Huck's perceptions and the truth

This simple list gives us a quick and effective way to assess students' knowledge and understanding of the book. We learn more about their understanding of the personalities and dialect of the boys through their creation of 1-minute monologues. Once again, we keep the assessment instrument simple, giving them a list of criteria for a successful monologue:

- Accuracy of detail
- Ability to reflect the character's personality
- Accuracy of voice and dialect

We create similar criteria for assessing their caricatures, dialogues, charts, and presentations. However, if we assign an analytical essay, such as a comparison between Twain's treatment of human vices and contemporary parallels, we create a formal rubric, not only to help students in the creation of their compositions but also to give us an evaluative instrument (Fig. 3-9).

Because the synthesizing project for this unit is the literary talk show, we spend time throughout the study of the book preparing students for an evaluation of this aspect of their learning (Fig. 3-10). Even before student groups begin to work on their talk show scripts, we discuss with them the characteristics of an effective talk show in general and of a literary talk show specifically, at least as they can imagine it. The characteristics they identify, along with the details of the assignment, become the basis for the rubric. We provide the categories: content, process, and presentation. As students begin to develop their scripts, they also identify the specific characteristics of a successful literary talk show. Not surprisingly, students identify under *content* the need for the talk show guests from the book to be faithful to the satiric spirit of the novel and the language of each character. They also say that it is important for each show to reveal some in-depth understanding of themes and literary techniques. Under *process* students always

Figure 3-9. *Rubric for Assessment and Evaluation of Essays*

QUALITY	Expert	Craftsman	Journeyman	Apprentice	Novice
Meaning: the extent to which the essay exhibits sound understanding, interpretation, and analysis of the text	Selects significant vice satirized by Twain and parallels it perceptively to a current news story; reveals insight into Twain's satire; describes completely the difference between a news story and Twain's satirical narrative.	Selects important vice satirized by Twain and parallels it effectively to a current news story depicting that same vice; conveys a clear understanding of the ways in which Twain satirizes the vice and the difference between a news account and Twain's.	Selects a vice satirized by Twain and connects it accurately to an appropriate news article describing a similar vice; shows an understanding of Twain's satire and of elements of news style.	Provides some understanding of a vice described by Twain but doesn't discuss satire; makes a weak connection between vice in Twain's narrative and a news article; relies on summary.	Exhibits little or no understanding of Twain's attack on a human vice and fails to connect that vice with a parallel news story; contains inaccuracies of fact.
Development: the extent to which ideas are elaborated through the use of specific, accurate, and relevant evidence from the sources	Supports thesis with abundant, significant facts, incidents, details, and relevant direct quotes from both Twain and the news article; contrasts satire of Twain with news approach with convincing specific examples.	Supports thesis with sufficient appropriate facts, incidents, details, and relevant quotes from both Twain and the news article; contrasts Twain's satire with news approach with effective specifics.	Supports ideas with appropriate, if not the most significant, facts, incidents, details, and some quotes; deals with satire with at least one example; presents parallel vice without contrasting to Twain.	Supports ideas with some references; includes few facts and incidents from the novel and the news article as support; limited quotes; details may be irrelevant or inaccurate.	Conveys vague or unsupported ideas, or presents random list of details; includes inaccurate and/or irrelevant references from the novel and the news story.
Organization: the extent to which the essay exhibits direction, shape, and coherence	Introduction has sophisticated discussion of issue in general statement, provable thesis; body pages develop aspect of thesis in a logical clear way; appropriate topic sentence for each body page; conclusion infers larger connection to real world.	Introduction has a relevant general statement, significant provable thesis; body pages develop thesis logically; appropriate topic sentence for each body page;conclusion infers larger connection to the real world.	Introduction has a general statement and provable thesis; body organized logically; conclusion summarizes content.	Some attention to thesis in introduction and attempt to organize discussion, but organization is simplistic or formulaic; conclusion vague and may be misleading or not follow from discussion.	No provable thesis. Shows little evidence of organization and is difficult to follow; weak conclusion.
Language Use: the extent to which the essay exhibits effective use of words, sentence structure, and sentence variety to convey ideas and information	Conveys ideas and information in original and precise language, with a noticeable sense of voice. Makes effective use of sentence structure and length to convey ideas; uses transitions effectively.	Conveys ideas and information in original and precise language. Shows consistent use of sentences that are varied in length and structure; consistent use of transition for coherence.	Uses ordinary language or language from the source to convey ideas and information. Some sentence variety but little variety in sentence beginnings; some attention to transitions.	Uses ordinary, often imprecise, language to convey ideas and information; sentence flow choppy; relies on sentences that lack variety in structure and length; may contain syntactical errors.	Includes vague, inappropriate, and/or incorrect language. Contains mostly simple sentence structures, marred by run-ons and/or sentence fragments that interfere with meaning.

Figure 3-10. *Rubric for Assessment and Evaluation of Literary Talk Shows*

Content (50)   Score _____

  Accuracy Re-creates characters from the book, keeping faithful to
            the spirit of Twain's novel and its satiric intent.

   Insight Makes significant comment on the book and demon-
            strates an in-depth understanding of themes, character,
            and techniques.

Originality Reflects unique approach to presenting that insight.

Creativity Develops presentation in interesting, inventive ways.

Process (20)   Score _____

Each group member contributes consistently to group effort.

Students work together to create an outstanding final product.

              Detailed written script

              Working outline

              Progress reports

              Rehearsed and memorized performance

              Edited final product

              Product completed on time

Presentation (30)   Score _____

Performance

              Polished

              Coherent

              Articulate

              Interesting

              Visually engaging

                Total Score _____

Commendations

Recommendations

---

want each group member to be held accountable for contributing to the project and for working cooperatively. Under *presentation* they identify an interesting, rehearsed performance as most important, whether the talk show is presented on video or live.

We formalize the rubric as appropriate before we distribute copies to each group to guide their creations and to remind them of the need for self-assessment along the way.

To celebrate the accomplishment, we invite other classes who have been reading or have read the novel and other teachers and administrators to be the audience for the literary talk show presentations.

CONCLUSION

Exploring *The Adventures of Huckleberry Finn* as social commentary, culminating in a literary talk show, not only provides a motivation for studying a novel written a century ago but enables our students to discover the relevance of the book in contemporary society. In their reading, writing, speaking, and listening activities, students can recognize the tragic consequences of hypocrisy, bigotry, greed, pretentiousness, and self-righteousness in the 1850s and today. These discoveries are the result of their journal writing, entry tickets, discussion of issues raised by their exploration of the novel, and the collaborative preparation of creative presentations. These kinds of activities, coupled with the opportunity for students to use sophisticated video and computer equipment in their individual and group productions, engage students of various intelligences in the study of the novel. This approach also enables them to reveal a deeper understanding of the nuances of meaning in *Huckleberry Finn* than is likely with more traditional approaches that culminate only in analytical compositions. This is not to suggest that we eliminate analytical exposition from our literary studies; rather, it is only one of many strategies through which students can understand and relate to what they read.

The format of the literary talk show and the activities that provide the scaffolding for its creation are suitable for the study of many texts, both classic and contemporary, especially those complex texts that might otherwise be inaccessible to our students.

ADDITIONAL TEXTS

Additional texts for which the literary talk show is effective include the following:

Antigone by Sophocles: The personalities and events of this complex text are made more easily comprehensible through the format of the literary talk show. By interviewing Creon, Ismene, and Antigone, students can explore the complexities of their motivations for their actions. Students can also examine the issues raised by the play, such as the conflict between obedience to state laws and one's individual moral conscience and/or religious principles.

A Thousand Acres by Jane Smiley: This novel lends itself to the talk show format because the novel raises so many questions about the parallels to Shakespeare's *King Lear.* Author Jane Smiley can answer questions, not only about the parallels of the book to *King Lear* but also about the accuracy of her description of family life on a Midwestern farm to reality. This format requires students to formulate questions and know the book well enough to create a lively dialogue and come up with credible answers to those questions.

Prince of Tides by Patrick Conroy: This book has a number of complex and interesting characters, whose interactions can provide the material for a lively roundtable discussion. Students need to know the book well enough to write a scenario that reveals the dynamics of the interpersonal relationships that make Conroy's book relevant to our students.

The Joy Luck Club by Amy Tan: This story intrigues students because of the universal intergenerational conflict. However, because of the structure of the book and the clash of cultures, the talk show format enables students to make meaning of the book by creating interviews with Amy Tan and the major characters from the book.

Things Fall Apart by Chinua Achebe: Students often have difficulty following the organization of Achebe's story of the impact of Western culture on African tribal life and traditions. The talk show requires them to lay out the events of the book in a chronological sequence that will enable them to understand the events and the characters well enough to create a dialogue.

I Know Why the Caged Bird Sings by Maya Angelou: As with the other titles we have mentioned, the talk show format provides an author lens through which the students look at characters and events and raise questions about why Maya Angelou chose those particular events from her life to dramatize. In creating the scenario for the talk show, students explore the author's belief that family support and faith in oneself, coupled with hard work and tenacity, can enable individuals to overcome any adversity.

CHAPTER 4

The End Justifies the Means and Other Campaign Strategies

Voting for our leaders is a basic exercise of our rights as citizens of a democracy. An examination of the process, both in deciding for whom to vote and in campaigning for the candidate of our choice, offers rich possibilities for bringing the real world into our classrooms. Moreover, it offers us the opportunity to involve students in authentic tasks that mirror real life and extend student learning by taking an interdisciplinary approach. Closely related to the topics covered in literature are the essential questions and curricula of the social studies classrooms. Our study of *Lord of the Flies* by William Golding, for example, has always been shaped by the consideration of issues of leadership and the concerns raised about the seeming impotence of democracy in the face of a determined totalitarian threat. Therefore, it is logical to make explicit the connection between our work and the study of government in social studies. We review our ideas with the social studies teachers and look for opportunities to make that connection, correlating our curriculum and scheduling with theirs.

To initiate our studies, we ask our students to describe the characteristics of a good leader—perhaps a student whom they would like to have represent them on the school board. They say, facetiously, that they would like someone who could lobby for free periods, no homework, and exemption from final exams. But then, in all seriousness, they say that they would like a student leader who has enough respect among adults so that their legitimate concerns would get a fair hearing. Recently, one student, Jennifer, said that it would have been good to have had a student on the school board last April when girls' tennis was being cut as part of an economy measure. John agreed and added that a student representative would also have been helpful when Coach Smith's job was in jeopardy because of budget concerns. Although students did successfully petition to keep him on staff, an actual advocate on the school board could have made a crucial difference, the students agreed. As a result of this discussion, the students decided that an important quality of a good leader is the ability to get results, to accomplish what those who elected that leader wanted. They identified many other qualities, too, such as being an articulate speaker and being persuasive, principled, and honest.

As we list these qualities on the board, we ask students whether, in the past, they have taken these qualities into account when voting for student leaders. Students have no trouble recognizing that, as a limitation of democracy, attractiveness and popularity more often than not determine who gets elected in school and in the larger community. They consider the reasons for this, focusing on the power of the media, particularly television, to influence the outcome of elections in ways that often work against the candidate who has the best qualifications but the poorest media presence.

This discussion is even more relevant when social studies teachers are also focusing on issues of leadership, either from a historical perspective, such as exploring the kind of leadership that was required for the Continental Congress to agree on the Declaration of Independence, or from a contemporary perspective, such as examining the leadership styles of recent political leaders, including Bill Clinton, George Bush, Al Gore, Newt Gingrich, and Bob Dole.

We then pose the essential questions of our study: (a) What are the limitations of democracy? and (b) What are the requirements for leadership in a democracy?

To consider the answers to these questions, students identify some advantages of democracy, focusing primarily on the election of leaders and their ability to govern effectively. Students spend several days in the library and on the Internet researching democracy and preparing themselves to grapple with these essential questions. After completing their research, they reassemble as a class to share perceptions and understandings. Part of the conversation in one class illustrates the nature of student inquiry on this issue:

> **Carolyn:** To me, free and open elections are the heart of democracy. I see only strength in being able to choose your own leaders.
>
> **Anthony:** Yes, but what about money? Unless you have a lot of money, you can't run successful campaigns for most offices. Remember Ross Perot in the 1992 election? He got 20% of the vote, but he spent a fortune of his own money for television time that no one else had enough money to buy. He really bought a lot of those votes. How is that democratic?
>
> **John:** Okay, so one of the limitations of democracy is that it takes big bucks to be a candidate, and that has nothing to do with qualifications.

Carolyn: But public access stations and equal air time laws for major candidates help, don't they? And don't forget the forums of groups like The League of Women Voters.

Chrissy: And I especially like the trust placed in us common everyday folks. How neat to be given all that control over our own government. I remember the last school board election. Mrs. B. won by only three votes. Imagine, if three people had stayed home or four others had gone to vote, her opponent would have gotten elected. So my vote really counts. It makes a difference whether we vote or not.

Anthony: Yeah, and how many people actually *do* vote, especially in local elections like for the school board? My research shows that only 3,500 votes were cast in the last school board election, out of a possible 25,000. That's ridiculous! So, if I'm one of those nonvoters, the winning candidate certainly doesn't represent me.

Carolyn: But that was your free choice! In a way, by not voting, you *did* influence the outcome of the election, in this case for Mrs. B.

Students go on to discuss the other problems they have uncovered as they researched democracy: selecting the best candidates, often having to choose between two candidates they don't really like or know, getting anything done by elected officials once they *do* get into office, and other limitations of a democratic system, in which the majority rules.

ENGAGING STUDENTS IN THE NOVEL

At this point, we introduce *Lord of the Flies* by telling our students that the very limitations of democracy that they have identified in their discussions are at issue in this book. However, the novel is not a political treatise; it is an adventure story containing all the elements of excitement that make reading enjoyable. When we ask them to identify those elements, they mention action, violence, humor, suspense, and, of course, conflict. We list the elements on the board and tell our students that they are going to have the opportunity to plan an adventure story that incorporates all these characteristics.

To accomplish the task, we ask students to organize themselves into groups of three. Each group is to devise a story plan that includes the following five plot elements gleaned from the book:

- Plane crash
- Remote deserted island
- Twenty survivors, ages 6–14
- Tall, attractive, pleasant boy with fair hair and brown eyes

- Muscular, intense, authoritative boy with well-groomed, short, red hair, and blue eyes

Each group drafts an opening for the story. Students are quick to see that the survivors will need to organize in some way and that the two boys who have been described may compete for leadership of the group. One group created the following opening for its story:

> Troy hated to fly. He had hated it ever since his father was killed in a plane crash. Now here he was, flying over the ocean with a bunch of other kids from his boarding school, going to Bermuda to compete in a soccer tournament. Suddenly, the plane dropped and began to shake violently. The seat belt sign flashed on as the pilot apologized for the sudden turbulence and tried to reassure the passengers that all would soon be well. Troy was scared, but he felt really sorry for the littlest kids, who looked terrified. He reached over to the child next to him to try to comfort him, but as he did, the plane dipped to the right and began to nose dive and shake violently. That was all Troy remembered until he came to, still strapped in his seat but no longer in the plane, which was now a wreck mired in the sand of a beach.
>
> Troy struggled to loosen his seat belt and get to his feet. Painfully he lifted his body and looked around. The small boy that had been next to him on the plane lay unconscious in the sand. Hovering over him was a tall, dark-haired, pleasant-looking boy whom Troy recognized as David, one of the senior boys who had always been kinda nice to him. Just as Troy started to call out to David, he noticed Jason standing nearby. Jason was saying something to David and looking red-faced and angry. His blue eyes glared intensely at David, who was trying to revive an injured child.
>
> "Leave him alone," snarled Jason authoritatively. "We gotta figure out where the hell we are and how we're gonna get outta here."
>
> "Where's the pilot?" David asked.
>
> "Dead along with the rest of the crew." Jason ran his hand through his red hair. "It's just you and me and a bunch of little snot-nosed kids."
>
> "How many?" David wanted to know.
>
> "As far as I can tell, there are twenty of us. Which means one of us, being the oldest, has to take charge. And it better be me because you'll spend your time wiping noses instead of finding us a way to get out of here."

The students who created this introduction outlined their plans for the story to include a major conflict between David and Jason. Actually, this is the general direction of most groups' story ideas, a result that we count on to engage our students in reading the novel and in exploring the dynamics of leadership. With that goal in mind, we ask students to examine the two protagonists in their stories and to describe what they envision as the leadership style of each boy. Invariably, the tall, attractive, pleasant boy is characterized as compassionate and concerned with the welfare of others, whereas the muscular, intense, authoritative boy is characterized as manipulative ("bossy," students say, "gotta be in charge"), unconcerned with the feelings of others. This contrast, our students predict, will result in conflict, more often than not characterized by violence.

Our students are quick to recognize that this contrast between the two boys and their approaches to leadership is common in real-life politics and historically manifests itself in power struggles, sometimes bloody, even in democratic societies. We point out that this universal struggle for leadership is the subject of Golding's novel and the focus of our study as we explore the appeal and limitations of two very different kinds of leaders. The framework of our exploration is an election campaign. "You," we tell them, "are going to select candidates, create party platforms, and run an election campaign to put your person in charge. Golding's novel and your responses to his story will help you to create your campaign to elect a leader—either a 'David' or a 'Jason.'"

MAKING MEANING OF THE TEXT

Journals

Once the purpose of our study is established, students read the book. We allow them approximately 2 weeks to read it and to gather the material they need to select their candidate and formulate an election platform. To help students organize the information from the text and think about it, we have them keep a four-column response journal. In column 1 they cite key events. In column 2 they assume the persona of Jack and respond to each event; in column 3 they assume the persona of Ralph and respond to each event. In column 4 they comment as themselves to both the events and the characters' responses, keeping in mind two questions: (a) What does Golding have to say about the kind of leadership necessary for effective governance and (b) what are the implications for democracy, in Golding's view?

The first three chapters of the novel focus on the boys' attempts to form a democratic government and to organize themselves for survival and rescue. The issues considered here invite comments in students' journals on freedom, the characteristics of good leadership, the limitations of democracy, and the inherent nature of humanity.

When we are coordinating with social studies teachers, we often select two candidates for one elected office, either on a national or local level to track. The four-column journal process works well here; in place of events, students list campaign issues and then respond first as one candidate, then the other, and then add their own thoughts, questions, and reactions in the fourth column. Social studies teachers find the four-column journal to be an effective technique to get students to hone in on the key issues of an election and to do some real thinking about each candidate.

Figure 4-1. *Sample Journal for* Lord of the Flies, *Chapter 1*

Event	Jack	Ralph (pronounced *Rayf*)	Personal Reaction
Young boys are apparently alone and on a deserted tropical island after a plane crash.			I don't think this so great. I'd be afraid if I were abandoned on a deserted island. How will they survive? How will they be rescued?
Ralph finds a big pink shell; Piggy identifies it as a conch and tells Ralph how to sound it as a way to call all the boys together.	Rats, it's a kid who blew that horn; there are no grownups here after all, just that kid with the shell horn and a bunch of little brats. I guess I'll take charge.	This is cool, no grownups. I do whatever I want. That fat kid Piggy is a pain. "Ass-mar, my Auntie says . . ." what a wimp, but he has some brains. He knew how to blow that conch shell—neat.	
At the meeting, the boys realize they need to organize; they hold an election and elect Ralph as leader instead of Jack because he had the conch and was attractive.	I should be leader. Stupid kids. Even my own boys voted for Ralph.	Wizard! I like being chief. I know Jack thought he should be chief, but I had the shell. I made him happy 'cause I put him in charge of the hunters.	Kids in charge of kids! They chose Ralph as leader just because he's good looking and has that conch. Those aren't reasons to elect anybody. Yet isn't that what happens all the time in a democracy . . . we elect the most popular or best-looking people for office, even for president of the United States.
Ralph asserts his leadership and puts Jack in charge of hunting and the choirboys as his army of hunters; he gives Piggy the job of taking everybody's name.	Anyway, I am the leader of the hunters. I like that, chief of an army of hunters. And nothing is more important than meat.	Piggy wanted to explore the island with Jack and me, but I didn't want him to . . . he'd just be in the way. I know he felt bad; that's why I told him to take everybody's name.	Ralph made a smart move by putting Jack in charge of the hunters. Jack could have been big trouble, but Ralph made him an ally. I wish he were kinder to Piggy, but Golding is being realistic in his depiction of kids, maybe of human nature. We always seem ready to pick on the most vulnerable.
Ralph, Jack, and Simon explore the place, see that it's an island, see that it's deserted, and decide it belongs to the boys.	Yes! It's our island and Ralph and I are in charge. We're gonna have a great time.	Wacco! This is great! It's all ours.	
Jack tries to kill a pig, but cannot bring himself to do it.	Next time I'll kill that pig and lots of pigs. I'll show 'em all.	What's a matter with him? Some hunter! Didn't he know you're supposed to stick a pig? These littluns have got the crazy idea that the creepers are snakes at night, beasties that'll get 'em . .	Of course he couldn't kill the pig. It's not so easy to take a life, any life. But living in this uncivilized setting, I suspect Jack will kill pigs and even take pleasure in it.
Little boy confesses fear of the "beastie," the snake-thing. Boys make a fire in the night to attract rescue. Piggy's idea, but no one notices. Fire goes out of control. Jack and Ralph begin to disagree with each other.			

To get them started, we model a journal entry for chapter 1 (Fig. 4-1).

This four-column journal enables students to make meaning of their reading and prepares them for the project. By taking on the personae of Jack and Ralph, students get close to the reactions of those characters and begin to gather the data that will enable them to develop their campaigns to elect one of the boys as leader. The personal-reaction column prompts students to think about the nature of leadership in a democratic context and the pitfalls of a process that is subject to the vagaries of individuals.

Students then use the model to help them create journal entries for chapters 2 and 3. These entries form the basis for a class discussion of those chapters that will focus on the actions taken to organize the boys into a society that can survive and help to effect their rescue. Students comment on Jack's cleverness in using Piggy's specs to start a fire. They are not surprised that initial efforts to create a signal fire lead to disaster, with the fire going out of control. Many are appalled that one of the children is apparently killed in that fire. They often predict that this is a very bad sign of what is to come. Reacting to the third chapter, students comment on Jack's preoccupation with tracking pigs and the introduction of conflict with Ralph over priorities. Ralph values shelter and rescue, whereas Jack values the immediate need for meat. Students also note that the "littluns" are afraid of the "snake-thing" or what they begin to call the "beastie," the unseen terror that they fear. These responses give us an opportunity to identify the needs that must be addressed if a society is to flourish: food, shelter, and security or safety. They notice that Ralph is having difficulty providing all three because he is unable to galvanize the boys to follow through sufficiently to complete any one project.

Dramatizations

Because chapter 4 introduces a major conflict between Ralph and Jack, we have students concentrate their attention on this conflict and its implications for the survival of this fragile democratic society. In their journals, students predictably comment on the enormity of the consequences of Jack's neglect of the fire in order to kill a pig just as a ship that could have rescued them was passing within sight of the island. They also comment on Ralph's lack of authority and Jack's confidence and assertiveness during the conflict over the fire. They sympathize with Jack's frustration in being unable to share his triumph with Ralph, and they are impatient with Ralph's obsession with the fire.

To dramatize the conflict and focus student attention on the potential for disaster, we initiate a psychodrama in which students decide to play either Jack or Ralph. We select one primary "Jack" and one primary "Ralph" who improvise the beginning of the confrontation. Students are invited to interject arguments, either as Jack or as Ralph, at any given moment. Our role as teachers is to keep the confrontation in play by prompting students with appropriate questions, such as

"What really bothers you about the way that Ralph is ignoring your gift?" and, for Ralph, "What are you worried about now that Jack has let the chance of rescue go by?"

After the psychodrama, we ask students to remain in character but deal in a nonconfrontational way with the reasons behind their words and actions. From this discussion, the students develop a better understanding of Jack as someone whose intentions are initially admirable and who justifiably feels unappreciated in this situation. We see him acknowledging his responsibility for letting the fire go out and showing a willingness to meet Ralph halfway by apologizing. We also understand Ralph's position as a leader whose primary responsibility is to effect a rescue. The psychodrama highlights just how precarious their society is now that Ralph and Jack no longer seem to be working together.

For their journals, students consider chapters 5, 6, and 7 together because in these chapters the children must face their fears and Ralph must assert his leadership or lose it. We organize students into groups of three to share their journals and to identify and list the problems that threaten this fragile democratic society. We ask them to be prepared to cite textual references in support of the problems they have identified. A portion of one group's list follows:

- Carelessness of their sanitation (p. 80): "We chose those rocks beyond the bathing pool as a lavatory . . . the tide cleans up the place . . . now people seem to use anywhere . . . that's dirty."
- Failure to build adequate shelters (p. 80): "The shelters might fall down if the rain comes back. We'll need those shelters then."
- Allowing the fire to go out (pp. 80–81): "The fire is the most important thing on the island. How can we ever be rescued except by luck without the fire . . . Can't you see we ought to—ought to die before we let the fire out?"
- Fear of the unknown that is causing things to break up (p. 82): "We've got to talk straight . . . about this fear and decide there's nothing in it . . . then we can start again and be careful about things like the fire."
- Tension between Jack and Ralph (p. 91): "And you shut up! Who are you anyway? . . . Just giving orders that don't make any sense. . . ."
- Jack's hostility toward Piggy (p. 90): "Who cares what you believe— Fatty!"
- Threat of order by rule (p. 91): "The rules! You're breaking the rules . . . because the rules are the only thing we've got!"

Discussions

Student-generated lists prompt class discussion about the universality of these problems and the kind of leader necessary to cope successfully with such threats to the stability of the social structure. While most of the problems cited are evident in chapter 5, we encourage the groups to explore the ways in which these problems play out in chapters 6 and 7. Students are quick to see the focus on the problem of fear in these chapters. Jack and Ralph appear to put their rivalry aside in order to confront the common external threat, particularly after Sam and Eric describe the beast they have seen on the mountain. Together, Jack and Ralph set off to confront the "beast."

We ask students to consider historical examples of such temporary reconciliation between rivals. Depending on their work in social studies, they may cite such alliances as those between the allies (Roosevelt and Churchill) and Joseph Stalin during World War II as well as the temporary alliance between the Catholic and Protestant Irish to fight for Irish independence in the early part of the 20th century.

Visual Representations

The focus of chapters 6 and 7 is on the increasing open antagonism between Jack and Ralph as well as the dread the boys express as they search for the beast. We ask students to meet in their groups and create a visual representation of the two forces that drive the action in these chapters: fear of the unknown and the increasing conflict between Jack and Ralph. Students have the opportunity to fulfill this task in a variety of ways; they may draw a picture, create a collage, or design some kind of three-dimensional sculpture. We provide poster paper, assorted magic markers, and magazines. Students display their products to the class, explaining the symbolic significance of their creations and the evidence in the chapters that prompted their representations. Their oral descriptions of their visual creations become a springboard for class discussion of the ways in which Ralph tries to exert his authority in the face of these fears and this antagonism.

Exploring Thematic Ideas

Chapter 8 is so rich that we ask students to review it, share their journal entries within their groups, and jot down whatever questions are generated by their review (Fig. 4-2).

Student discussion focuses primarily on their questions about the last section of the chapter, in which Simon talks with the pig's head. Most students have difficulty understanding that section, and their personal responses in their journals reflect that confusion. To help them make sense of this crucial episode, we convene the class as a whole and have students read from pages 143–144 aloud. As they read, we chart what the pig's head is saying on the board, revealing the clear connection among the "Lord of the Flies," the beast, and the boys. This connection becomes clear to them when they read aloud ". . . I'm part of you. Close, close, close! I'm the reason why it's no go? Why things are what they are? . . ." To clarify the meaning of title "Lord of the Flies," we tell them that it is a transla-

Figure 4-2. *Sample Journal for* Lord of the Flies, *Chapter 8*

Event	Jack	Ralph (pronounced *Rayf*)	Personal Reaction
Jack calls a meeting to discuss their having seen the beast.	Who does Ralph think he is? He's not any kind of leader—he can't hunt and get us meat. All he does is talk and say things like Piggy. It's time for me to take over and be chief.	I don't understand Jack. All he cares about is hunting. I'm just as brave as Jack. I went to find the beast like a good chief should.	Obviously Jack is using this meeting as a way to make Ralph look bad in front of the others. That's a pretty sick move, something you see in politics anytime.
Jack calls Ralph a coward and asks for a new election. When no one votes for Jack, he quits the tribe and goes off by himself.	What a bunch of losers! I don't play anymore. I don't need anybody. I'm a hunter, and I can take care of myself.	I'm still the chief. Who needs Jack? He'll come back.	I expected Jack to win the election; I thought the kids would vote for him because he is the hunter and might be able to protect them from the beast. Jack's going off by himself means the beginning of the end of their democratic society.
Piggy and Ralph try to decide what to do. Piggy encourages Ralph to build the fire on the beach.		I don't know what to do. We can't go back up on the mountain and build the fire because the beast is there. I can't even think straight anymore. Thank God for Piggy; he always has an idea.	Piggy and Ralph can't do it all by themselves. The only help they have is from "Samneric," which isn't enough.
They kill the sow, cut off her head, and put it on a stick. They say it is a gift for the beast.	I did it! I killed the sow! What a kill—she was huge and wild and I killed her. I cut off her head. It was grinning and black with blood. The beast won't bother us anymore.		That was gross. In the beginning they couldn't even touch blood, now they cover themselves with it. Cutting off the head and giving it to the beast is like some kind of primitive religious ritual. It's so hideous that they even frighten themselves. Totally uncivilized!
Jack becomes a dictator and flaunts his power over his savages.	I told 'em all they could join me and my hunters and live along the beach. We hunt and feast and have fun. They'll come, probably Ralph and Piggy, too. Maybe I'll let 'em eat and maybe I won't. I love it when my hunters call me "chief" and raise their spears and shout, "The chief has spoken." They'll do anything I want.	I don't understand what's happening to me. I can't think. I'm scared and I don't know what to do.	Jack loves power. He lords it over the kids and makes them do anything he wants. He's a total dictator compared to Ralph, who has tried to be democratic.
Jack invites the boys to a feast on another part of the island. Ralph is becoming disoriented, even forgetting why the fire is so important.			The boy's tragile civilization is coming apart. Jack splits from the group, and Ralph seems to be losing it. Only Piggy has some sense. This is really bad. Without Ralph these kids have no hope of surviving and being rescued.
Simon talks to the pig's head.			I don't get this. How can the pig's head talk to Simon? And why is it the "Lord of the Flies"? Is he saying the beast is the boys? Why does the voice of the pig's head start to sound like Jack? What is going on here?

tion of the Hebrew name *Baal-Zevuv* (*Beelzebub* in the Greek translation of the Bible), a Philistine god whose name became synonymous with the Christian Devil. According to critic E. L. Epstein, [the] "name suggests that he is devoted to decay, destruction, and demoralization, hysteria, and panic" (see Perigee edition for his comments).

Students have trouble accepting that all the boys are really the beast. They connect quickly, however, with the idea that Jack is the beast, recognizing the "voice" of Jack in the lines on page 144: ". . . We are going to have fun on this island. Understand?" We point out that Simon seems different from the others. He alone is able to understand who the beast really is. It is so upsetting to him that he loses consciousness.

Now that the students have begun to understand the concept of the beast being present *within* the boys rather than as an outside threat, we have the groups discuss chapters 9 and 11 in terms of this idea. How does the inherent evil in humanity manifest itself in these chapters? They note the mob psychology of the reenactment of the killing of the pig and the frenzy that results. They are appalled by the death of Simon and invariably read the passage aloud that shows the depth of bestiality that is revealed in the boys when they attack Simon, believing him to be the beast. "Kill the beast! Cut his throat! Spill his blood . . ." as they leap on Simon screaming, striking, and biting. "There were no words . . . [only] the tearing of teeth and claws" (pp. 152–153). We point out that, despite the horror of this act, the boys haven't reached the depth of bestiality that allow them to kill a human being consciously. When they kill Simon, they are too far gone to realize what they are doing. However, when Piggy is killed, Roger deliberately and knowingly unleashes the boulder that crushes him. Students are riveted by the graphic description of this savage act: from Piggy's head, "stuff came out and turned red. Piggy's arms and legs twitched a bit, like a pig's after it had been killed." Students note the simultaneous destruction of Piggy, the thinking man, and the conch, the symbol of order and civilization, and realize that there is no hope for the boys as they succumb to all that is bestial within them. Once this occurs, the students no longer have trouble with the exchange between Simon and "Lord of the Flies" in chapter 8.

ESSENTIAL QUESTIONS

Students are now ready to deal with our essential questions: (a) What are the limitations of democracy? and (b) What are the implications for leadership (and, we add, of humanity) as characterized by Golding in a democracy?

They deal with the first question by tracing the fate of the democratic society established by Ralph. Then they look at the second question by tracing the evolution of Jack's rise to power, focusing on chapters 9–11 but not limited to those chapters. They review their journals for chapter 8, in which they noted that Jack quit the tribe and formed his own group, over which he exerted tyrannical powers

They also consider the earlier parts of the novel, in which Jack struggled with Ralph over leadership and temporarily accepted the role as head of the hunters and second in command to Ralph.

Evan's group traced the fate of the democratic society established by Ralph.

Alex: There was no way Ralph could control that group of kids. They did whatever they wanted.

Kerry: They weren't taking any of it seriously. It was just a game. They thought the conch was neat, so they came at first whenever it was blown.

Evan: But don't forget, Ralph got to be chief just because he was holding the conch and seemed to represent power.

Alex: Yeah. They even listened to whomever held that conch, at least just as long as it seemed fun to do.

Kerry: But when Piggy had the conch, they didn't listen. I guess that's when their democracy started to crumble.

Evan: Well, maybe but the real problem came when Jack left the group, upset that he hadn't been elected chief. I guess our democracy would fall apart, too, if people who lost elections acted like Jack.

Alex: So, that means that a limitation of democracy might work only when everybody plays by the rules, even when they don't like them.

Shamika's group focused on the second question and talked about the implications for democracy of Golding's negative view of humanity.

Daniel: You know, I kind of like Jack. I'd go with him, too. At least he promises fun, and he's doing something other than building huts that fall down, anyway.

Shamika: Hey, don't forget what he made everybody do, though. What about all that—ordering the boys to do what he wanted? They made servants out of them. Remember that he had them raise their spears and say, "The chief has spoken . . ."

Sandra: And he decides who gets meat and who doesn't.

Daniel: OK. I remember, too, how he was going to beat that guy, what's his name?

Shamika: Wilbert, I think.

Daniel: Look at this! On page 150, he's ordering all these kids around, and they have to listen, and Golding says, "Power lay in the brown swell of his forearms: Authority sat on his shoulder and chattered in his ear like an ape."

Shamika: They are apes, dancing around the fire singing that stupid song, "Kill the beast! Cut his throat! Spill his blood!"

Sandra: Ugh! That's why they killed Simon, probably. They were so worked up from that old dance that they just tore him to pieces when he crawled out of the forest.

Daniel: He got things done all right, with all that power. But we learned in social studies from Mr. Faigle that too much power isn't good. Our democracy works because a Jack couldn't do what he does here. We have checks and balances so that no one person gets total power indefinitely.

Shamika: Golding doesn't seem to have much faith in people, does he?

Sandra: No, even these little choir boys, who should know better, go off the deep end when they get the chance. They end up killing each other for the thrill of it.

As a closure activity, we ask each group to write a summary of what it discovered about the kind of leader necessary to govern successfully, given the limitations of democracy and the inherent nature of humanity as characterized by Golding. What students generally recognize is that humanity's inherently savage nature requires a strong leader, one who can control that savagery. Jack, they say, certainly is a strong leader, but there is something wrong with the leadership. We help them to see what is wrong: Instead of controlling the boys, Jack exploits their latent savagery to become a tyrant and a murderer. Students also identify that it is admirable that Jack knows how to appeal to the boys because he understands how to satisfy their immediate needs—in this case, meat and adventure. Students insist that this is an essential quality of leadership. However, we remind them that Jack also knows how to intimidate the boys by playing on their fears, by making the beast an imminent danger from which only he can protect them. Jack's power over the boys goes unchecked, and he himself becomes the murderous beast they fear.

Students see in Ralph some of the good leadership qualities that Jack lacked, but they acknowledge that these qualities, without the power to make what he says stick, doom him to failure. Ralph, at least, recognizes that they must be rescued, and until then they need food and shelter and some sort of organization. Students jokingly comment that Ralph needs a police force; then everything would be fine. They usually conclude their summaries with the idea that maybe Ralph needed some of Jack's qualities to be successful. We acknowledge that as a possibility, but we also point out that Golding shows us that a strong leader by himself is not enough. In a democratic society, unless every member takes responsibility for preserving that democracy, it will fail; this is what happens in the novel.

Students are appalled by what they see happening to the boys as they become more and more savage. They find the murder of Simon repugnant, but they can understand that it was done in a frenzy. However, they are horrified by the deliberate murder of Piggy and the primitive hunt for Ralph, which they recognize as resembling the hunt for the pig. They invariably ask whether the boys really intended to cut off Ralph's head, as they had done to the sow, and eat him. We send them back to the book to look for evidence to answer that question for themselves. Most of them conclude that Golding did indeed want the reader to believe that Ralph would have been treated like another sacrifice for the beast. They can't however, accept this as a realistic possibility, believing as they do that civilized humanity would never become that savage. They remain confident that somehow the right leader will emerge and that the boys will, under that leader, regain their civilized demeanor.

THE ELECTION CAMPAIGN

We tap into this optimism as we ask the students to imagine the boys 5 years after their rescue. They now attend a private boys' school in the United States, where Ralph and Jack are rivals once again, this time vying for president of the school's student body. To get the campaign underway, we organize the class into groups of five. Each group is to form a political party and accomplish the following:

- Choose a candidate
- Give the party a name
- Create a party platform (students identify five guiding principles— that is, what the party wants to see accomplished in the school, and a rationale for each principle)
- Create a motto that epitomizes the party philosophy
- Create a visual metaphor that reflects that philosophy
- Write an election speech for its candidate, one that contains reasons to vote *for* the candidate and reasons *not* to vote for the opposing candidate
- Present their campaign to the class, either live or videotaped
- Collect their products into a portfolio to be submitted to the teacher for evaluation

Students may also add any components to the requirements in order to enhance their campaign and their grades.

Ralph's Campaign

Because of the work that students have already done in studying the book, they are not only ready for this activity but respond to it enthusiastically. Most groups tend to want Ralph as their candidate, but, with some encouragement from us, Jack is well represented. Students especially enjoy naming their political party and creating the visual metaphor. However, to do that they must develop the party platform that provides them with a political philosophy for their candidate. One group, who called themselves The Liberty Party, chose a bell with a crack in it for their visual symbol and declared as their motto, "To make the right choice, pick the right voice: Ralph." They chose The Liberty Party because they believe that equality and freedom are the key to good government. Another party that favored Ralph called themselves The Eagles. Their visual metaphor was blind justice balancing a scale. They said that they chose the name The Eagles because it is a symbol for American democracy and the metaphor blind justice because democratic leaders must be fair to everyone. Their motto was: "If you want a say, vote my way." This slogan was chosen for Ralph, they explained, because he recognizes that in a democracy, everyone should have a voice in governance.

Typical of the party platforms for Ralph was the one created by The Liberty Party:

- Students will have freedom of speech and press. They should have the right to run a school paper and say whatever they want in it.
- Students will have a say in curriculum and homework policies.
- Students will have a student-run court to hear grievances and make judgments.
- Students will have a say in the evaluation of teachers.
- Students will participate equally with teachers on district committees.

The Liberty Party also wrote the following speech for Ralph:

> I believe that all students should be equal, that everyone should have a say in what happens to them in school. I always listen to the ideas of other people and I always try to treat people with respect. As your president, I will try to make a government that is by the students and for the students. My opponent, on the other hand, wants all the power for himself and won't pay any attention to you.
>
> I believe that you, the students, have the right to run your school paper as you wish. I will fight for your right to put into it any articles you want without the principal or superintendent stopping you. You should be allowed to voice your opinions, whether they be favorable or critical, without administrators trying to control what you say.
>
> I also believe that we should have a student court to handle our complaints and deal with us in a fair way. We should have a voice in what happens to us. Right now we don't have anyone except the principal, who makes decisions on his own, without consulting us. He can't really understand the pressures we face and deal with us impartially.
>
> As your president, I will make sure that your voice is heard in evaluating teachers. After all, who knows better than we do what is really going on in the classroom? My opponent, Jack Merridew, says he will hire and fire teachers. That's a ridiculous promise that he can never keep. And even if he could, you wouldn't want one person, Jack Merridew, to decide for you what kind of teachers you're going to have.
>
> Besides having a say in evaluating our teachers, I believe we should have a voice in curriculum planning and homework policies as well. As students, we know best what we need to learn and how much homework we can handle. If you listen to

Jack Merridew, he'll be telling you that you don't need any homework. This might sound great, but you're too smart to fall for it.

Finally, what I propose is that we be a part of all district committees. They need to hear from us. After all, we are the ones they are supposed to be serving with these committees.

As you can see, I believe you should have a say in all parts of school life. Unlike Jack, I know that school is not just about having fun. I like to have fun, too, but I know as you do that school is for learning, and we have to do some work to learn. But we can have a lot more to say about what we learn and from whom we learn, and we can have a good time doing it, too. So vote for me, and make your choice give you a voice!

Jack's Campaign

A group campaigning for Jack called itself The Bolts. They chose the lightning bolt as the party symbol because it strikes fear into the hearts of people, like Jack did. Their motto for Jack was, "Play it my way; it's the best way!" This slogan, they said, reflects Jack's assertiveness and his belief that he has all the answers. Another group favoring Jack focused on his promise of good times for the boys and called itself The Good Times Party. Their motto was, "A vote for Jack is a vote for fun." Their visual metaphor was confetti, which represents parties and celebrations. Typical of the party platforms for Jack was the one created by The Good Times Party:

- One man will rule. This is the most efficient way to get things done.
- Sports and other "fun" activities will take precedence over academics—a way to raise school spirit to an all-time high.
- Students will be free to leave the school grounds at any time.
- No homework will be assigned and no tests given.
- Student president will have the power to hire and fire teachers.

The Bolts' speech for Jack reads as follows:

I, Jack Merridew, am running for school president. I'm sure that many of you are wondering why you should vote for me. It's because I'm the man for the job. I know what this school needs. When all my ideas are put in place, we will enjoy ourselves a whole lot more. We will even have fun at school.

But what are my ideas, you're now asking yourselves. I'll tell you. For one, I say that over all, the school president needs much, much more power. Elect me president and give me the power I want, and you'll see all sorts of exciting changes in this school, changes you'll like because things will work more efficiently. I will make sure that the things you want done get done.

What changes do I have in mind? I'll tell you. I will hire and fire teachers in this school. If a teacher is giving you a hard time, I could stop it. I would see that this teacher changes his or her ways or is out of here.

I will make the lunch period longer. Right now it's too short. In 43 minutes you can't enjoy your lunch and still have enough time to play a little basketball or just hang out with friends. After all, we're here to have fun, not be slaves to classes. I'd give you two full periods for lunch. Adults have as much time as they want. Just look at how much time off our teachers have. They don't work as hard as we do, but they get plenty of time for eating lunch and relaxing.

As president I will outlaw homework and tests. Hey, when you think about it, why is it that we get so much homework now? I say, forget it. We can learn all we need to in class. Besides, I've heard people say that we learn best by doing, anyway.

And speaking of that, let's spend less time in school and get out in the world where we can do real things. As president, I will make sure that we have an open campus and can leave school whenever we want. Even better, I'll shorten the school year by giving you longer holidays.

Let's face it. School should be fun. These adults don't know what we want. Only I can give you more fun. I'll make sure that you don't have homework or tests, that you have all the time you want for lunch and sports, that you have an open campus and lots of long holidays, and I'll hire teachers who will understand that you're really here just to have a good time. So remember, a vote for Jack is a vote for fun, for good times.

EVALUATION

Critical to the success of this study of *Lord of the Flies* is the functioning of the groups. To assess each group's performance and each student's contribution to the group effort, we have each student summarize his or her contributions to the campaign and rate the group's work on a scale of 1–10. One group's self-evaluation included the following:

Overall Performance Grade: 9

Rationale: Our group worked very well together. We shared ideas, created the platform together, got our work done on time, helped each other with constructive criticism, and rehearsed our class presentation outside class.

Lindsay: Created the visual metaphor as a collage representing Ralph's character. During the presentation she carefully explained the meaning of the collage and its relevance to Ralph's personality and his campaign. She also contributed to the philosophy of the party, and ideas for the platform, the name, and the motto.

James: Created the governing principles for the party and in the presentation carefully explained the rationale for each governing principle. He contributed to the philosophy of the party, and ideas for the platform, the name, and the motto. He played Ralph in the video.

Shimika: Came up with the idea of a video for the group presentation and decided on a Jack figure to participate in a debate between Jack and Ralph. She was the mediator and wrote the rationales for the platform. She also contributed to the philosophy of the party, and ideas for the platform, the name, and the motto.

Patricia: Wrote the campaign speech for Ralph, videotaped the debate, made up questions and responses for the debate, and contributed to the philosophy of the party, and ideas for the platform, the name, and the motto.

Each member of the class evaluates the products and performances of the groups, using the form in Figure 4-3.

Figure 4-3. *Evaluation Sheet for Group Projects*

(Evaluate on a scale of 1–10)
Party Participants_____
Candidate _____
_____   Party platform—guiding principles
_____   Visual metaphor
_____   Motto
_____   Speech
_____   Overall presentation
Individual Grades:

Our teacher evaluations of the student work on the election campaign are based on a combination of student self-assessments, peer evaluations, our own observations of student preparation and performance, and our assessment of student portfolios. We consider the completeness of the portfolios and the quality of the thinking reflected in the products contained in them. We assign each student a group grade and an individual grade.

To evaluate the journal projects, we create a rubric (Fig. 4-4). Because students need this evaluative guide in the writing of their journals, we develop it early in the study of the book, after students have had some experience in the journal process. We begin creating the rubric by asking for input from the students, who tell us what they believe should be valued in the work. They express concern that several different tasks are demanded from them. For that reason they want the rubric to reflect the different types of responses they are asked to make. To address their concerns, we create a four-dimensional rubric, one for each col-

Figure 4-4. *Rubric for Evaluation and Assessment of Journals*

DIMENSIONS	4 This section	3 This section	2 This section	1 This section
EVENTS: the choice and accuracy of the depiction of key events.	Presents the most significant events accurately and reveals keen insight about their importance, both in and of themselves and for the larger issues surrounding them.	Presents most of the key events with accuracy; shows an understanding of those events; reveals some awareness of the larger implications of those events.	Presents events accurately but may not select the most important ones; reveals a limited awareness of the larger significance of those events.	Presents events that may not be accurately described and are of limited significance; leaves out key events.
JACK'S PERSONA: the extent to which the journal exhibits insight into the complexities of Jack's character and accurately depicts his actions and his voice.	Reveals in-depth, insightful understanding of Jack's personality and the implications of his behavior; remains true to Jack's actions and thoroughly captures his voice in choice of phrasing and rhythms of speech.	Reveals an understanding of Jack's personality, some of the implications of his behavior but not all of them; accurately portrays Jack's actions and captures some of his tone and the rhythms of his speech.	Reveals some understanding of Jack's personality; fails to consider the implications of his behavior; may depict some of Jack's actions inaccurately; has a limited ability to convey Jack's voice.	Reveals little or no understanding of Jack's personality; often inaccurate; fails to capture Jack's voice.
RALPH'S PERSONA: the extent to which the journal exhibits insight into the complexities of Ralph's character and accurately depicts his actions and his voice.	Reveals in-depth, insightful understanding of Ralph's personality and the implications of his behavior; remains true to Ralph's actions and thoroughly captures his voice in choice of phrasing and rhythms of speech.	Reveals an understanding of Ralph's personality, some of the implications of his behavior but not all of them; accurately portrays Ralph's actions, captures some of his tone and the rhythms of his speech.	Reveals some understanding of Ralph's personality; fails to consider the implications of his behavior; may depict some of Ralph's actions inaccurately; has a limited ability to convey his voice.	Reveals little or no understanding of Ralph's personality; often inaccurate; fails to capture Ralph's voice.
PERSONAL REACTIONS: the extent to which the journal shows interaction with text; ability to connect events and characters' responses with essential questions.	Reveals a significant personal interaction with the text; insightful connections into the larger implications of the text; depth of perception.	Reveals a clear interaction with the text; makes some valid connections; some insight into the larger implications of the text.	Interacts with the text but on a superficial level; few connections with questions; little or no insight into the larger implications of the text.	Exhibits minimal interaction with the text; few or no connections; lack of insight.

umn of their journal: Events, Jack's Persona, Ralph's Persona, and Personal Reactions. With students' help we identify the elements to be considered within each dimension. We then flesh out the details and the gradations of performance for each level within the rubric and share it with our students to guide them through the completion of their journal. Of course, we use it to evaluate their completed journals.

CONCLUSION

Studying a book as an exploration of the limitations of democracy and the challenges for effective governance as a result of the nature of humanity offers students the opportunity of a meaningful interdisciplinary study. They can recognize the immediate significance of their studies in the world around them. The journal project provides a format for students to explore the novel as a microcosm of the larger world as Golding sees it and to draw conclusions about the limitations of democracy and the inherent nature of humanity. The election campaign synthesizes their learning in a realistic format that requires them to produce a comprehensive product.

Throughout their studies, students develop their abilities to read, write, speak, and listen critically and analytically.

- They analyze the nature of the characters in the novel and the kinds of leaders that emerge as a result of that nature. They identify the qualities of a leader that appeal to an electorate and exploit those qualities.
- They investigate the limitations of democracy and its implications for governance.
- They select details, evidence, and arguments to influence the electorate to vote for their candidate.
- They determine oral and written strategies for their campaigns to influence their audience. This process requires them to select rhetorical devices appropriate for persuasive argument.
- They participate orally in a variety of contexts, including group discussions, individual presentations, and debates.
- They are active participants in the evaluation process, listening carefully to presentations and making judgments about the value of each aspect of those presentations.

This rich, integrated study focused on *Lord of the Flies* provides the opportunity for students to develop essential language skills in an authentic context and makes academic use of the competitive nature of our students. The result of this approach is an exciting, productive learning experience for students of diverse abilities and learning styles.

ADDITIONAL TEXTS

Additional texts for which an election campaign is effective include the following:

Julius Caesar by William Shakespeare: The political chaos that followed Caesar's assassination resulted in a climate that caused competing factions to vie for power. The election campaign requires groups of students to study the play in depth to devise a multifaceted election campaign to promote their particular candidate.

A Separate Peace by John Knowles: As a result of his experiences with his friend and rival, Finny, Gene absorbs Finny's philosophy and becomes a pacifist. This naturally puts him in opposition to Brinker and the forces drawing him into World War II. The election campaign is a natural way for students to get in touch with those opposing forces and understand the historical context of this war.

Animal Farm by George Orwell: By its very nature, this book is political satire. Therefore, it lends itself to an exploration of competing ideologies, culminating in an election campaign reflecting these different positions. In studying the book for the campaign, students not only learn about the nature of satire, they also learn of Orwell's contempt for communism and the totalitarian state.

1984 by George Orwell: Like *Animal Farm, 1984* satirizes conformity and the totalitarian state. To explore the meaning of this novel through an election campaign requires a slight revision in the ending—Winston must be able to withstand the pressures of the state and challenge its authority; however this format provides students with a vehicle for in-depth study of the characteristics of totalitarian society that Orwell attacked in this book.

CHAPTER 5

Paradoxes and Paradigms

It was the best of times, it was the worst of times.

As our students face the prospect of studying Charles Dickens' *A Tale of Two Cities*, they might very well feel the conflict suggested in the opening lines of the text. They have been told of the richness of Dickens' writing, but they also have feared the difficulties that they know to be part of his 19th-century style and syntax. Many of them come to the text believing that they will not be able to understand it and will need the assistance of some commercial guidebook to help them through their impending ordeal. Realizing how often, despite teacher admonitions, students resort to such guidebooks—not as aids to their reading but as a substitute for a firsthand encounter with a text perceived to be difficult—we make a virtue out of their "crutch" and invite them to create an original guidebook for the next group of students required to read *A Tale of Two Cities*. In fact, we frame our entire study around this project. As they read the text, they think of what would help them make meaning more easily. Their ideas will become the basis of a handbook, perhaps computerized, and study guide, the ostensible purpose of which is to facilitate the reading and comprehension of the book for the classes that follow. In the process of creating this guidebook, they enhance their own understanding of what they have read. With the motivation of a real-life task and a real audience for the work they produce, students pay closer attention to the intricacies of Dickens' plot and structure, which they might otherwise avoid or gloss over.

GETTING STARTED

Initially, we engage students by confronting the guidebook issue head on, bringing in copies of assorted commercial notes for titles students may have already studied, such as *Of Mice and Men* and *Lord of the Flies*. Because our creation of handbooks for *A Tale of Two Cities* must of necessity be a collaborative effort, we take this opportunity to form the groups that will work together throughout our study of the text and eventually produce a guidebook. We divide students into groups of three to insure maximum individual effort, being careful to place students of multiple talents and abilities in the same group. Our classes are heterogeneous, so wherever possible we place at least two academically strong students together with one who may be weaker. Their task is to analyze the contents of the sample guidebooks for the texts they have already read. They consider questions such as the following:

- What is the content of the commercial notes?
- What elements do they think might have been helpful in their reading?
- What are some of the negatives?
- What topics or elements from the books studied are *not* contained in these guides?
- What else might you want to know that is not contained in the samples?

These and other questions prompt students to explore both the reason for resorting to commercial guidebooks as aides and the limitation of doing so. An excerpt from a typical group discussion illustrates the value of this exercise:

Jessica: I don't believe that she is really asking us to look at commercial notes seriously.

Lisa: Right! I remember last week when she caught John with a copy under his notebook and threw it in the trash.

Bob: Hey! Don't knock it. Maybe we can convince her it is okay to use these!

Jessica: It certainly beats reading all this stuff.

Lisa *(thumbing through some commercial notes)*: Okay, first we're supposed to list the contents as advantages. They all seem to give us a background of the author's life. That should help us to understand why the author wrote the book.

Bob: Yeah, but does it? Who cares what else he wrote or what he did or didn't do as a kid? How do you get through all these pages about him and find the part of his life story that has anything to do with the tough parts of the book?

Jessica: Good point! Why don't we do two of these questions at the same time, then? I'll write down the negatives of using these

guides, and Lisa will write down the positives. I'll start with
what you said, Bob, about how the biographical stuff doesn't
focus on what we need to know to understand the book but just
has a lot of irrelevant facts about the writer's life.

When Jessica and her group, like most groups, continued to explore the sample
notes, they found that they could get a basic overview of the story from them, but
they were unhappy that the summaries gave away too much of the story, spoiling
any element of surprise. They found the time line and historical background
material to be helpful but thought that what was included about each character
was not enough to have helped them in the essay assignments they had been
given. For example, they had to discuss the ambiguity of George's relationship
with Lennie in *Of Mice and Men* and write a statement of George defending
himself against a charge of murdering Lennie. The commercial notes were too
superficial to be of much help with such an assignment, they decided. They also
objected to what they saw as a bias of interpretation, which their own readings of
the book might cause them to reject. Even more to the point, they found that the
commercial notes were lacking anything that would help them deal with the actual language of a text, particularly with the difficulties of a Dickens' novel. As a
result, they decided to include in their own handbooks aids on the stylistic techniques of the novel. Jessica's group is typical of those who identified the need to
deal with the following questions:

- What keeps the reader going? How does the author build interest?
- What does he include, what does he leave out, and what is the
  effect of each on the reader?
- What ideas or themes (if any) underlie the story?
- What images or symbols does he use and why?

When groups of students come together, they usually decide that an ideal
handbook contains only limited plot summaries but rather includes leading questions that will force the reader to discover certain key points without giving too
much away too soon.

INTRODUCING THE TEXT

Once we have looked at the sample commercial guidebooks together and analyzed what is helpful in them, or lacking, we are ready to confront the text of *A
Tale of Two Cities* itself. We tell the students that as they read they are to keep a
reader's log to help them obtain material for the handbooks they will write for
next year's class. Until we are well into the book, we can't structure the format for
the log, but we do ask students to go beyond the traditional summary available in
commercial guidebooks and include the kind of information they found missing
from the sample guides they reviewed.

We brainstorm with the class ideas about the kinds of details that they think should be included in their logs. One class group of students decided that, rather than a plot summary, an appropriate quote from a chapter would provide the essence of the meaning of that chapter and also help students to confront the language and syntax problems of the book. They agreed to list the quotes in one column, and in a second column they deal with the implications or problems arising from or suggested by this quote, as well as their personal reactions to what they had read so far.

Jessica's notes for chapter 1, "The Period," reflect how she began to handle both the book and the need to gather material that would help her and her group develop a handbook to go beyond the standard guides and avoid the pitfalls they had discovered in their study of the samples:

Chapter 1: "The Period"

Key Quote	Implications, reactions, and possible activity for the study guide
"It was the best of times, it was the worst of times, it was the age of wisdom, it was the age of foolishness, it was the epoch of belief, it was the epoch of incredulity, it was the season of Light, it was the season of Darkness, it was the spring of Hope, it was the winter of despair, we had everything before us, we had nothing before us, we were all going direct to Heaven, we were all going direct the other way—in short, the period was so far like the present period, that some of its noisiest authorities insisted on its being received, for good or for evil, in the superlative degree of comparison only."	Good grief! An 11-line sentence? It took me many readings before I could figure it out at all. I think this quote sets me up for the way the book will be written. First of all, all isn't as it seems if it is both "the best and worst of times," etc. I find it interesting that this is a book about two cities and two contrasting ways of looking at events. Maybe the book will be made up of paradoxes or contrasts. I also find it interesting that Dickens mentions that the time he writes about isn't all that different from the time he lives and writes in. I wonder if that connection will be important.

After meeting with Bob and Lisa and discussing their entries for this chapter, Jessica added the following possible activity for the group's study guide:

> Perhaps we could ask students to list the ways in which the period is the "best of times" and also make a list of the ways in which the period is "the worst of times." Maybe they shouldn't do this until they read more of the book, or they could begin it after reading this chapter and come back to it later and add additional items to their lists.

After reading the next chapter, "The Mail," and identifying "recalled to life" as a quote important to that specific chapter, Lisa wrote this observation:

> I don't get it. How can anybody be recalled to life? Who's dead? Why does Dickens just drop this in and not even give us a clue of what he is talking about? It's weird that the characters in the chapter themselves spend so much time and energy talking about how *they* don't understand what is meant, either. Give me a break!

Sharing her puzzlement with her group led Lisa to include the suggestion in her log that the handbook they create have a list of tips for readers to help them avoid or get beyond the initial frustration she was experiencing by Dickens' habit of posing a question and not answering it until much later. The group decided that this might be an important technique that Dickens used to get people hooked and make them want to read on. At this point in the study, we ask our students to include in their readers' logs a list of unanswered questions as they discover them and then see where, how, and if Dickens answers those questions.

STRUCTURING THE READER'S LOG

Collecting Ideas for the Study Guide

As a result of this discussion, Lisa, Jessica, and Bob began a folder of material for their group's handbook with a piece entitled "Reading Tips" or "How to Survive the Best and Worst of Times." The first tip they included was the following:

> Do not become too preoccupied with things you are not sure of. Just continue with the book. The beginning has many unanswered questions, but they are unanswered on purpose; it's not that you missed something. The author is deliberately holding back key information. Don't worry, though, he comes back to it later; all the loose ends will be tied up. Above all, don't become frustrated! Just keep a list of the questions you can't yet answer. Then leave space so you can come back later in the reading and write in the answers to those questions. It's actually kind of cool how he does this.

When students read chapter 3, "Night Shadows," they focused in on the hints they were given that would eventually lead them to understand the "recalled to life" comment. Bob included the following dialogue as his quote for this chapter:

> "Buried how long?"
>
> "Almost eighteen years."
>
> ". . . to be buried alive for eighteen years!"

His comment and reaction section read as follows:

> Okay. So this character has been buried alive and now has been rescued. How could he live in a grave for 18 years? Wait!!

Maybe he wasn't dead at all but just as good as dead, cut off
from everybody—maybe in exile or in prison, where nobody
could visit him or even knew he was there???

As a result of Bob's speculation, his group added another idea to its folder for
the handbook: to create an activity chart of Unanswered Questions. They decided
that they would model the activity by beginning it for the students, filling out the
clues and answers to the first unanswered question once they figured it out themselves:

Unanswered Question	Clues (chapter, page)	Answer to the Question
Who or what was recalled to life?	Someone has been buried alive for 18 years and has now been dug out (chapter 3, pages 24–25; Signet Classic).	

After reading chapter 4, Bob wrote the following in his reader's log:

I called it. This guy *was* in prison; he was a doctor or something
in France. Chapter 4 has Mr. Lorry meeting a Miss Manette and
telling her that her father, missing for her whole life, has been
"recalled to life," and they are going to Paris to meet him and
bring him back to England. But now I have a new question, or
maybe several. Why was he in prison, and how does he
suddenly get free after all this time?

Armed with this new information, Bob and his group revisited their activities
chart and filled in the rest of their sample question, clue, and answer:

Unanswered Question	Clues (chapter, page)	Answer to the Question
Who or what was recalled to life?	Someone has been buried alive for 18 years and has now been dug out (chapter 3, pages 24–25; Signet Classic).	Dr. Manette, imprisoned in a French jail on the authority of a powerful enemy for an as yet unknown crime (chapter 4; page 34).

Despite the focus by most students on trying to resolve their first unanswered
question, at least one group is bound to become interested in another issue raised
by chapter 3. For example, Carl focused on the opening of "Night Shadows" and
quoted the following lines:

"A wonderful fact to reflect upon, that every human creature is
constituted to be that profound secret and mystery to every
other . . . every one of those darkly clustered houses encloses
its own secret; that every room in every one of them encloses

its own secret; that every beating heart in the hundreds of
thousands of breasts there is, in some of its imaginings, a
secret to the heart nearest it . . . in any of the burial places of
this city through which I pass, is there a sleeper more
inscrutable than its busy inhabitants are, in their innermost
personality, to me, or than I am to them?"(p. 21)

In his comments, he reflected upon the strangeness of this chapter in confus-
ing him instead of getting the story going and clearly introducing the major characters or the problem underlying the plot. He then went on to speculate as follows:

I wonder if secrets have something important to do with this
story, I mean beyond the questions that we have to wait till
later to get answers to. Maybe part of what will happen is that
we will be misled about a character and only later discover that
he or she has an important secret and, like the unanswered
questions, we will find the truth behind the secret only after
reading much further into the story. I think our group should
keep a list of secrets by an appearance or reality chart or even
by making this an activity for our handbook that students could
work through as they read the novel.

His group then added this activity idea to its folder:

Keep a list of possible contrasts that might reflect secrets
important to the story. Organize your list around "What You
Know" and "What Is Hidden," or *Appearance* and *Reality*. For
example, as you meet a new important character, write down
what this person appears to be like and save room to go back
later and maybe find out that he or she was really different from
your first impression. A sample first secret might involve the
reason for Dr. Manette's imprisonment. We know that he was in
a French prison for 18 years, but we don't know why. Although
this could be an unanswered question, it might also be a secret
if the answer to the question either hides or reveals other
important facts.

With an activity such as this, students can consider Carton's appearance as
opposed to his reality, or Darnay's false English identity versus his real identity as
an Evremonde. These issues may or may not be perceived by students as unanswered questions to be resolved later. They formulate a chart like the following:

Secrets ". . . every human creature . . . [is a] profound secret and mystery to
every other." (p. 21)

What We Know	What Is Hidden (Secret)	Truth Behind Appearance
Dr. Manette was in a French prison for 18 years.	What did he do to get such a harsh punishment? Why has he been released, and how? (chapter 5)	???

After encountering some reading frustrations as they try to work their way through the initial chapters of the book, students may decide to include a reading tips section and begin to draft ideas that they think are important for classes to know before they go too far into the book. One such tip sheet read as follows:

1. Pay attention to the titles of the books and especially of the chapters. They tell you what the chapter will be about.

2. Be patient. It takes time for the story to start. But some of the description is important and gives clues to questions you will want to answer later. Also, don't treat this like some stupid English assignment. If you do, that is what it will be, and you will bore yourself to death. Enjoy reading the story. Once you get into it, it is actually good. Have a good time and try to get involved with the characters' feelings—the reader's log will help you do this and follow what is happening.

3. Keep a good reader's log. The quotes from each chapter and the reactions you have at the time you read it will help you remember what is going on later.

4. The vocabulary in *A Tale of Two Cities* can sometimes be difficult. If you encounter a word you do not know, try to finish the paragraph and see if you can discover from the context what the word means. Most often you will find that you can!

5. If a word is giving you a hard time even after you've finished the paragraph, and you're worried that you're missing an important point because of it, *Look it up!* Whatever you do, do not forget about it. If you don't have a dictionary with you, make a list so that you can look it up when you do have a dictionary. Vocabulary is very important. You will find that most of these words come up in other books that you read, not to mention SAT tests!

6. Most important, make sure that you understand what you read. Don't just skim this book. Read it carefully—it is a classic known by all learned people. If you find that even after class and group discussions you do not understand something, talk to your teacher. Do not put this off; trust me, you can't fake your way through just by reading guidebooks on the chapters, not if you have a really good teacher who makes you think for yourself.

7. For your reader's log, make sure that your reactions are twice as long as your quotes. You can talk about unanswered questions, coincidences, metaphors, things that puzzle you, feelings about what is happening or not happening, and even predictions about what you expect to happen. These entries might seem to be a pain when you have to do them, but they sure come in handy later.

(Note: Sometimes groups decide to keep a running list of such words themselves and include a vocabulary glossary of difficult words and their meanings, keyed to pages and chapters. As they offer help to future classes who are reading the book, they are also improving their own vocabularies.)

WAYS OF MAKING MEANING

Book 1

At this point in their study, students are sufficiently aware of the approach that Dickens takes in this book to read the next two chapters quickly and complete their reading of book 1. We ask them, in addition to continuing their readers' logs with quotes and reactions from these two chapters, to write entry slips to class that incorporate prior knowledge of the conditions leading to the French Revolution with a creative response to the conditions revealed in chapter 5. They take on the persona of an on-the-spot reporter witnessing the event of the breaking of a cask of wine and the reaction of the impoverished people of St. Antoine. One student wrote the following:

> Last evening a large group of poverty-stricken peasants was whipped into a violent frenzy over a cask of wine that was dropped from a passing carriage. Eyewitnesses say that 70 or 80 men and women gathered around the spilled wine, lapping it up off the cobblestone. This lasted until the muddy pavement was licked dry and everything on the street corner was stained red. One of our reporters, John Barsad, was unable to get a comment from Monsieur Ernest Defarge, owner of a wine shop and witness to the fiasco. However, Barsad reports seeing a very tall man smear the letters B-L-O-O-D on the wall of a nearby building. One citizen, known only as Jacques, was overheard saying, "It is not often that many of these miserable beasts know the taste of wine, or anything but black bread and death" (p. 41). Despite the size of the crowd and the lack of restraint in getting as much wine as possible from the muddy cobblestone streets, there were no casualties this time. We fear, however, that if a barrel of wine can cause a disturbance like this, it would be very easy to provoke mass hysteria in such a crowd of peasants if the provocation were any greater. We urge the ruling aristocracy to take steps to prevent such a catastrophic possibility.

After students complete book 1, they meet in their groups to process what they have learned from their reading, share the information in their readers' logs, and get new ideas for their handbooks. We encourage them to keep track of what they have learned about each of the characters they have met so far—Lorry, Lucie Manette, the Defarges—by taking notes on how they are described by the author. This again engages them in exploring Dickens' use of language and encourages them to dig more deeply into the characters and the book than they would with the one-sentence overview of the characters found in the typical guidebook. Their readers' logs contain not only a quote from each chapter and a reaction to that quote but also a description of a major character introduced in that chapter and a comment on the behavior of that character. For example, Kevin's log for chapter 5, "The Wineshop," included the following entry about the Defarges:

> Defarge: bull-necked, martial-looking man of 30; "implacable, set purpose" (p. 40)—I wonder what he will do. It is strange that he should be described this way, yet what we see him doing first is helping out an old employer in the most compassionate, friendly way. There is something more here that I don't get yet.
>
> Madame Defarge: "a stout woman . . . with a watchful eye that seldom seemed to look at anything . . . a steady face, strong features, and great composure of manner" (p. 40). How can she have a watchful eye if she doesn't look at anything? What is all that stuff about her toothpick, lifting her eyebrows, coughing? An awful lot of detail about nothing, it seems to me, unless . . .

In discussion with his group, Kevin shared his impressions of these two characters and added to his notes when Danielle said that those motions sounded to her a lot like some kind of signal or shorthand, because just after Madame Defarge did something with the toothpick and her eyebrows and coughed, Mr. Defarge noticed the presence of Mr. Lorry and Lucie Manette in the wineshop. Danielle was also curious about why so many people in this chapter were named Jacques and were so interested in spying on Dr. Manette, who, for some strange reason, was still locked up in an attic room in the wineshop. They decided to add to their chart of secrets the possibility that there was some secret behind this wineshop and all the "Jacques."

In the meantime, Lisa, Bob, and Jessica were mostly preoccupied with Lucie's strange behavior and with the condition in which Lucie found her father when she finally entered that small attic room. Lisa shared the following entry from her reader's log with her group:

> Lucie Manette: "a short, slight, pretty figure, a quantity of golden hair, a pair of blue eyes that met his own with an inquiring look, and a forehead with a singular capacity of lifting and knitting itself into an expression that was not quite one of perplexity, or wonder, or alarm, or merely of a bright fixed attention . . ."(p. 29). She seems awfully fragile to me. The first thing she does when she hears about her father is faint. Then, when she is about to meet him, she needs to be lifted into the room, and she talks to him in such a weird way, with that sappy "weep for it, weep for it" stuff. She hardly seems like the kind of character I would want for the female lead in my story!

To her criticism of Lucy, Bob interrupted, "I dunno. It sounds kind of nice to me. I would want to help or protect somebody like that. Maybe that's what Dickens wants us to feel for her. Let's cut her some slack before we decide." They then went on to talk about Dr. Manette and to speculate on why he calls himself "105

North Tower" and keeps making the same pair of shoes over and over. Jessica made the following comment:

> Hey, if you were alone all that time, you'd forget who you were, too. Maybe "105 North Tower" is like your social security number or something, like the number of his prison cell. His whole world for 18 years was that cell. I bet that his jailers called him that, so after a while he thought that was who he was. I wonder if he'll be okay now that Lucie has found him.

Lisa added, "Well, at least we know the answer now to 'recalled to life.' His imprisonment must have seemed like a death if it made him forget who he is!"

Book 2

Although students have been able to come to such insights for these last two chapters with little direction from the teacher, with the introduction of book 2, "The Golden Thread," we find it necessary to give more direction to the class to help the students make meaning of some particularly difficult chapters involving Charles Darnay's English trial and surprise acquittal. We begin by speculating about the meaning of the title, "The Golden Thread." Generally, students have no idea what that is, but they are predisposed not to worry too much about it yet. Their experience with book 1 and the unanswered-question technique has prepared them to be secure that eventually Dickens will help them to discover the meaning of the title and even to enjoy the aspect of his technique that keeps them guessing. What they *do* know is that this title has some significance to the meaning of the book. Invariably, given their view that Dickens is a writer who got paid by the word, and so added more words than were necessary, they are surprised by the fact that book 2 begins 5 years after the close of book 1.

Danielle complained, "Hey, not fair! Here we spend pages just on somebody's arched eyebrows and picking her teeth with a toothpick, and then suddenly—bam!—we lose five years? How could *nothing* of importance have happened in all that time?"

Their frustration is compounded as they learn that they have been dumped right into the middle of a trial involving a character they haven't even met yet. To capitalize on their interest in what went on in those lost years, we often ask them to fill in the blanks and write a scene or two of what might have gone on during the intervening 5 years. They note that Dr. Manette has changed, that he now seems restored to good health and good memory, so their stories often revolve around Lucie's care of him that led to the renewal of his ability to function normally. They also note the sudden introduction of a new major character, Charles Darnay, and speculate on how he came to know the Manettes and how he got in so much trouble with the English government that he is now on trial for his life. They often invent interesting stories, suggesting that Lucie and Darnay first met on the trip back from France and subsequently became involved in an incipient romance. This explains Lucie's deep concern when it looks as if Darnay will lose his life because of some real or imagined treachery on behalf of France and against England. These stories grow out of the brief testimony at the trial of Lorry, Lucie, and Dr. Manette (pp. 77–80).

Rather than assign students to read these chapters on their own, we often read aloud the first part of the book, particularly the description of Tellson's Bank, inviting the students to listen in their groups and collaborate on sketches of what they see from the words we read to them. Their sketches remind us of the imposing neoclassical bastions of power characteristic of the banks of 19th-century England rather than modern banks. After they sketch their vision of the bank and the people who work in it, we invite the groups to discuss the purpose of this description, posing the question: What is Dickens telling us about England and about English justice? We invite them to find words and phrases that reveal Dickens' mocking, ironic tone. Then we ask them to focus in particular on the discussion of punishments (beginning on p. 62), and on the encounter between Jerry Cruncher and Mrs. Cruncher, to try to make some sense out of it.

After wrestling with chapter 1 of book 2, Kevin's group added a note to the folder for their handbook to remind them to go back later and devise some activity or write an article discussing Dickens' use of irony, satire, and humor. Lisa's group added a new unanswered question to their list: "Why are Jerry Cruncher's fingers always so rusty, and why does he get so angry at his wife for praying?"

We alternate reading the next chapter, "A Sight," as a play and assigning it as homework for students to consider collaboratively before making entries in their readers' logs. Most students focus on Charles Darnay, worrying about the terrible punishment in store for him for treason (quartering). They express disbelief that the Manettes could possibly serve as witnesses against the defendant. Students expect, if anything, that the Manettes' involvement would be for the defendant, to protect him from such a barbarous sentence.

Because of the difficulties that students have in reading the text of the trial, we ask them first to read it silently and then, in their groups, to script the trial for a TV production of the scene. This requires them to translate sections of it into dialogue. To do this, they must figure out who says what. That is not always clear at first. Each group is given one portion of this task to complete. When they finish, we re-create the entire scene for the class. This has the added advantage of clarifying problems with the way the chapter is written and also of making absolutely certain that students understand what happens to Darnay and why. Following is an excerpt from Lisa's group on the introductory charge to the jury:

> **Attorney general:** Gentlemen of the jury; it is my sad duty to inform you that this prisoner, now facing you and looking so young and innocent, is old enough to have committed the terrible treason for which you have no choice but to condemn him to death. We will prove beyond a shadow of a doubt that his correspondence with our hated enemy, France, was long-

standing and full of grave danger to the health of our country, that the prisoner had for a very long time traveled back and forth between England and France on secret business for which he could have had no honorable purpose. It is fortunate for us and for the survival of our great country that his wickedness and guilt in this traitorous business was discovered and put to an end before it was too late. We are indeed fortunate to have a patriot willing to come forward and denounce this man and his hated activities to save this great country of ours from a terrible fate at the hands of our enemy.

The indictment goes on to outline the case and mention the kind of testimony that would be provided by the various witnesses that the attorney general intended to produce as evidence to prove his case against Darnay.

Another group worked on clarifying the testimony of John Barsad and Roger Cly as they were cross-examined by Darnay's attorney, who is referred to only as "the wigged gentleman." Students often have difficulty, when they read the original text, separating the questions from the responses because of the way Dickens writes, so scripting helps them to make the distinction. From page 75, where Darnay's attorney proves that Barsad is a liar and a paid spy, with an ulterior motive to testify against Darnay, students created the following script:

Attorney: Mr. Barsad, have you ever been a spy?

Barsad: Absolutely not. What a base insinuation.

Attorney: How do you earn your living?

Barsad: Through my property.

Attorney: Where is your property?

Barsad: Well; I can't say exactly. I don't remember.

Attorney: Have you ever been in prison?

Barsad: Absolutely not!

Attorney: Not even debtor's prison?

Barsad: What's that got to do with anything?

Attorney: Come, come now Mr. Barsad; *never* in a debtor's prison?

Once the performance of the reconstituted trial is over, we summarize as a class exactly what has happened and then convene our groups to discuss what is worth putting in the readers' logs for this chapter and what, if any, new ideas for the handbook have emerged. Lisa's group was intrigued with the eagerness of the crowd to convict the defendant and the number of people who came to witness what they thought would definitely be a terrible execution. They noted the title of the chapter, "A Disappointment."

Jessica: How could they be disappointed that he got off? Look at that last line, as the crowd leaves the courtroom: "A loud buzz swept into the street as if the baffled blue-flies were dispersing in search of other carrion."

Bob: What's *carrion*?

Lisa: Flesh, victims, stupid! I really am grossed out by that picture. I hate flies. Just imagine them swarming around a dead body. Yuck! They were looking forward to swarming around Darnay's cut-up body!

Jessica: Maybe we better add something to our folder that will let us explain stuff like the blue-flies. What do you call it?

Lisa: Imagery, I think. Yeah, write down *blue-flies* and say that Dickens uses this as a way to talk about the people's sick interest in seeing people die.

Bob: Yeah, and don't forget coincidence, too. Imagine, that Carton dude looks just like Darnay, enough to get him off. Man, Dickens must really be hard up to pull that one out of his hat just to save his hero! This is beginning to sound more and more like a soap opera to me.

Jessica: Well, I like soap operas. I listen to them every day after school.

Maintaining the Focus

Once we have helped students to understand the facts of the trial and begin to deal with the complexities of Dickens' style as he works through his story, we are ready to give students a little more independence in reading the next section of the book, chapters 4–6. In these chapters they learn much more about Sydney Carton and his relationship to Stryer. They also pick up on the importance of still another technique that they add to their folder of ideas: foreshadowing.

However, once they get to chapters 7 and 8, "Monseigneur in Town" and "Monseigneur in the Country," we usually find it necessary to slow the reading down and to bring them together as a class to read all or significant parts of these difficult chapters aloud. Usually we read it to them to help them understand, in particular, the parts of chapter 7 that deal with the overall situation in prerevolutionary France and only tangentially deal with characters and situations important to the novel. Then the Marquis Ste. Evremonde is introduced (p. 115), where he drives away in anger from the reception at the Monseigneur's and runs over a little child who has the temerity to be in his way. Students who have studied the French Revolution in their social studies classes are invited to contribute their knowledge to a discussion of the conditions in France that led to the revolution. These conditions are depicted quite graphically and satirically in these two chapters. Other students are assigned the task of doing some research on the period, either in the library, from their history texts, or with the commercial guidebooks that we have so far disdained. One of the strengths of these books, identified by students at the start of their study, is providing historical background information. We encourage them to make use of that strength at this point in our work.

While we read the opening pages of chapter 7 to them, we ask them to jot down examples they find of sarcasm, instances in which Dickens seems to be highly critical of the French aristocracy's behavior. We also ask them to list any evidence found in these pages of reasons that might explain or justify the peasants' revolt against this aristocracy. During discussion, students are quick to throw back words and phrases from the text that particularly struck them, such as "leprosy of unreality" and the "holiest of holies" (p. 112) in which the Monseigneur took his chocolate, assisted by an entourage of no fewer than four servants.

Often they confuse the Marquis with the Monseigneur and need to be prompted to go back and key in on his description (p. 114) after he runs over Gaspard's child, and they begin to realize that he will play an important role in the story. To highlight his importance, we ask students to create a monologue with his words and reactions to the accident and its aftermath. Because he has such a violent response, students have a field day with this assignment. Cathy wrote the following:

> Damn! What the . . . fool, why are you stopping? What nonsense! Why can't these idiots take better care of their urchins! One or the other of them is always in my way. Here now! See to the horses; how do I know what injury that b—d child may have done to my horses. I can't replace these beauties easily, you know . . . [*under his breath*] dogs, pigs. look at them swarming over there, staring at me, but too cowardly to do more than grovel disgustingly before me, their superior in every way. I would cheerfully exterminate all of them from the face of the earth if I could have my way. [*aloud*] Who threw that? If I knew which one of you threw that, I would crush him happily beneath the wheels of this carriage. [*undertone*] How dare they reject my coin! They should be grateful. That child wasn't worth half the value of that coin to his father. I shouldn't have wasted my money on them! Bah! Look at them, slinking away like rats to their holes, not a man among them! How I loathe the very sight of them! I don't see why we have to put up with them. The world would do far better without all these worthless mouths to feed at our expense.

After Cathy shared her monologue with the class, Bob muttered, "I don't like that guy. He spells trouble. I bet we haven't heard the last of him." Danielle recognized the name Gaspard, the father of the dead child, remembering that he had smeared the word BLOOD on the wall of the wineshop back in the chapter where the wine cask had broken in the street in front of Defarge's shop. "What will he do now?" she asked.

Students read chapters 8 and 9 and convene in their groups to discuss their readers' logs entries for these chapters. Most have trouble understanding the title, "The Gorgon's Head" until we ask them to reread the first paragraph of chapter 9, in which the word *stone* is repeated over and over. We encourage them to tap into their previous knowledge of mythology to define the gorgon for themselves. One group added mythological references to its list of techniques to be included in their handbooks, either as an activity or spelled out to save future readers the trouble of having to research those clues.

The focus of discussion for most groups is their surprise and dismay that Darnay is related to the Marquis Ste. Evremonde. We guide their discussion by asking them to focus on the conversation between Darnay and his uncle and discover what is the nature of their relationship. Each group goes back over the chapter, especially pages 126–129. We urge the students to reread to the end of the chapter. They will submit an exit slip explaining the final line of chapter 9, "Drive him fast to his tomb. This, from Jacques." The exit slips will be worth a quiz grade and will be either a 10 or a zero for the entire group. The students are to explain the quote, tie it in with what happens to the Marquis at the end of the chapter, and speculate on who may have been responsible and why.

When we discuss the exit slips the next day, we clarify for those who are uncertain that the Marquis has indeed been murdered, that Darnay did not do it but is now the rightful owner of a title he has despised and renounced. Again, we invite students to speculate on who may have committed the crime and why. Many are quick to notice that *Jacques* was the name of the man in Defarge's wine shop and the name on the note attached to the knife that killed the Marquis, so they assume the revolution has begun, or at least that Gaspard has somehow extracted blood vengeance for the death of his son. They wonder what Darnay will do now, and they express impatience that the book switches at this point to England and a seemingly unrelated subject, Lucie Manette and her courtship by a host of suitors, including Charles Darnay. We ask them to fill in the blanks with a charge to the caretaker, M. Gabelle, on what to do with the Marquis' estate.

> My dear M. Gabelle,
>
> As you know, I never sought any profit from my uncle's estate, nor do I want any. I hated everything he stood for, and with every fiber of my being I reject reaping any reward from it. My mother's dying wish was that I show mercy to the people from whom my uncle and my father took all this, and so I charge you with using the money from this estate to redress the wrongs of the past—let the people live here free of any payment of rent or taxes. Make certain they want for nothing. Feed them, give them medical care and whatever else they need. I don't care if every cent is used up in doing so. I don't ever intend to come back or to spend a sous on myself. For these services, you will be paid well, you may be sure. Goodbye and farewell, M. Gabelle. We will not have occasion to meet again. I intend to marry and live in England.

Concluding Book 2

At this point in their study of the novel, students have usually overcome their initial difficulties in reading it and are curious enough about what will happen to Darnay, Lucie, and Dr. Manette that they can handle larger chunks of the novel as homework and meet in their groups to share log entries and resolve any lingering concerns. Accordingly, we assign the rest of book 2.

Chapters 10–13 focus on the courtship of Lucie and Darnay. For this section, we guide them to look at character development through the technique of contrast and to keep track of questions still unanswered as well as secrets (determining what the secrets are and why they are being kept as secrets). For example, Manette has suspicions of Darnay's real name and background but makes him promise to keep it a secret from him until the day of Lucie and Darnay's wedding. When Darnay *does* tell Minetta the truth, the scene is not recorded by Dickens, but we see a seemingly inexplicable reaction on the part of Dr. Manette, who suffers a relapse and once again believes that he is the shoemaker in 105 North Tower.

Chapter 14, "The Honest Tradesman," reintroduces Jerry Cruncher and resolves unanswered questions about the rust on his fingers. This chapter can be assigned separately or as part of the chapter 10–13 grouping.

Chapters 15–16 reintroduce Madame Defarge and explain her knitting.

Chapter. 17–21 pose no serious difficulties for students and further the romantic attachment of Lucie and Darnay while also resolving the problems Manette has experienced upon first learning that Darnay is an Evremonde.

Chapters 21–23 move so rapidly through events, such as the start of the revolution and the inexorable tide of events that forces Darnay to return to France, that students should be allowed to read it with little interruption for assignments and discussion, unless they seem to be experiencing difficulty following the thread of events. When they complete their reading of book 2, students may meet for several class periods to consider the ways in which the two cities of the book are becoming intertwined and the way in which the puzzle pieces are coming together. They may find it especially fruitful to examine examples of foreshadowing, such as echoing footsteps, and imagery, such as the sea and fire rising, as well as the allusion to the lodestone rock. Jessica's group, having determined early in their study of the book that they would include a list of such terms and their explanations in their handbooks, take the class time that is available now to make significant progress. Part of their list reads as follows:

> **Golden thread**: Lucie, who has golden hair, weaves the threads of her love around all whom she loves and who love her—Darnay, Manette, Carton, her children, Miss Pross, even Mr. Lorry.
>
> **Echoing footsteps:** Passing of years that Lucie found soothing and sweet; also menacing echoes of the revolution coming from across the sea in France. Suddenly, in the middle of chapter 21, we are in France, and the footsteps become "headlong, mad, and dangerous . . ." The echoing footsteps of the revolution are said by the author to be rushing into Lucie Darnay's life to disturb her peace and security.
>
> **Sea rising:** The peasant uprising of the French Revolution is described as a sea "of black and threatening waters." It becomes more and more violent and bloodthirsty as the leaders of the revolution, especially the Defarges, behead the enemies listed in the register kept in the knitting.

Fire rises: Another image for the spread and increasing violence of the revolution, but also real fires as the peasants burn the hated chateaus of the aristocracy, including Evremonde's chateau.

Lodestone Rock: Reference to the magnet that is drawing Darnay closer to return to France; that is, the letter he receives from Gabelle begging him to return to save his life as he is now a prisoner of the revolutionary authority.

Although we let the group discussions proceed with only limited guidance by us, we do make sure to have them look closely and analyze Darnay's behavior by posing the following question:

What is it in Darnay's character that influences his decision at the end of chapter 23? Write him a letter in which you give your opinion/feelings about his decision and the extent to which you agree or disagree with it.

We also ask them at this point to make some predictions about what they believe will happen next, once Darnay reaches Paris.

To reinforce students' earlier judgments of commercial guidebooks as not being sufficiently helpful and often biased in their treatment of characters, we invite students to consult a description of Charles Darnay found in one of these notes as they prepare to write their letters to Darnay. They read a description of him as a "phlegmatic, passive" character who means well but is ineffective. The discussion of Jessica's group was typical of student response to this characterization of Darnay:

Jessica: What's *phlegmatic* mean?

   Lisa (*looking it up*): Sluggish. I guess they mean that he is slow to act, doesn't get excited enough about anything to do anything about it. I don't see him like that at all. After all, on the strength of that letter, he does decide to go back to France when he probably shouldn't.

   Bob: Look here, on page 240, "he saw hardly any danger . . . that glorious vision of doing good . . . he even saw himself in the illusion with some influence to guide this raging revolution that was running so fearfully wild." I don't see him as too passive. If anything, he's too reckless here, unrealistic.

Jessica: I agree. The letter we should write is one telling him what a stupid idea it is to risk everything to go to France. There is nothing he can do to help Gabelle, and he will probably get himself killed, as well.

   Lisa: And what about Lucie and her daughter? He's not being fair to them at all.

   Bob: I think I'd rather write a letter to notes and argue with them about Darnay's being phlegmatic and passive. That's just flat-out wrong!

Book 3

Because chapters 1 through 7 of book 3 contain no major reading problems, we often assign them to be read as homework, either in several chapter chunks or as a whole.

Students then meet in their groups to work on their readers' logs for these chapters and to see if any information gleaned from their reading can be useful in fleshing out ideas they have already started in their folders for their handbooks. Danielle's group became interested in the title of the first chapter in book 3, "In Secret," and the suspicion that Dr. Manette's imprisonment might also have been "in secret." They decided to explore the idea of prisons and imprisonment wherever they found it in the book, noting that Darnay was imprisoned first in England and now in France. They noted that the parallel between Darnay's imprisonment and Manette's wasn't all that far-fetched since Darnay paces his jail cell (p. 255), saying, ". . . five paces by four and a half . . . he made shoes, he made shoes, he made shoes." Kevin's group was more interested in exploring the sense it had that early scenes were being repeated here, but with a sinister and different spin on them. They particularly were interested in the echoes of the breaking of the wine cask scene (book 1, chapter 5, "The Wineshop") in the scenes describing the bloody activities of the revolutionaries at their awful work in "The Grindstone" (book 3, chapter 2). Lisa's group also saw parallels, but instead of focusing on imprisonment or early and late scenes of the revolution, they focused on the similarities and differences between Darnay's plight in England, where he was on trial for treason, and in Paris, where he was on trial on the charge of being a returned emigrant. They noted in both cases that the odds were terribly against him and the punishment was to be cruel and fatal, but he was rescued at the last possible second against all odds, first by the coincidence of looking like his lawyer and second by the sympathy that Dr. Manette evoked in Parisians aware of his own suffering at the hands of the aristocracy. We caution them against being too certain that they are ready to explore that parallel yet. After all, the last chapter they read, "A Knock at the Door," placed Darnay in jeopardy once again.

Because chapter 8, "A Game of Cards," has generally proved difficult for some students to follow, we encourage a classwide dramatized reading of it with a deck of cards actually being laid out as Carton articulates his case against Solomon Pross, a.k.a. John Barsad (pp. 296–297) and attempts to gain access to Charles Darnay in prison through the intervention of Barsad, now a "sheep" of the prison for the revolutionaries.

We also read chapter 10, "The Substance of the Shadow," and urge the groups to outline it and include a copy of the diagram of the relationships inherent in that chapter in their handbooks. This chapter contains the crucial information on why Dr. Manette was imprisoned as well as the reason for Mme. Defarge's excessive vendetta against the Evremonde family, explaining her eagerness to make certain that Charles Darnay and all those connected to him become victims of La Guillotine.

After we complete this chapter, and students understand the secrets revealed as a result and the many previously unanswered questions that have been resolved, they are eager to finish the book and find out what happens to Darnay and what comes of Carton's visit to the prison. They are unwilling to meet in their groups at this point because they just want to get on with the reading.

Concluding the Book

Once students have completed the entire book, we process their understanding of the ending by asking them to complete an entry slip explaining Carton's final words: "It is a far, far better thing that I do, than I have ever done; it is a far, far better rest that I go to than I have ever known!" In class discussion, we note that Carton's behavior seems much more understandable and acceptable to the girls than to the boys. Bob, for example, said, "That's lame! Why would he give up his life like that, just for a woman?" Lisa, on the other hand, argued that she would really like to meet someone who was so in love with her that he would do literally anything to make her happy. All agreed that such behavior was hardly typical and not very believable. Some just saw it as a convenient way for Dickens to wrap up his story, although Danielle argued that Dickens must have had this in mind all along, since Darnay was saved the first time by the coincidence of looking like Carton.

Students meet in their groups to discuss their feelings about the last scenes of the book. Kevin's group was particularly intrigued by the way all the secrets come unraveled.

Danielle: I really think it's neat that from the beginning, when Manette was freed, Dickens had this secret letter in mind. That must be what Defarge was searching for in the Bastille scene when he went through 105 North Tower.

Kevin: I think I remember something Darnay said about a prisoner writing a letter in prison and hiding it in a wall somewhere so the wrong people wouldn't find it.

Carl: Yeah, but there are secrets inside secrets. Not only does Manette have a secret reason to hate the Evremondes, but so does Mme. Defarge—that was her sister who was raped by that Evremonde guy.

Danielle: What about the coincidence of it all? I can buy all that about the Evremondes and even that Darnay is secretly an Evremonde, but of all the families in the world for Lucie Manette, given her father's past, to have married into! That's really too much of a coincidence for me.

Carl: That doesn't bother me. What gets me is this sudden business with Barsad or Solomon Pross or whatever his name really is. That comes from left field.

Danielle: That's true, and the ending depends a lot on that too, 'cause without that ace, Carton would have had nothing to bribe

Barsad with to get him into the prison so he could switch places with Darnay.

Kevin: Talk about coincidences! Doesn't that one bother you? How would he have pulled any of this off if he hadn't been, like, Darnay's double? And he frees him twice that way, too!

Danielle: Well, without that, though, there wouldn't have been a book!

CREATING THE STUDY GUIDE

After students have aired these and other reactions to elements in the story, they are ready to undertake the task of reviewing their idea folders for work they might use in their handbooks. At this point, we formalize the handbook project into an assignment with very specific requirements for each member of the class and for each group as a whole. We remind students that they are to develop a handbook or study guide for next year's class so that their reading of the text will be easier than it was for this year's class, but not so easy that students need not read the book. The students' challenge is to avoid the pitfalls that they noted in the sample commercial guidebooks. To assure accountability and contributions from each member of each group, we specify that, at a minimum, the handbook must contain three completed pieces from each group member and three pieces on which they collaborated. Each student is expected to deal extensively with at least one serious issue that the group found in the text—whether it be a discussion of secrets, balance and contrast, or thematic ideas, such as what the book has to say about the limits of power, problems of mob rule, the nobility of sacrifice, or the need to temper one's idealism with a touch of realism, even cynicism.

While we value artistic contributions from those with artistic talent, we want to frame the assignment so that no one's total contribution to the creation of the handbook can be so one-sided. We remind them that many of the collaborative pieces might already be started or even completed, as the *Tips for Reading* or activity sheets on unanswered questions and/or secrets. We encourage them to work together devising a cover with a catchy name for their group and on an introductory page that sets the stage for students who are reading the book. This introduction might contain a statement of purpose—what the group wants students to get out of reading the handbook and the book.

Carl's group discovered in their folder an activity on the secrets in the novel:

Secrets: ". . . every human creature . . . [is a] profound secret and mystery to every other." (p. 21)		
What We Know	**What Is Hidden (Secret)**	**Truth Behind Appearance**
Dr. Manette was in a French prison for 18 years.	What did he do to get such a harsh punishment? Why has he been released and how? (chapter 5)	????

They decide to work on this activity and include it in their Handbook. Rather than make a list of secrets for students and give them the answers, something that commercial guidebooks might do but that they wanted to avoid, they decided to make a list of leading questions or hints about where they might look to find secrets and leave it to the students who read the handbook to discover for themselves the details of those secrets. So they added to their chart as follows:

Secrets: ". . . every human creature . . . [is a] profound secret and mystery to every other." (p. 21)

What We Know	What Is Hidden (Secret)	Truth Behind Appearance
Dr. Manette was in a French prison for 18 years.	What did he do to get such a harsh punishment? Why has he been released, and how?	???
Charles Darnay has a French connection, one that leads to his accusation in England that he has committed treason on behalf of France.	What is Darnay's French identity? (book I, chapter 9) What does it have to do with the Manettes?	
Mme. Defarge is a leading figure in the revolution. She knits all the time, seeming to notice everything and nothing.	What does she knit? What is sinister about the the knitting? Why does she especially hate the Evremondes?	???
Jerry Cruncher is an odd-job man working for Tellson's Bank.	Why does he return at night with muddy boots and rust on his fingers? Why does he attend Barsad's funeral? And what does he discover that is important later?	???
Carton is a drunken lawyer who helps Darnay at his English trial.	He loves Lucie but doesn't feel worthy of her. What importance will his secret love have for the lives of the main characters in the story?	???
Barsad testifies at Darnay's English trial. Stryver discredits him as a spy being paid by the Crown.	No one in France knows the truth of why he left England. What else does Carton learn about his true identity? How does he use that information?	???

The table of contents for one very typical handbook was as follows:

The table of contents is followed by the introduction:

> From our experience of reading *A Tale of Two Cities* by Charles Dickens, we learned what a hard book it is and how difficult it can be to comprehend. Therefore, we have put together this handy booklet to help you in your reading. By breaking the study into the parts discussed in this booklet, we have tried to anticipate and resolve any problems you might face in trying to understand what is going on and Dickens' style of writing. We have given you hints of what to look for as you read, and we hope that this will be helpful to you.

One of the faults students often find when they study sample notes is that biographical material is not specifically targeted to *A Tale of Two Cities*. To correct that and make the biographical information more helpful, Bob's group wrote the following article for their handbook:

Dickens' Life and His Writing

Many believe that Dickens' form of writing and the feelings expressed in his writing were influenced by many of his own experiences. Dickens was born in 1812 and lived until he was 58 years old. During his life he was an inspirational English novelist. In his work he combined storytelling, humor, pathos, and irony with sharp social criticism and acute observation of people and places. *A Tale of Two Cities* was a significant novel that showed Dickens' concern with social issues, revealed his understanding of the psychology of human nature, and demonstrated how well he constructed a complicated story around a key historical occurrence. In looking at *A Tale of Two*

Cities, you can see that Dickens incorporated a lot of personal things into it. For examples, his father was imprisoned for debt in 1824. This left him alone to support himself. In *A Tale of Two Cities*, he has a number of scenes that revolve around imprisonment and jails. His knowledge of what the effect of imprisonment was on people must have come from his own experience. Another link may be found in his relationship with a young actress, which later destroyed his marriage.

ASSESSMENT AND EVALUATION

As students begin to organize their guides, determining what work to include, expand, revise, or delete, they return to their initial notes to review the desirable and helpful features of commercial notes and the additional features they created. For the pieces they find most useful, they identify elements of content and presentation. Taking time to describe these elements not only helps students to compile, revise, and copyedit their material but also to begin to create a rubric to assess and evaluate their final products. We ask them to include in this rubric the process of creating the guides. Of course, we are always ready to suggest additional elements that we think are essential, such as those dealing with insight and originality. Incorporating our students' ideas with ours, we then create a final version of the rubric (Fig. 5-1) to distribute to each group to remind them of the criteria that we have established together for evaluating a literary guidebook.

Figure 5-1. *Rubric for Assessment and Evaluation of Guidebooks*

---

4   Conveys a comprehensive and perceptive analysis of the key elements of the novel.

Presents a thoughtful integration of the information gathered by all members of the team.

Presents a persuasive and fully developed point of view.

Contains an insightful treatment of the themes, characters, events, and language.

Clearly exploits the format chosen for the guidebook to increase the reader's interest in and understanding of the novel.

Shows originality.

Reveals an organization that is coherent, logical, and most effective for the reader.

Conveys ideas and information with use of varied and complex sentence structure, fluent and precise language, a noticeable sense of voice, and few or no errors in spelling, punctuation, grammar, or usage.

---

3   Contains an in-depth analysis of some of the significant elements of the novel.

Integrates the information gathered by all members of the team.

Presents a persuasive and fully developed point of view.

Contains a treatment of the themes, characters, events, and language.

Reveals an understanding of the format chosen for the guidebook.

Shows originality.

Reveals an organization that is coherent and logical.

Conveys ideas and information with use of sentences of varied structure and length, appropriate and specific language, and few errors in spelling, punctuation, grammar, and usage that do not interfere with communication.

2   Contains a consideration of some elements of the novel, but not necessarily the most important ones.

Partially integrates the information gathered by all members of the team.

Presents a point of view and develops it with accurate but limited detail.

Includes limited treatment of themes, characters, events, and language.

Reveals some understanding of the format chosen for the guidebook.

Shows some originality.

Organizes pieces into a beginning, middle, and end but may not have selected the most effective organization to gain the reader's interest in or understanding of the book.

Conveys information with some variety of sentence structure and length, language that is appropriate and accurate, and some errors in spelling.

1   May omit treatment of some aspects of the novel, such as theme, characters, events, and language.

Shows little or no originality.

Includes little variety in structure and length of sentences, uses language that is vague and inappropriate with errors in spelling, punctuation, grammar, or usage that interfere with communication.

CONCLUSION

Studying a text such as *A Tale of Two Cities* within the context of creating a handbook for future readers has several advantages. Students know from the outset that the work they do as they make meaning from their reading of the text will culminate in a real product to be read and used by a real audience of other young people. As such, the task and the study has intrinsic authenticity and value for them. The attempt to clarify problems that they anticipate others might have with the reading enhances their own understanding and appreciation of the book. They are encouraged to think independently as they go through the book. No two groups focus on the same issues in the text, nor do any two handbooks look all that much alike. They make connections and discoveries in their groups and are empowered by these discoveries to have more confidence in their own ability to grapple with complex material, written so long ago. In the end, they enjoy the story more than they ever thought they would, and they also have a good grasp of key elements of Dickens' craft in writing the book. This understanding will help them with the next book(s) they read, whether for assignments or on their own. One student, Jessica, was overheard commenting the following to her group.

> I hate to admit this, but I never read a book now without having a pencil in my hand to jot down some idea that occurs to me as I am reading. No one despises these journal things more than I do, but I have to admit that I'm doing some of this stuff on my own now.

Creating a handbook for future classes of students is a project that can be a valuable aid in the study of any number of texts. Students from one school might want to send such a handbook to another school via e-mail or "snail mail" and to institute dialogue with a school, even one in another country, on differing perceptions of such a book. For example, how different is it for a class in an English school to study *A Tale of Two Cities*? Students in another school or another country might be willing to share an analysis of what they found helpful in the handbook and what they would like to see added, as well as what they agree with and what they disagree with in students' interpretations of various aspects of the book. In any event, the primary value of the handbook is in its creation.

ADDITIONAL TEXTS

Additional texts for which a handbook or guide would be effective include the following:

Beloved by Toni Morrison: To follow the intricacies of Toni Morrison's contemporary classic requires a considerable knowledge of history and mythology. The creation of a handbook for a student audience requires a close study of the historical context and the mythological allusions that give the book depth and meaning.

Moby Dick by Herman Melville: The handbook format helps students to comprehend the complexity of the characters, events, and ideas of this book. Students need to make sense of the symbolism, the details of whaling, the vastness of the themes, the richness of the allusions, and the language. In putting together a handbook, groups of students must focus on these key elements in such a way as to make them accessible to other students.

Billy Budd by Heman Melville: This book is so rich in symbolism and biblical allusions that for students to make meaning of this text requires careful study. The handbook format affords individual students the opportunity to concentrate on a particular element of the novel and working with colleagues to create a handbook that reflects their understandings and is helpful to other students reading the book.

Portrait of the Artist by James Joyce: This challenging narrative has the potential to speak to many different kinds of students. The book's focus on a young person's self-identity and purpose in life engages students, but the complexity of its many layers of symbolism and allusion often make the reading difficult. However, the preparation of a handbook provides both the focus and the assistance for making meaning that students need.

CHAPTER 6

The American Dream and All That Jazz

The Great Gatsby is a multidimensional novel that gives students an opportunity to explore a literary masterpiece rich in imagery and symbolism, as well as complex characters and relationships. It is also rich in vivid details of the Jazz Age, that seminal decade of the 20th century that began with the end of World War I and ended with the Great Depression. America changed forever in those years, and so did the American Dream. The enlightened belief that individual happiness was the result of moral integrity and honest, hard work was replaced by a hedonistic commitment to self-indulgence characterized by shallow relationships based solely on immediate gratification.

For this era and the ideas in Fitzgerald's novel to come alive for students, we structure our study around the creation of a film version of the novel. The film is a perfect vehicle for study of the false values of the Jazz Age because film, by its very nature, is illusionary.

ENGAGING THE STUDENTS

We begin by creating an activity around Nick's final judgment of the callous actions of the Buchanans. Students consider this description: "They were careless people, . . . They smashed up things and creatures . . . and let other people clean up the mess they had made . . ." (pp. 180–181, Scribners edition) We have students organize themselves into groups of three to write a movie scene for which this could be the epithet. They are to imagine who these "careless people" are, what and whom they "smashed up" and how, and what kinds of "messes" other people had to clean up. We give them time in class to get started and encourage them to complete their stories outside class.

For groups having some initial difficulty, we suggest that they consider the carelessness of drunk drivers, greedy land developers, unscrupulous investment brokers, or others who care only about themselves, without regard for anyone else.

The scenarios begin to emerge, some of them domestic narratives of selfish boyfriends, girlfriends, or family members, others more general stories on abuses of the environment or the public trust, and still others historical indictments of robber barons, dictators, and conquerors. What students create depends upon the knowledge and experience they bring to the task. As each group shares its scenario about "careless people," we begin to make notes highlighting some common characteristics of these people:

- Self-centered
- Self-indulgent
- Indifferent to the effect they have on others
- Irresponsible
- Manipulative
- Aggressive
- Self-righteous

We consider this list in a discussion exploring the impact that people with these qualities have on others, especially those who try to live morally responsible lives that reflect the ideals of the American Dream. For example, we look at a particularly appropriate story, such as the one created by Norman's group.

The Dreamboat

Bobby was a hunk. All the girls said so, and even the teachers liked to look at him. Of course, Bobby knew that he was good-looking; he worked at it. He lifted weights, wore great clothes, and even had his wavy black hair cut by a stylist. So it was no wonder that every girl in school was ready to drop dead for him, but Bobby played it cool. He was nice and friendly to all of them, but he never had a special girlfriend—at least not until he met Emily, the smartest girl in school.

Emily was a real brain and kind of a nerd, too. She was in the advanced math and science classes, Advanced Placement English, fourth-year French, and the orchestra (she played the flute). She wasn't exactly shy, but she never hung out much and would be the last person in the whole world who'd ever pierce her belly button or get a tattoo.

Anyway, Bobby started talking to Emily. You'd see him sometimes, standing at her locker like he was waiting for her, or going over to her in the cafeteria. And then he started gong to her house after school. That didn't seem right for Bobby. Nobody could see him hangin' out with somebody like Emily. He was just too cool for her.

Fred asked him one time what was up with him and Emily, and Bobby just said, "Hey man, Emily's okay, so lay off."

After that he was spending a lot more time with Emily, which was really weird because it was May and the weather was nice and warm, good for the beach. Instead of playing beach volleyball every afternoon, old Bobby was with Emily.

Bobby was really different, and Emily was, too. She seemed friendlier and even said "hi" to some of Bobby's friends. She told Jennifer in the girl's room one day that she was going to the prom and that her mom had bought her a beautiful dress. Jennifer said, "I guess you're going with Bobby." Emily smiled and said, "Yes."

As prom night got closer, the guys began to rent tuxes and hire limos, and the girls made appointments at beauty shops and nail salons. Fred asked Bobby if he wanted to share a limo with him, but Bobby said that he and his date were coming by themselves.

The night of the prom, everybody looked great. All the guys were in tuxes and the girls were like magazine models, except some of them weren't too steady in their high heels. One couple was missing, though: Bobby and Emily. Everyone especially wanted to see what Emily would look like.

Then, in came Bobby, looking like John Travolta in a white tuxedo, and with him was a knockout girl in a black satin evening gown cut so low in the front that every guy's eyes were popping out of their heads. This babe was drop-dead gorgeous, but she wasn't Emily. Bobby introduced her as Nicole. Jennifer found out later from Bobby that Nicole went to school in the city, and that she and Bobby had been dating for over a year. Jennifer didn't say anything about Emily. Nobody did, at least that night.

The Monday after the prom, Emily wasn't in school. In fact, she didn't come back to school before summer vacation began. One day Fred asked Bobby what had been going on with Emily. Bobby just laughed and explained that he had been failing math and had got a warning notice in English, so he had to do something. So he started seeing Emily. He pretended he was interested in her, and yeah, he did say something about the prom, even though he knew all along that he was taking Nicole. "Women will believe anything they want," he said. "Let's face it, Emily got something out of it. I gave her my time and made her feel like a woman, and I got through math and English. She got what she wanted, and I got what I wanted. No big deal. Emily'll get over it."

After students have listened to the story, we ask them to consider the ways in which Bobby's behavior reveals the characteristics of careless behavior, which we have listed on the board. Angry at the betrayal of Emily by Bobby, the girls in particular are quick to point out that Bobby's manipulative, self-centered behavior reflects his complete indifference to Emily's feelings. The girls are outraged by Bobby's justification of his actions: claiming that Emily had nothing to complain about because she "got something out of it" just as he did. Of course, she didn't get what she wanted, which was for Bobby to be her boyfriend and escort her to the prom. Instead, her dream was shattered, and she was humiliated and heartbroken. Students like to speculate on what happened to her after the prom, wondering if she even showed up for graduation and what psychological effects Bobby's behavior might have had on her. Almost any story that students produce will provide similar opportunities for a discussion of the effects of the behavior of careless people on the lives and dreams of others.

INTERACTING WITH THE NOVEL

The Screenwriter's Notebook

We introduce *The Great Gatsby* as the story of a man who devotes his life to the fulfillment of a dream. So obsessed is he with his dream that he succumbs to the corruption of careless people. To follow the unfolding of Gatsby's story, we ask our students to think of themselves as filmmakers who are reading the novel with an eye to filming it. To that end, they are to keep a screenwriter's notebook of ideas for the following:

- The setting of each major scene
- An elaboration of scenes that are only vaguely sketched in the text
- In-depth analyses of major characters, including their values, motives, gestures, and clothing
- Casting ideas

We instruct students to include the following elements in their screenwriter's notebook: (a) a summary of a key scene for each chapter, (b) a description of the setting of this scene, (c) a description of the characters in the scene, and (d) a description of the action to be filmed. Our purpose here is not to teach filmmaking but to provide a context for engaging students in visualizing the characters and the action and for making meaning of the narrative.

Anthony's notebook for a scene from chapter 1 is characteristic of a thoughtful student response to this assignment:

> **Summary:** In the first chapter, Nick is disgusted by the marriage problems he sees at his cousin Daisy Buchanan's house.
>
> **Setting:** A beautiful house in East Egg on Long Island Sound. Obviously, very rich people live here. The house has large, open French windows at each end of the living room. Pale curtains blow "like pale flags twisting towards the frosted wedding cake of the ceiling and then rippl[ing] over the wine-

colored rug." Two young women in white dresses look like they're "floating" above an enormous couch. They go out onto a rosy-colored porch, where four candles flicker on the table. It is sunset.

Characters: Tom is a large man, a guy with a "muscular, cruel body." He has a gruff voice and talks down to others, even to Daisy. Daisy is ditsy. She is dressed in white. She has an "absurd, charming little laugh" and doesn't know what to talk about. She says such things as "I'm p-paralyzed with happiness" and "I always watch for the longest day of the year and then miss it." She is also very beautiful. "Her face was sad and lovely with bright things in it, bright eyes and a bright passionate mouth . . ."

Lights, Camera, Action: Camera is on Daisy, Tom, Nick, and Jordan Baker at the dinner table on the porch as the sun sets. They are drinking wine and discussing a book that Tom has read, when the phone rings in the house. The butler comes to the porch to tell Tom to take the call, and he goes inside. The camera comes in on Daisy's face. She isn't happy. Suddenly she throws her napkin on the table and runs into the house. The camera stays on Nick and Jordan Baker as they hear in the background the voice of Daisy saying something to Tom. Nick looks embarrassed. He doesn't know what to do or say. He gets up and makes some excuse and leaves.

The Cast of Characters

After students have read the first three chapters of the novel and completed their screenwriter's notebook for those chapters, they meet in their groups to refine their visions of Nick, Tom, Daisy, and Gatsby. They create visual representations of these characters, including an appropriate quote for each picture. Each group presents its pictures to the class and defends its judgment about the personalities of Nick, Tom, Daisy, and Gatsby.

At this point each group is eager to make casting decisions. We have discovered that students have an easier time creating scenarios when they can envision a specific actor in each of the various roles. To facilitate the group casting process, students review their analyses of the major characters and select actors for each role.

For Nick, students rarely have strong feelings about who should play him because they see him as the narrator and not the focus of events. Some students say that he is not very exciting, but nevertheless they want the actor to convey his earnestness and sensitivity. Jimmy Smitts and Noah Wylie are frequent nominees for this role.

For Tom, students look for a villain type. Alec Baldwin is often mentioned. He has the physical attributes, but some girls think he is too gorgeous. Tommy Lee Jones is another popular choice because of his ability to look menacing and convey latent cruelty.

For Daisy, some students like Sarah Jessica Parker or Drew Barrymore, but others want someone more fragile and prefer Julia Roberts, who has Daisy's charming little laugh, her low, thrilling voice, and an expectant, wide-eyed look about her.

For Gatsby, students look for someone who is good-looking, has a sincere smile, and possesses a compelling vitality. They want someone who can, as Gatsby did, "concentrate on you with an irresistible prejudice in your favor and believe in you as you would like to believe in yourself." With this description in mind, students consider Harrison Ford, Nicholas Cage, Brad Pitt, and sometimes Robert Redford; the latter amazes us, because rarely do we have a student who is familiar with the 1974 movie *The Great Gatsby*.

Key Scene 1

Students' pleasure in casting a movie version of the novel compensates for the difficulty that some of them may have in getting involved in the initial chapters of the book and in coping with Fitzgerald's sophisticated language. Building on their interest in visualizing characters, we ask them to imagine and describe a scene that introduces Nick and would immediately engage a viewer's interest. We encourage students to be as creative as they wish and to play with the words and actions of the first few pages of the book.

To help them in writing camera direction for their scenes, we review some filming vocabulary, such as *zoom, pan, close-up, medium close, long-shot,* and *fade out*. We also remind them that a voice-over narrator can convey what characters are thinking.

Andy's group worked diligently and enthusiastically to produce the following scenario:

> The setting is a Manhattan street in the 1920s. People are bustling back and forth, weaving between the automobiles in the busy street. In the background you can hear the sound of the train whistle and see the steam rising from drainage holes in the street. You can hear the beeping of the car horns and the shouts of paperboys and vendors advertising their wares. Slowly the camera turns to the doors of a high-rise building and then slowly pans up the face of the building.
>
> The camera focuses in on a tiny office on the 16th floor. The walls are an ugly green color, and on one wall is a painting of a beach scene. The room is furnished with an oversize desk and an old, beat-up leather chair. In that chair, pouring over a mound of papers, is a tall, thin, young man: Nick Carroway. We zoom in on his face just as he removes his glasses, rubs his eyes, and lets out a tired sigh. He is thinking about visiting his cousin Daisy and her husband, Tom Buchanan. In the voice-over he says to himself, "I hope I'm up for this after the day I've had! But I can't wait to see Daisy again. What a sweetheart she is, but I don't know what she sees in Tom Buchanan. I've never

liked him. He was so conceited, so pushy . . . a real s.o.b. even when I knew him in college."

The scene shifts to Nick on a train, on his way home to West Egg, after work. Nick thinks to himself about how much he needs a vacation. The voice-over comes on, and we hear Nick saying, "God, I can't remember when I've been this tired. I'll be lucky to keep my eyes open during the long train ride home and then be able to be good company for Daisy. Maybe they'll invite me to stay for the weekend at their swanky house in East Egg. That would sure be a relief from this sweltering heat and the drag of the Bond market routine." We hear the clanking of the train wheels and pass a number of stops very quickly; finally, the train slows down and comes to a stop at a station marked West Egg. Nick Carroway jolts himself awake just in time and stumbles off the train.

It's twilight now. Nick gets into an old Dodge and drives about 3 miles down a road to a cramped, old white house. Near it is a huge mansion. This house is a "factual imitation of some Hotel de Ville in Normandy, with a tower on one side, spanking new under a thin beard of raw ivy, and a marble swimming pool and more than forty acres of lawn and garden." You can hear the sound of the ocean in the background and the waves lapping at the shore. Nick stares at his neighbor's house, shakes his head, and then walks into his little house. The camera follows him as he walks slowly up his walkway, opens the front door, enters the house, closes the door, and pours himself a glass of milk from the icebox. He takes his glass out to his porch and stares at the shoreline. Across the small bay is East Egg and more palacelike mansions. Nick thinks, "My house is an eyesore next to places that rent for $12,000 a season."

The students reflect their careful reading of the text and their attention to the elements that will translate into visual images and make the narrative come alive on the screen. We applaud their appropriate inclusion of direct reference.

Continuing the Cast of Characters

Now that the image of the affluence of the Eggs is established in the opening scenarios, we direct students to visualize the valley of the ashes where "ash gray men swarm up with leaden spades and stir up an impenetrable cloud, which screens their obscure operations from your sight." We want them to see the bleakness of this desolate area dominated by the eyes of T. J. Eckleburg and inhabited by George and Myrtle Wilson. We ask them to review their screenwriter's notebook entries for chapter 2 and share with the class their portrayals of the Wilsons. Many of the students have described George Wilson in Fitzgerald's words as a "blond, spiritless, . . . anemic, and faintly handsome" pathetic little man. Myrtle, on the other hand, is described as a forceful presence, in her middle 30s, "and faintly stout, but she carries her surplus flesh sensuously . . . she has a perceptible vitality about her as if the nerves of her body were continually smoldering."

Students have difficulty casting George's role because he is so bland. They consider Anthony Edwards (from *ER*) Dave Barry (from *Dave's World*), and Luke Perry. For Myrtle, they consider Raquel Welch and an overweight Sharon Stone with dark hair.

Exploring Characterizations

Once all the major players have been introduced and cast for a film version of the book, students need to see the connections between these characters and their dreams. With the exception of Nick, each character is searching for the fulfillment of an unattainable dream with a singleness of purpose that leads to an indifference to the effect of one's actions on other people. The result of this repeated indifference to others is an acceptance of the philosophy that "the end justifies the means." To help our students discover this truth, we send them to their groups and have them examine one of the major characters that they have analyzed for casting. We do not assign Nick for this project, since he is the interpreter of the action and the moral conscience of the author. (Students examine his role in another context later in the study of the novel.)

We ask each group to develop a chart in which they identify each of the following items for its assigned character:

- The dream of the character
- What the character is willing to do to attain the dream
- The effect on others of the character's pursuance of the dream
- The consequences of the pursuit on the moral integrity of the character

With each entry on their charts, students must cite references from the text to support what they list in each category. At this point in their study of the text, students can identify the dreams of the major players, describe some of what the characters are willing to do to attain their dreams, and begin to indicate some of the effects on others as they pursue those dreams. As the students continue their reading and discussing of the novel, they will add to the character charts, revealing their insight into the consequences of the pursuit of the dreams on the moral integrity of the characters.

For example, a group working on Myrtle produced the following entry for its chart:

Dream	Actions to attain the dream	Impact on others	Consequences
To be a grand lady and live luxuriously (pp. 29–31)	Cheats on her husband, lies, calls Tom at his home, is abused by Tom (pp. 15, 26, 38).	Hurts Tom's and Daisy's marriage, treats her husband like dirt (pp. 15–16, 25–26).	Sells herself to Tom, is a tramp and breaks her marriage vows (pp. 23–38).

Each group shares its initial chart entries with the entire class. Obviously, some charts are more detailed than others, partly because the impact of some characters on others in pursuing their dreams may not be felt as early in the novel as it is with Myrtle. But at least all the students begin to get a more detailed picture of each character, which will be useful as they continue to develop their screenwriters' notebooks and create their film scenarios.

The next assigned scenario is based on a close reading of chapters 4 and 5. This section of the novel gives students an opportunity to get to know the mysterious Gatsby. To help their classmates with their scenarios, the group charting Gatsby needs to extend its work and share the results with everyone.

Dream	Actions to attain the dream	Impact on others	Consequences
To have Daisy and the classy life she has.	He builds a mansion across the bay from Daisy's house. He gives huge parties for people he doesn't even know or care about just because he hopes that someday Daisy will show up. He lies about his background to make himself sound like a big shot. He does business with a crook. He uses Nick to get together with Daisy. He tries to impress Daisy with his possessions. (pp. 21–22, 39–56, 65–67, 69–74, 91–94)	Impresses Daisy and Nick. He's used by people who gossip about him. (pp. 43–46, 68–69, 91–94)	We don't know enough yet to say.

Key Scene 2

To help students select scenes to script, we suggest scenes from chapters 1–5 that are only alluded to in the novel and would have to be written for a film version. Some students focus on Gatsby's party and want to picture Gatsby as he observes his guests and dreams about Daisy. Other students like to create scenarios dramatizing Gatsby's encounter with Tom in the restaurant (chapter 4). Still others are intrigued by Daisy's romance with Gatsby in 1917, when they met in Louisville, and her supposed behavior on her wedding night, when she drunkenly bemoans her decision to marry Tom and clutches a letter from Gatsby (chapter 4). Perhaps the most popular scene to dramatize is the one in Nick's house after Gatsby and Daisy are left alone (chapter 5). Students like to imagine the conversation that leads Gatsby from being nervous to glowing with delight at being with Daisy. Adrian's team, obviously influenced by romance novels, wrote the following for that imagined scene:

We are in Nick's bungalow. It is raining very hard as a crew of gardeners is mowing the lawn, trimming the hedges, planting flowers, working steadily despite the rain. A huge truck drives up to the house delivering loads of fresh flowers (assorted types), and a dozen vases to put them in. Gatsby is talking to Nick inside the living room. Gatsby is dressed in a white flannel suit, silver shirt, and gold tie. He is very pale and has dark circles under his eyes. Nick is wearing a blue turtleneck and gray pants. Gatsby paces back and forth, looking at his watch.

Gatsby: I'm going home. Nobody's coming to tea. It's too late! I can't wait all day.

Nick: Don't be silly. She isn't even due to come yet. It's not quite 4.

Gatsby sits down again, looking forlorn and miserable. Suddenly a car motor is heard, and Nick goes outside to greet Daisy and protect her from the rain with his big yellow umbrella. Daisy steps out of her car looking very happy. She is wearing a big lavender hat, a thin white sleeveless dress, white shoes and stockings, with a strand of pearls at her throat.

Daisy *(in her low, thrilling voice):* Is this absolutely where you live, my dearest one? I'm p-positively delighted to be here alone with you, Nick. Are you in love with me? Is that why I had to come alone?

Nick: Ah. That's my secret. I have a very special surprise for you, my dearest cousin. Send your chauffeur far away and tell him not to come back for at least an hour or more.

Daisy: Come back in an hour, Ferdie. *(To Nick)* His name's Ferdie.

Nick hurries Daisy into the house, guiding her by her arm and taking care to keep her as dry as possible. As they enter Nick's living room, Nick looks startled as he sees that the room is empty.

Nick: Well, that's funny.

Daisy: What's funny? Are you expecting someone else?

They hear a knock at the front door. Nick goes to the door, opens it and we see Gatsby, "pale as death, with his hands plunged like weights in his coat pockets, with a puddle of water around him and his eyes glaring tragically" at Nick. He enters the room "as if he were on a wire" and stares at Daisy.

Daisy: J-Jay, my God, Jay! I can't believe it? I can't believe it's you. Is it really you? I'm so-so glad to see you, so awfully glad to see you again.

Gatsby says nothing, just stands in the middle of the room staring at her. Nick goes out of the room. Finally after a long silence, Gatsby takes her hand in his and holds it tenderly.

Gatsby: Daisy, oh, my Daisy, you are even more beautiful than I remembered you.

Daisy (*looking away from him and in a low, thrilling voice*): Oh, Jay. Do you really think so? I'm p-paralyzed with happiness that you think so. It's been so long, so very long. I've missed you so, I really have. I felt abandoned when you left.

Gatsby: Oh, Daisy, I hated to leave you. How could you have married anyone else, especially Tom Buchanan?

Daisy (*moving nervously to the window away from Gatsby*): Oh. Please, Jay, let's not talk about that. Let's not spoil this beautiful moment.

Gatsby (*following her and then taking her in his arms*): But you knew that I loved you, loved you more than anything in the world, and that I would come back for you.

Daisy (*turns towards him, looks up into his eyes and whispers*): And you have, Jay; oh, yes, you have.

He kisses her.

Daisy (*breathlessly*): Oh, Jay. I'm overcome with happiness. (*She begins to cry.*)

At this point Nick comes back into the house; Gatsby is glowing, Daisy is smiling through her tears.

Gatsby: Why, hello, Old Sport!

The scene ends.

Exploring the American Dream

Students share the highlights of their scenarios and explain the understanding of the characters that led them to embellish the novel in the ways they did. Understanding Gatsby's obsession with Daisy and some of its ramifications, they are curious about his background. They wonder about those rumors and how many of them might be true. Chapter 6 gives students the answers they are looking for and also provides an opportunity to discuss Gatsby's understanding of the American Dream as being rooted in money. We give them time in class to review the chapter in their groups and continue their screenwriters' notebooks, and the Gatsby group can receive class help in fleshing out the chart with significant details from chapter 6.

We guide students in understanding the relationship between James Gatz and Dan Cody and in recognizing the significance of Gatz's transformation into Gatsby, calling their attention to key passages on pages 98–102. After students have completed their work with this chapter, we assign the reading of the rest of the novel, if they have not already completed it. Because these final chapters are so rich in action and character detail, we divide our consideration of them into several sections. Students share their screenwriters' notebooks with the class and focus on the confrontation in the hotel room, the accidental death of Myrtle, the killing of Gatsby, and Gatsby's funeral.

Brooke's notebook included the following:

> **Summary** (hotel confrontation): Gatsby wants Daisy to say that she has always loved him and not Tom, so he goes to lunch at the Buchanans'. Nick and Jordan are also there. It's very, very, hot so Daisy suggests that they all drive to New York City to the Plaza Hotel. Tom drives Gatsby's car, and Gatsby drives Tom's. In the hotel room, Tom starts criticizing Gatsby's past and suggests that he is involved with gangsters. Daisy gets more and more upset until she finally begs Tom to take her home. Tom knows that he has won over Gatsby, but he insists that she drive home with Gatsby. He says to Daisy, "Go on. He won't annoy you. I think he realizes that his presumptuous little flirtation is over."

> **Setting**: Plaza Hotel, 4 p.m. Stifling heat; large room, windows are open; gusts of hot air blow in. There's a mirror on the left as you come in. There is a flowered carpet on the floor. The walls are papered in a pale beige print. A crystal chandelier hangs from a high wedding-cake ceiling. The two windows on the far wall are almost floor to ceiling and the windows are covered with see-through white curtains. In the room are two small sofas and several chairs arranged close together so that people can sit in them and talk.

> **Characters**: Tom seems to enjoy what's happening and making Daisy and Gatsby uncomfortable. He doesn't pay any attention to Jordan and Nick. He doesn't care how they might feel about all of this.

> Gatsby gets more and more nervous. He keeps trying to get Daisy to say that she will go off with him and that she never loved Tom. When she can't do that, and Tom calls Gatsby a bootlegger and makes Daisy afraid of him, Gatsby "looked to Nick as if he had killed a man." Daisy seems helpless and unable to handle the situation. She always wants to run away or stop anything unpleasant from being said or happening. First she wants to run into the city, and then later she wants to run away from the hotel. She can't bring herself to say what Gatsby wants her to say or even what Tom wants her to say. "It was as though she had never, all along, intended doing anything at all." She seems about to fall apart.

> **Lights, Camera, Action**: The camera pans the hotel room, focusing on the curtains to show that no air is moving and then on the red, perspiring faces of the characters, especially Tom and Gatsby. When Tom and Gatsby are trying to make Daisy say what they want her to say, the camera should move up close on Daisy to show her reactions until she turns to her husband, sobbing, and he says, "I'm going to take better care of you from now on."

As students share notebook entries on this and other scenes from chapters 7, 8, and 9, we guide them to come to certain understandings about the four characters:

Gatsby believes that he can re-create the past, that Daisy will renounce Tom and be his forever. Even after the confrontation in the hotel room and the death of Myrtle, he refuses to acknowledge that his dream of possessing Daisy is over. Gatsby deludes himself and embraces a dream in the form of Daisy, who he believes is attainable only if he is rich enough. Ironically, she is not worth having; she is all false promise. For this illusion, Gatsby becomes a gangster, a bootlegger, a liar, perhaps even a murderer; he sacrifices his integrity and ultimately, his life.

Daisy is a shallow, empty person, not worth having, a woman who has no real feelings for anyone—not her daughter, her husband, her lover, or Gatsby. There is no purpose in her life; she is, as we see her in the beginning of the novel, one who "floats" from one experience to another, untouched by any deep emotion.

Tom is an accomplice in Gatsby's death and is completely indifferent to the effect of his actions on the Wilsons. He is willing to run off with Daisy after Myrtle's death and Gatsby's murder with no moral compunction, feeling blameless of any responsibility for the deaths of three people. He is morally corrupt.

Nick, the moral man in the immoral society, is left to deal with the results of the messes of careless people. He alone cares enough to arrange a respectable funeral for Gatsby. He alone recognizes the shallowness of his cousin Daisy and the illusory nature of Gatsby's dream. He rejects the meaningless, amoral life of the rich Eggs by returning to the Midwest where family, tradition, and respect for the individual remain important.

Completing the Character Charts

To synthesize these understandings about each character, we ask each student group to complete its chart for its character. Natalie's group presented its findings for Daisy:

Dream	Actions to attain the dream	Impact on others	Consequences
To be the adored princess.	Marries Tom. Surrounds herself with beautiful, expensive things, avoids unpleasantness of any kind. She is coy and flirtatious; has a romantic affair with Gatsby but wants to stay married to Tom. Rejects Gatsby when she finds out that he is connected to crooks. Fails to take responsibility for killing Myrtle. Goes away on vacation to escape the mess she created.	She leads Gatsby to believe that she loves him and will divorce Tom and marry him. She causes Tom to try to destroy Gatsby's reputation. She's directly responsible for the death of Myrtle and indirectly responsible for the deaths of Gatsby and Wilson. She lost Nick's love and respect.	She exposes her empty, shallow, self-centered, self-indulgent nature. She leaves Nick disgusted with the way of life she represents. Her life has no purpose or meaning.

Once the groups have completed their charts, they display them for all the students to study as they script their final scenarios and plan their video versions of *The Great Gatsby*. For their final scene we encourage them to select incidents toward the end of the book that are not fully realized. For example, they may script what happens when Daisy goes home to Tom after she has run over Myrtle. Students imagine what she would say, determine if Tom knows the truth, what the couple decides to do, and what happens next. Or they might write about Wilson tracking down the killer car, going to Tom's house, and then heading for Gatsby's to kill Gatsby, then himself. What goes through Wilson's mind; what does Tom say to him? Another possibility is the scene in which students describe Myrtle's accidental killing. Students write the dialogue between Gatsby and Daisy before and after the accident. A popular scene to script is Nick's observation of Tom and Daisy in their kitchen "conspiring" after the death of Myrtle. What do they actually say and plan? Some groups dramatize Nick's efforts to arrange a proper funeral for Gatsby.

Key Scene 3

Anthony's group, especially interested in how the film would end, produced the following scenario based on its reading of chapter 9:

> In the driveway of Gatsby's house are several police cars and the coroner's van. A rope is stretched across the driveway. A policeman is standing guard to keep away the sightseers. The camera shifts to the front foyer. The house used to be full of laughing people and music, but now it is full of low murmuring voices and men in trench coats. The men are scribbling on their notepads. In the background a uniformed policeman is snapping pictures of Gatsby's body and the pool area. As all this is happening, the voice-over (Nick) says: "I remember the rest of that day, and the night and the next day, only as an endless drill of police and photographers and newspapermen in and out of Gatsby's front door."
>
> The camera flashes back to Nick holding a newspaper. The camera is now looking over his shoulder. We can see that the headline says, "Jay Gatsby Shot to Death." Nick reads aloud in a half whisper to himself, "Love triangle catches up with millionaire Jay Gatsby." Nick slowly shakes his head in disgust and sighs as he turns and walks into his house.
>
> Then the camera switches to Nick's house. We see Nick sitting in the chair in his kitchen, and he's on the telephone. He is speaking to a maid at Daisy's house.
>
> **Nick:** Hello. Is Daisy there? Well, when will they be back? Do you know where they went? Auggh. [*Slams down the receiver in disgust, then gets on the phone again.*] Operator, will you ring Mr. Wolfshiem's office again?
>
> **Operator:** Sorry sir, I've already rung three times. I'm afraid that no one is there.

Nick slams down the receiver for a second time. Music comes up, something slow and thoughtful. The camera fades out and then fades back in to the next morning. There is a knock on Nick's door. Nick comes to the door, opens it to a message-boy with a telegram.

Message-boy: Please sign.

Nick signs the paper, the boy leaves, and Nick reads the telegram. The voice-over (Wolfshiem) comes on as his eyes scan the page. "Dear Mr. Caraway: This has been one of the most terrible shocks of my life. I can hardly believe it. Such a mad act as to kill Jay Gatsby. I cannot come out to West Egg right now as I am tied up with some very important business, I'm sure you understand. If there is anything I can do a little later on, let me know. Yours truly, Meyer Wolfshiem."

Nick (*crumpling the telegraph*): Yeah. All bullshit!

The camera is in Gatsby's foyer. There is a knock on the door and Nick opens the door. Standing on the porch is an old man with a gray beard. He looks up; his eyes are red and bloodshot.

Old Man: I'm Henry C. Gatz.
   Nick (*inviting him in*): Hello, Mr. Gatz. I'm Nick Carraway. I was . . . I was your son's friend.
   Gatz: I saw it in the Chicago newspaper. It was all in the Chicago newspaper. I came right away.
   Nick: I didn't know how to reach you.

The camera moves away from them as they continue talking, but we don't hear them. They get up and walk into the drawing room where the coffin is sitting. Nick waits in the foyer. After a moment Mr. Gatz comes out, his eyes filled with tears. The voice-over (Nick) says, "I guess he had reached an age where death no longer has the quality of ghastly surprise."

The camera is now at a cemetery. It is raining. We see a few people standing by a gravesite. A minister is speaking. Nick's voice-over says, "I felt a shame for Gatsby. I called everyone in his phone book, but no one cared that he had been killed. One man I phoned implied that he got what he deserved. However, that was my fault, for he was one of those who used to sneer most bitterly at Gatsby on the courage of Gatsby's liquor, and I should have known better than to call him."

We switch to a view of Nick's house on a cold fall morning. Nick is walking out to his car with the last of his bags. We can see that the car is packed full. Nick puts the bags in the car and then turns around to walk back and lock up the house. He pauses and turns to look at Gatsby's house. He walks slowly over to Gatsby's lawn. Music fades in: ghostly, half-invisible images of guests dancing, singing, and drinking on Gatsby's porch appear. Nick stands with his hands in his pockets and remembers those summer parties. Nick walks over to the white marble steps. He walks up and opens the door into the foyer and takes one final look around. Then he walks out, closes the door, and begins the walk back to his car. As he does so, the voice-over (Nick) comes on: "And as I walked back to my car, I thought of Gatsby's wonder when he first picked out the green light at the end of Daisy's dock. He had come a long way to his blue lawn, and his dream must have seemed so close that he could hardly fail to grasp it. He did not know that it was already behind him, somewhere back in that vast obscurity beyond the city, where the dark fields of the republic rolled on under the night. Gatsby believed in the green light, the orgiastic future that year by year recedes before us. It eluded us then, but that's no matter—tomorrow we will run faster, stretch out our arms further . . . And one fine morning. . . . So we beat on, boats against the current, borne back ceaselessly into the past."

PRODUCING THE FILM

To prepare their three scenarios for filming, student groups must review what they have already created and determine what concept about the novel they want to convey in their film. To find that concept, they reread the scenes, review the charts, and study their screenwriter's notebooks. The concepts that emerge tend to focus on the lifestyles of the Buchanans and Gatsby and the corruption of the ideals of the American Dream. Groups decide to make statements in their films such as "The end doesn't justify the means," "You can't live a lie," "Money doesn't necessarily buy happiness," "Romantic dreams can never be fulfilled," and "Careless people destroy lives without regret."

When the groups have stated their unifying concept of the novel, they are ready to write the narration that will introduce that concept and link it to their scripted scenes. Their scripts complete, they must annotate them with directions for blocking so that the actors know where to be and how to move, and for filming so that the camera crew will know when to pan and when to have a wide-angle shot, a close-up, or a medium close-up. We are not emphasizing cinematography here, only trying to give students some help so that their filming will be successful. Many of our students are skilled in using their video cameras and enjoy the opportunity to apply that skill to an academic project. Our best strategy is to give minimum direction and maximum latitude for students to film their scenarios.

Key Scene 1 was annotated as follows:

auto noise " horns train whistle	The setting is a Manhattan street in the 1920s. People are bustling back and forth, weaving between the automobiles in the busy street. In the background you can hear the sound of the train whistle and see the steam rising from drainage holes in the street. You can hear the beeping of the car horns and the shouts of paperboys and vendors advertising their wares. Slowly the camera turns to the doors of a high-rise building and then slowly pans up the face of the building.	<u>wide angel</u> <u>shot</u> <u>slow pan</u> up high-rise building <u>Pan up</u>

slow fade
of sound

sound out

voice-over

The camera focuses in on a tiny office on the 16th floor. The walls are an ugly green color, and on one wall is a painting of a beach scene. The room is furnished with an oversize desk and an old beat-up leather chair. In that chair, pouring over a mound of papers, is a tall, thin, young man: Nick Carroway. We zoom in on his face just as he removes his glasses, rubs his eyes, and lets out a tired sigh. He is thinking about visiting his cousin Daisy and her husband, Tom Buchanan. In the voice-over he says to himself, "I hope I'm up for this after the day I've had! But I can't wait to see Daisy again. What a sweetheart she is, but I don't know what she sees in Tom Buchanan. I've never liked him. He was so conceited, so pushy . . . a real s.o.b. even when I knew him in college."

medium
close-up

focus
on Nick.

close-up

With their scripts annotated for filming, we send them out to create their mini-movie versions of *The Great Gatsby*. In each group, at least one student usually has a video camera, but in case a group does not have access to a camera, we arrange for students to work with school equipment. We don't allow class time for filming, which means that students must schedule time after school, something they are willing to do because they enjoy the activity of "making a movie" and getting credit for it.

We monitor student progress on the filming by having student groups periodically submit completed progress charts. We comment on their responses and make suggestions that we expect them to incorporate into their final projects. We collect all their progress charts along with their annotated scripts at the end of the project.

Even if filming the scripts is not possible, the study of *The Great Gatsby* within the context of creating a movie script is still engaging and valid. In fact, just imagining the filmed version of the script has some advantages in that students can envision a big-budget Hollywood production of their versions of the novel. That ability to visualize images based on the written word is a critical reading skill and in itself a considerable achievement for many of our students.

EVALUATION

As in all project-based literary studies, the success of studying *The Great Gatsby* by creating a film script is dependent on our students' willingness to work productively on their own, in this case on their screenwriters' notebooks, and with others in their groups, in this case on scenarios and scripts. To evaluate their screenwriters' notebooks, we created a rubric with student input (Fig. 6-1). We begin the development of this evaluative instrument early in the study of the novel so that students can use it to guide them as they work on their notebooks. Their involvement in creating the rubric makes it meaningful to them, because as they contribute to it they gain a sense of what excellence looks like and what they must do to strive for it. To encourage that effort we model a screenwriter's notebook

Figure 6-1. *Rubric for Assessment and Evaluation of Screenwriters' Notebooks*

DIMENSIONS	4	3	2	1
Summary: an accurate, incisive, and focused description of the events on which the scene is based	Presents a complete and accurate description of events; reveals an in-depth understanding of the significance of events in the scene.	Presents an accurate description of events; reveals an understanding of the significance of events in the scene.	Presents events with limited accuracy; reveals some understanding of the significance of events in the scene.	Presents events that may be inaccurately described; reveals little or no understanding of the significance of events in the scene.
Setting: a description of the significant physical elements in the scene	Clearly and accurately describes all essential physical elements of the scene.	Accurately describes most essential physical elements of the scene.	Describes some physical elements of the scene.	Inadequate or inaccurate description of the physical elements of the scene.
Characters: an accurate, insightful description of the characters, their behaviors and their dreams	Reveals perceptive understanding of all characters and their dreams; shows insight into the effect of their behavior on others.	Reveals an understanding of most characters and their dreams; shows the effect of their behavior on others.	Reveals some understanding of most characters and their dreams; may not accurately show the effects of their behavior on others.	Reveals little understanding of the characters and their dreams; does not address the effect of their behavior on others.
Lights, Camera, Action: specific direction of camera focus that reveals an understanding of the significance of the scene	Demonstrates particularly effective use of camera to capture the drama and significance of the scene.	Demonstrates generally effective use of camera to capture the drama of the scene.	Demonstrates limited use of camera for its effect.	Demonstrates no understanding of the camera's potential to tell the story.

Figure 6-2. *Film Project Progress Chart*

Date: _____
Group names: _____
_____
_____
_____

Work completed before this class (specify who did what):_____
_____
_____
_____

Work accomplished during this class (describe contribution of each
group member): _____
_____
_____
_____

Work you need to do after this class (specify who will do what): _____
_____
_____
_____

Group grade _____
Individual Grade _____

entry and apply the rubric to it. This process also challenges us to be clear and specific in defining the gradations of performance for each level within the rubric. Of course, we must acknowledge the element of subjectivity in all evaluation, but the process of developing detailed rubrics with our students, coupled with experience in applying them, enables us and our students to judge their work more objectively than a holistic overview would allow.

To assess each group's progress on the film project we have the groups periodically submit progress charts (Fig. 6-2).

To evaluate their final film projects, we create another kind of rubric, one that is easier for students to help design but that has more meaning for them after they have contributed to the notebook rubric. Because of the nature of the film project, the diversity of group and individual experiences, we give students two grades: one for their group contributions to the products and one for their individual accomplishments. Figure 6-3 addresses what we and our students understand as the essential elements in designing and executing their film versions of *The Great Gatsby.*

Figure 6-3. *Rubric for Assessment and Evaluation of Film Projects*

	4	3	2	1
Accurate, complete chart for a character				
Well-developed scenes				
Believable scenario revealing knowledge of the way the characters function in the book				
Clear articulation of a thematic idea from the book dramatized by the scenes				

Preparation for video performance
    Set creation
    Knowledge of lines
    Connecting narration
    Blocking of scenes
    Appropriate music				

Participation in the group				
Performance, contribution to film product				
Group grade _____				
Individual grade _____				

CONCLUSION

The most obvious advantage of approaching *The Great Gatsby*, or any novel, as a potential screenplay is that it engages students' interest by appealing to their love of movies. They know from the beginning of the study that they are not going to be reading a book in order to write an essay and pass a test. Instead, they are thrust into the role of screenwriters, looking at a text through a filmmaker's lens, examining characters, events, and settings as a way to tell a story and make a statement about some aspect of the human condition. It gives them the opportunity to do the following activities:

- Read actively by visualizing, questioning, connecting, responding, and inferring

- Write for a variety of purposes and audiences by keeping a screenwriter's notebook, writing scenarios, and contributing to a screenplay
- Think critically by selecting key scenes on which to focus, deciding on a thematic idea to convey visually and linguistically, and evaluating their individual and group performances
- Work productively with others by listening to each other, sharing their thinking with each other, and making significant contributions to the group effort
- Take responsibility for their own learning and their commitment to the group

Occasionally when we share this approach to the study of a novel, some of our colleagues will comment on the absence of an analytical essay in the unit. Our response is that the essay is only one mode of writing and certainly a valuable one, but we believe that our students can learn to be better readers, writers, and thinkers by having experiences in a variety of modes, such as the screen scenario. The need for clarity, coherence, and correctness of expression is as important, if not more so, in a written product designed to convey an abstract idea through characterization and action for a visual medium than in an analytical essay. The student samples we have included here reveal a depth of understanding and insight based on a close reading and a thoughtful study of *The Great Gatsby* that exceed, in many cases, what we would expect in a literary essay. And equally important, our students enjoy the learning experience.

ADDITIONAL TEXTS

Additional texts for which the film script is effective include the following:

Angela's Ashes: This Pulitzer Prize–winning contemporary novel is eminently suited to the film medium. The visual clarity of Frank McCourt's narrative begs for dramatization. The challenge for students is to select those vignettes that give insight into the complex characterization and reveal the thematic motif that runs throughout the memoir. In selecting scenes and writing a script, students gain a deeper understanding of the forces at work on the characters and the significance of the narrative.

Catcher in the Rye by John Steinbeck: This book has never been made into a film because of J. D. Salinger's opposition. Nevertheless, our students can enrich their understanding of this American classic by bringing the character of Holden Caulfield to life in a dramatized version of the novel, particularly when the focus of their scripts is on the nature of Holden and his contradictions, speech, dress, dreams, and relationships.

When the Legends Die by Hal Borlandi: This story engages students, but not necessarily through its imagery. Author Hal Borland creates powerful symbolic scenes that reveal the extent of the loss of self experienced by Bear's Brother as he is forced to abandon his Native American culture to become Tom Black. When students translate this book into a film script, they discover that they must draw upon Borland's rich imagery in order to tell the story.

The Learning Tree by Gordon Parks: This book chronicles the childhood of an African American boy as he discovers and overcomes racial discrimination. The visual power of the narrative, particularly the description of the boy's dilemma during the trial of a White man falsely accused of murder, makes this novel ideal for a movie. In writing the script, students must select those scenes and focus attention on those elements that best reveal their understanding of the boy's character as influenced by his upbringing.

CHAPTER 7

Everything You Ever Wanted to Know About the Meaning of Life

No other work in the canon of world literature has been translated into more languages, studied by more scholars, generated more critical commentary, and fascinated more people than *Hamlet*. Certainly every professional or aspiring male actor has, in the almost 400 years since the play was written, envisioned himself as Hamlet. In each instance, the actor has made his own imprint on the role. So it's understandable that *Hamlet* is a prominent part of the high school literary canon, extolled by teachers but often feared by students. Its language, its length, the complexity of its characters, and the sophistication of its themes coupled with the mystique of its literary greatness can intimidate even the most committed students. Why, then, considering the challenges of *Hamlet*, do we keep it in the curriculum? The answer is simple: It's a powerful and uniquely relevant work for all kinds of students to study. The challenge for us as teachers is to take the awe out of *Hamlet* and let our students, as diverse an audience as that of London in 1600, discover the power and relevance of Shakespeare's greatest play.

What makes the play as relevant today as it was in 1600 are the universal topics that Shakespeare explores as he considers the meaning of life, including the following:

- Fear of death
- The role of fate
- Betrayal
- Revenge
- Moral corruption

These are difficult topics for people of any age to explore, but they are of particular significance for teenagers who are consumed with questions about the meaning of their lives, the inevitability of death, and the nature of human relationships. These concerns prompt us to scaffold students' study of the play to enable them to create modern analogues addressing these critical topics. This approach prompts our students to relate to the circumstances of the play and appreciate its thematic richness in the context of contemporary settings.

INTRODUCING THE PLAY

We introduce *Hamlet* by asking our students to tell us what they look for in a story, what interests them. Some identify such elements as humor, suspense, or the unknown. Others are intrigued by tragedy, love, and sex. Still others admit that they prefer blood and gore. And all students seem to be fascinated by the supernatural and that which is frightening. Because all of these are found in *Hamlet*, we can pique students' interest by telling them to watch for these elements as we read the play together. Once we have established that *Hamlet* has the potential to be a play they will like because it contains everything they look for in a great story, we prepare them for the opening scene by asking them to consider what they would do to create a foreboding tone. Students talk about *setting*, brainstorming various kinds of "scary" settings, such as old abandoned houses, dark and empty public buildings, cellars, and isolated cliffs. After some discussion many of them decide that any place can be made scary by lighting, music, and weather. Darkness, stormy or foggy weather, and eerie music can evoke a foreboding mood, one that indicates that something unnatural, even evil, is about to occur. Then we read the first 17 lines of act 1, scene 1, of *Hamlet*.

Bernardo: Who's there?

Francisco: Nay, answer me. Stand and unfold yourself.

Bernardo: Long live the king!

Francisco: Bernardo?

Bernardo: He.

Francisco: You come most carefully upon your hour.

Bernardo: 'Tis now struck twelve. Get thee to bed, Francisco.

Francisco: For this relief much thanks. 'Tis bitter cold, And I am sick at heart.

Bernardo: Have you had quiet guard?

Francisco: Not a mouse stirring.

Bernardo: Well, good night.
If you do meet Horatio and Marcellus,
The rivals of my watch, bid them make haste.

Enter Horatio and Marcellus

Francisco: I think I hear them. Stand, ho! Who is there?

  Horatio: Friends to this ground.

Marcellus: And liegemen to the Dane.

Francisco: Give you good night.

Marcellus: O, farewell, honest soldier!

Who hath relieved you?

Francisco: Bernardo hath my place.

Give you good night.

Exit Francisco

We ask them to examine the lines to pick up the language cues that help to create the foreboding tone. Right away, at least one student will pick up on Francisco's observation, "'Tis bitter cold, and I am sick at heart." Another student will note that it is midnight, the "witching hour." More astute readers will recognize the fear that causes the two guards to challenge each other's presence as Bernardo asks, "Who's there?" and Francisco answers, "Nay, answer me. Stand and unfold yourself," an unusually puzzling and even hostile response to a question from a comrade. We guide them to notice that Francisco challenges Horatio and Marcellus to reveal themselves, even though he knows that they are supposed to come on duty at this time. We direct them to see the connection between Francisco's apprehension and his confession that he is "sick at heart." They speculate on what is making him so fearful.

Having established the role of language in creating the foreboding tone, we ask students to determine concrete ways in which they could set the scene to enhance that tone. They suggest fog, as an effective way to obscure vision, and suggest a condition. They wrap their characters in heavy cloaks to indicate the cold and the resulting discomfort. Some students urge the inclusion of a slow muffled drum. Others like the low notes of a French horn, and others will suggest using an electronic keyboard to create all kinds of frightening sounds.

At this point, students want to learn why Shakespeare makes this opening scene so foreboding and what is about to happen. We read the rest of the scene and ask students to identify events that justify the setting. Students are quick to note the ghost that appears, refuses to speak to the guards, and then disappears. They also refer to the country's preparations for war and the threat of invasion from the Norwegians. We conclude students' investigation of this scene by asking them what they think the appearance of the ghost signifies. Modern students associate ghosts with evil, even though they don't really believe in them, saying that Shakespeare probably used the ghost just to get the audience's attention. We have to tell our students that Shakespeare's audiences believed literally in ghosts, both as threatening figures intent on evil and as unquiet spirits seeking expiation for their sins or seeking redress for sins committed against them.

Students rarely see the ghost as a threatening figure because he hasn't done any harm, at least not yet. They perceive the ghost as an unquiet spirit trying to make contact with the living. And since he resembles the dead king, Old Hamlet, the guards logically figure that he will communicate with young Hamlet.

Making Connections

Now that the play has been introduced and the conditions in Denmark established, students are ready to meet the main characters: Hamlet, his mother Gertrude, his uncle Claudius, the king's advisor Polonius, and his son Laertes. To make this meeting more engaging to our students, we give them the following assignment:

> Imagine that your father has died unexpectedly and, within 2 months of his death, your mother has decided to marry your father's brother. She writes to you at school asking you to take part in the wedding. Write your response to your mother.

Students need no further prompting to throw themselves into this task. Invariably, they are incensed at their mother's precipitous decision to marry and her request that they, in effect, endorse her decision. Michael wrote the following letter:

> Dear mother,
>
> I received your letter today, and the contents of it shocked me. I cannot believe what you want to do. It has been only 2 months since my father, your husband, died. It seems to me that the love you supposedly held for him went in the grave with him, for I would never have expected you to remarry so soon. Only a month ago you were in such a deep state of shock that you could not bring yourself to leave the house. And now, here you are talking about marrying again. What happened to you? I know you love your brother-in-law, and no doubt he helped you in your grieving, but why do you have to marry him? As to your request that I give you away at your wedding, I must decline. I cannot bring myself to shame my family, as you will do if you marry my uncle. Of all the men in the world, you have to marry him, my uncle, your brother-in-law? I can feel my father turning in his grave.

Susan wrote this letter:

> Dear Mother,
>
> Was it you who wrote me that letter? Have I been gone so long that I do not know my own mother? I must tell you that it took me days to read your letter again. How am I supposed to react to such a proposition? And how dare you ask me to do so? Though you may not be, I am still grieving for my father, not even 2 months dead.
>
> Your actions have made me question my reality. What I perceived to be love and happiness has taken on a different face. All those years, I thought that I was the product of something real, something true, and something strong. But your behavior has left me doubting myself and my world. I have

> encountered many false people in my life, but I have always
> been comforted by believing that those who were nearest and
> dearest to me were honest and true.

Considering their responses, we ask them to anticipate Hamlet's behavior toward his mother and his Uncle Claudius.

Jon: I'd be really mad. I wouldn't come home because I wouldn't want to see either one of them.

Janice: Oh, I'd go home, but I'd try to stop the wedding somehow.

Rich: Yeah, sure. How would you do that? I'd go after Claudius and get rid of him.

Janice: What do you mean? What could you do, kill him? Then spend the rest of your life in jail?

Debbie: I wonder why Hamlet isn't king. I mean, his father's dead. Shouldn't he be king?

This question affords us the opportunity to explain the process of selecting a king in the feudal society of the 12th century: The nobles "elected" a man from among themselves to be king. Even though a reigning monarch could name an heir (as King Duncan did in *Macbeth*), the court had to give its assent. The questions raised here include "Did Old Hamlet name his son his heir?" and "Why did the court overlook young Hamlet and approve Claudius as king?" We don't have the answers to these questions, but as our students explore the play, we remind them periodically to consider some possible answers.

INTRODUCING CHARACTERS AND CONFLICTS

Act 1

Now that students are personally invested in the family situation, they are ready to assume some responsibility for getting to know the characters. To that end, we organize the class into groups of five. Each group reads act 1, scene 2, assigning parts as they wish. At the end of the reading, each group is responsible for teaching a specific aspect of the scene. The tasks are as follows:

Group 1: Look at Claudius as a ruler, identifying the specific problems he has, how he deals with each one, and what they infer about Claudius based on his behavior in this scene.

Group 2: Look at Claudius as a parent (now stepfather to Hamlet), identifying the specific problems he has with Hamlet, how he deals with each one, and what they infer about Claudius based on his treatment of his stepson.

Group 3: Look at Hamlet, identifying the problems he has with his situation and his responses to each problem.

Group 4: Look at the language of Claudius, lines 1–38. Notice the pattern of opposites in the king's speech. What does this language reveal about the man and the state of the kingdom?

Group 5: Look at the language of Hamlet, lines 129–158. Notice the imagery of this soliloquy. What does this speech reveal about Hamlet's state of mind?

When we reassemble as a class, we process the group reports as a way of exploring the intricacies of this scene. To assess student comprehension, we have them write two diary entries, one in the persona of Hamlet and another in the persona of Claudius. In these entries, they react to the encounter between Hamlet and Claudius. These diary entries will be the first of a collection that students will create throughout the study of the play; they provide an ongoing assessment tool for us as well as material for students to use to scaffold their projects.

Robert wrote the following diary entry as Hamlet:

> There are few words that can accurately describe the hatred
> that is growing within me for my Uncle Claudius. Not only does
> he believe that I will tolerate him treating me as if I were a child,
> but he also sees fit to treat me as if I were *his* child. It simply
> makes matters worse that my mother stands idly by and allows
> this man to deceive both family and subjects alike. How dare he
> deny me my right to mourn the passing of my own father?
> Perhaps everyone else is fooled by his kingly manner, but I
> know that he does not belong on the throne that is rightly mine.
> Surely, I must find some way to deal with this horror before it
> consumes me.

As Claudius, Linette wrote the following:

> I can't believe how easy it has been to become king and marry
> Gertrude. Nobody challenged me when I took the throne right
> out from under my late brother's son. Speaking of him, Hamlet
> has shown himself to be the sole flaw in my otherwise perfect
> plan. His attitude and loyalty to his late father may cause me
> some difficulty in the future. Hopefully, the queen will be able to
> force him into line soon enough. After all, he isn't much of a
> man. However, if Hamlet becomes a real problem, I will know
> exactly how to deal with it.

Just as the students have taken an initial look at three major characters, they have an opportunity in scene 3 to explore the personalities of Polonius, his son Laertes, and his daughter Ophelia. We remind them that they learned in scene 2 that Laertes has the king's permission to return to France. We ask them to consider what kind of advice their parent(s) would give them if they were leaving home to live abroad. Students assume that their parents would tell them to choose their friends carefully, stay away from drugs and alcohol, work hard, be careful about their money, keep in touch, and have fun.

Students return to their groups to read act 1 scene 3, paraphrase Polonius's advice to Laertes (lines 59–80), and compare it with the advice they would expect from their own parents. We ask them to comment on the value of Polonius's advice and what the advice reveals about his character. We hope that our students will recognize Polonius for what he is, a pompous windbag; however, we realize that each piece of advice in itself sounds good, so we may have to help our students, through class discussion, to recognize the subtle genius of Shakespeare in creating this and other characters in the play whose appearances are deceptive. To help students recognize the hypocrisy and shallowness of Polonius's "precepts," we ask them to describe the qualities of a true friend and a good-hearted person. Invariably, they describe behavior that we label as evidence of compassion, trust, fidelity, generosity, and commitment. When students compare these characteristics with those encouraged by Polonius, they recognize for themselves the kind of self-serving, political creature that Laertes would become if he followed his father's advice.

To assess our students' understanding of the character of Polonius and his effect on his children, our students write two more diary entries, one in the persona of Laertes reacting to his father's advice and one in the persona of Ophelia reacting to her father's directive never to relate to Hamlet again. We have students share these diary entries with the members of their group and arrive at a group judgment on the nature of Polonius. The more perceptive students will focus on his hypocrisy, noting as Steven did, that "by the time he [Polonius] tells Laertes to be true to himself, he wouldn't even know how to be true to himself."

Because of the drama of Hamlet's first encounter with the ghost, we show a film version of *Hamlet,* scenes 4 and 5, on the VCR. (We especially like the BBC production with Derek Jacobi, available from Time-Life Television.) Before students view the scenes, we ask them to imagine themselves as Hamlet preparing to encounter the ghost of his dead father. In their diaries, they write their fears and concerns in anticipation of their encounter with the ghost. We share their responses and then show the scenes. After they have viewed these scenes, they return to their diaries and write a second entry summarizing what the ghost told Hamlet, Hamlet's reaction, and what Hamlet resolves to do. We use these entries as a way of discussing the scenes and making sure our students understand that the ghost is the ghost of Hamlet's father who accuses Claudius of murdering him and of seducing Queen Gertrude. He also instructs the young Hamlet to avenge his "foul and most unnatural murder." We also want them to see the problems that this information poses for Hamlet, who confesses his horror at this injunction when he says, "Oh cursed spite that ever I was born to set it right." Finally, we want to be certain that they understand that he will pretend to be mad to discover the truth of the ghost's indictment.

REVIEWING THE EVENTS

We ask each student group to create a chart identifying the universal topic (betrayal, corruption, revenge, fear of death, meaning of life) that it is exploring as it studies the play. We provide a template for the chart with the headings Event, Result, and Insight. Each group lists under *Event* those occurrences related to its topic; under *Result*, a description of the effect of the events; the *Insight* column remains blank until we have finished reading the play. To help the groups get started with this task, we work with the class to identify the major events of act 1, then leave the completion of the charts to each group. One class listed these major events for act 1:

- Ghost of Old Hamlet appears to the castle guards.
- Horatio fills in the guards on what's been going on in Denmark in the recent past.
- Claudius marries Gertrude, Old Hamlet's widow, and begins to rule Denmark.
- Claudius tells Hamlet to stop grieving the death of his father.
- Hamlet confesses to us that he hates his uncle and is furious with his mother.
- Horatio tells Hamlet about the ghost.
- Laertes goes back to France after his father Polonius tells him how to behave.
- Polonius forbids his daughter Ophelia to have anything more to do with Hamlet; she agrees.
- Hamlet learns from the ghost that Old Hamlet had been murdered by his brother Claudius, who wanted the crown and the queen.
- The ghost makes Hamlet promise to avenge Old Hamlet's murder.
- Hamlet decides to feign madness, except to Horatio.

A group exploring the topic of betrayal began its chart for act 1 as follows:

Event	Result	Insight
Claudius is named king of Denmark.	Hamlet is cheated out of the throne.	
Claudius marries Gertrude 2 months after Old Hamlet's death.	Old Hamlet is not properly mourned, certainly not by Gertrude.	
Polonius forbids Ophelia to have anything more to do with Hamlet; she agrees.	We don't yet know, but we can guess.	
Hamlet learns that his father has been killed by Claudius and that his mother and Claudius had been having an affair.	He believes the ghost and vows speedy revenge, but he also says, "Oh cursed spite that ever I was born to set it right." He decides to pretend to be crazy to confirm the truth of the ghost's story.	

Act 2

Having moved slowly through act 1 to establish the setting, the circumstances, the characters, and the conflicts, we move more rapidly through the rest of the play, focusing on key scenes. This is not to say that students don't read the entire play, only that we focus class attention on specific segments and respond to questions that students might have about other parts of the play as they arise. Students read act 2, scene 1 (lines 74–120) in their groups. Two of the students in each group read aloud the conversation between Polonius and Ophelia. We encourage them to read parts of the scene more than once to allow the other three students to create a visual of the "mad" Hamlet. As a caption for the picture, they summarize Polonius's interpretation of Hamlet's behavior. We post these pictures around the room (Fig. 7-1).

Figure 7-1. *The "Mad" Hamlet*

Hamlet is falling apart both literally and symbolically—or so he wants everyone to think. He gives the impression that his madness is driven by his love for Ophelia; at least this is the conclusion Polonius arrives at. However, Hamlet feigns insanity. He knows that he is truly in control of himself.

These visuals not only allow us to assess quickly students' abilities to make meaning of the reading but also to encourage less verbal students to demonstrate their understanding of what they have seen, read, and discussed.

Students read act 2, scene 2 (lines 1–188), on their own, then assume the persona of the king in their diaries and summarize their reasons for bringing Rosencrantz and Guildenstern to court and the plan concocted by Claudius and Polonius to test Polonius's explanation of Hamlet's "madness."

Students dramatize act 2, scene 2 (lines 189–456), in which Hamlet encounters Polonius and Rosencrantz and Guildenstern, and then work in their groups to review the scene in terms of Hamlet's evidence of madness and sanity in his encounters with these three people. Students assume the persona of Hamlet and record their feelings about Polonius, Rosencrantz, and Guildenstern, including their feelings about the nature of humanity, as revealed in lines 319–332. We review highlights from the diaries with the class, making sure that students have identified the insight Hamlet reveals about himself in his comments beginning, "I have of late—but wherefore I know not—lost all my mirth," lines 311–332. Robert wrote the following observation:

> My mind is disjointed, but I don't know, I have lost all my mirth and am so miserable that nothing on this earth gives me any comfort. Even the air I breathe is a foul and pestilent congregation of vapors. And I consider mankind, noble in reasoning ability, like an angel in form and motion, and a god in appearance. And yet, what difference does all this make? I am disgusted with all mankind, each of us the quintessence of dust.

We summarize for students the exchange between Hamlet and the players and note especially the intensity of emotion the actor displays when recounting Hecuba's grief at the gruesome murder of Priam. We show (with a VCR) Hamlet's response to the player's speech in "Oh, what a rogue and peasant slave am I," lines 556–613, and ask students to assume once again the persona of Hamlet and create a diary entry revealing his conflicting emotions as revealed throughout the speech. We encourage students to try to emulate Hamlet's language as much as possible. Andre's entry captures Hamlet's tone.

> The time is rapidly approaching for the tediousness of words to give way to the violent passions of action. What a coward I have been thus far, wandering the castle pretending madness in my pursuit of truth. For a cause far lesser than mine, men have gone to battle and died or killed brutally, yet I have stayed my hand and kept my sword unstained. Surely I need not be provoked any more than I have been already. If Claudius is truly the villain that the spirit describes, then he will feel the taste of my vengeance. Still, I must first confirm his guilt for myself. There is a simple genius behind my plot to reveal my uncle's true nature by confronting him with a play in all ways similar to the alleged murder of my late father. He will be unable to deceive me any further once this night has passed, for his reactions will tell all tales.

And Holly wrote:

> I wish I knew the truth...whether my uncle was indeed the villain responsible for my dear father's murder. Maybe then I could muster up the passion to avenge my father's death. I must be a coward! How is it that my father is dead, likely at the hands of my uncle, and I do nothing? My uncle mocks me, spits in my face, and still I do nothing? Where is my courage? This player tonight showed more passion in a scene from a play in which he has no personal involvement than I show in response

to my own father's murder. Have I really lost my mind? Is that
why I have been reduced to a mere dreamer, showing anger
only through my words rather than my deeds? Well, tomorrow I
will get my proof. I will observe my uncle's reaction to the
player's performance about murder. A murderer with a guilty
conscience cannot avoid flinching upon such a reminder. If he
shows any such reaction, I will know that he is guilty, and then I
will find the motivation to avenge my father's murder.
Otherwise, I will learn that this ghost has been the devil
taunting me all along. If that be the case, I will be grateful for
my weakness and indecision. Only tomorrow can tell.

In their groups, students share their diary entries and characterize Hamlet's
feeling now that he has determined a plan of action. Students say that Hamlet is
feeling relieved to have decided to do something, and he is hopeful that his doubts
about the "honesty" of the ghost will be resolved. Some students say that he is also
fearful that if what the ghost has said is true, he will have to take the action the
ghost demanded of him. We tell our students that Hamlet will execute his plan,
but that while Hamlet is laying a trap for Claudius, the king is conspiring with
Polonius to test Hamlet's supposed madness.

Act 3

Act 3, scene 1, dramatizes Polonius's test of Hamlet as the king and he spy on
Hamlet's meeting with Ophelia. Students view the scene (on video) to focus on
Hamlet's treatment of Ophelia. After they view the scene, students are eager to
complain about Hamlet's harsh treatment of Ophelia. They can see why he might
be angry that she has refused to see or talk to him, but they feel that he goes
overboard and seems to be criticizing all women when he says, "God hath given
you one face, and you make yourselves another. You jig, you amble, and you lisp;
you nickname God's creatures and make your wantonness your ignorance. Go to,
I'll no more on't—it hath made me mad…To a nunnery go." Students speculate
on whether Hamlet says this just to be cruel, or if it's for the benefit of the king
and Polonius, who he suspects are spying on him. In any event, they agree with
the king and Polonius that Hamlet is not mad for lack of Ophelia but is danger-
ous, and they understand the king's decision to send him to England get rid of
him.

Once students have explored the implications of Hamlet's confrontation with
Ophelia, they are ready to focus on lines 64–96, the "To be or not to be" soliloquy. Working in their groups, they re-create the speech in their own words but in
a way that reflects their sense of Hamlet's state of mind. One group wrote the
following:

To live or die, that is my question. Should I endure this agony
or put an end to it for myself? Certainly, death can't be worse
than life—death is like sleep, sweet, restful sleep. On the other
hand, perhaps not. What if, in my sleep of death, I dream of

> life's horrors? That is a fearful thought, one that may have
> caused other people to endure life's sufferings even into old
> age. The truth is, no one knows what happens in death. As a
> result of our fear of the unknown nature of death, we become
> cowards who put up with the slings and arrows of a miserable
> life.

Students present their dramatic monologues to the class, after which we help them characterize the feelings (e.g., despair, hopelessness, helplessness) that Hamlet is experiencing. Students recognize these as feelings that all people experience at some time in their lives and in various kinds of circumstances. The question then arises as to why, considering Hamlet's determination to take some action at the end of act 2, he is now in such a depressed state. Students offer various answers:

Carlos: This guy is really crazy, not just acting that way.

Heather: He is suffering from depression; he hates himself.

Jeff: No wonder he's depressed; his girl dumped him, and his father's been murdered by his mother's new husband.

Bobby: But that's the point; he doesn't know for sure that his uncle killed his father; he's not sure the ghost is a good ghost.

Trish: That's right. And if the ghost is telling the truth, then Hamlet has to kill Claudius, which is enough to upset anyone.

Jeff: Not necessarily. I could imagine killing someone who murdered a person I loved.

As students complete their charts for act 2, many begin to make notes on insights they may add later. We encourage this but ask them to hold off completing the Insight column until they have read through the play.

Now that students are thinking about the consequences of Hamlet's plan to "catch the conscience of the king," we show on the VCR act 3, scene 2. To explore the implications for each character of the "play within a play," students meet in their groups to create diary entries in the persona of one of the main characters: Group 1 as Claudius, Group 2 as Gertrude, Group 3 as Horatio, Group 4 as Polonius, and Group 5 as Hamlet.

When students present their diary entries to the class, they speculate on how well the plot worked for Hamlet and the degree to which he was trapped by knowing the truth. They want to know if he will finally take action against Claudius, and they worry about what Claudius is likely to do to Hamlet, whom he now recognizes as his enemy. To answer their concerns, we show act 3, scenes 3 and 4. Students return to their groups and react to the events of these two scenes. Once again, they assume the personae of their assigned characters, except for the group that examined Horatio, which now focuses on Hamlet's response to his mother. When they present their diary entries, we discuss the key issues in these scenes: (a) Hamlet's decision not to kill the king in scene 3, (b) Claudius's attempt to pray, (c) Hamlet killing Polonius, (d) Gertrude's reaction to Hamlet, and (e) Hamlet's reaction to his mother.

These samples inform our discussion of these two scenes and enable us to make sure that students understand the reasons that Hamlet did not kill Claudius at prayer when he had the chance, the irony of Claudius's attempt at prayer, Hamlet's disgust with what he considers his mother's incestuous marriage to Claudius, the contrast between Hamlet's unwillingness to act against Claudius and his precipitous killing of Polonius, and Hamlet's effect on Gertrude, not only by his actions but by what he says. Usually the diary entries fail to touch on a few critical issues, which we then need to raise for the class. For example, the political implications of the king and queen's personal corruption often go unnoticed by our students, as Hamlet reminds his mother (act 3, scene 4) of "rank corruption [that] . . . infects unseen," so that the moral sickness of the Crown contaminates all of the state, confirming Marcellus's observation in act 1, scene 4, "Something is rotten in the state of Denmark." Here is another opportunity for students to note the continuation of the metaphors for moral corruption that run throughout the play.

Act 4

Before considering act 4, we ask students to predict what the consequences will be for each of the major characters of Hamlet's actions in act 3.

> **Julie:** The king will have to kill Hamlet now. It's too dangerous for him to have Hamlet know the truth about him.
>
> **Jason:** Yeah, but how will he get away with that and still keep Gertrude's love? And don't forget, she loves her son.
>
> **Joe:** He said he's going to send him to England. Maybe he could arrange for him to stay.
>
> **Alice:** And what about Laertes? He's going to want to get back at Hamlet for killing his father.
>
> **Ida:** What about the queen? Do you think she'll tell the king what Hamlet told her?
>
> **Jason:** No, she won't. Remember she loves Hamlet; she'll protect her son.
>
> **Julie:** What about Ophelia? Maybe she'll be glad that Polonius is gone; now she can get back together with Hamlet.
>
> **Alice:** Oh, yeah, sure. How can she still love the man after he killed her father? Maybe she'll want revenge, too.

Students read act 4, after which they are full of questions, but they are also ready to boast about their predictions that were confirmed by the events in act 4. What puzzles them is the reappearance of Fortinbras, whom they almost forgot, from the beginning of the play. We explain that his purpose here is as a contrast to Hamlet. He takes drastic action even though his cause is at least questionable, and he grants his enemies no mercy. Hamlet once again berates himself for inaction and, inspired by Fortinbras' example, vows that "from this time forth my thoughts be bloody or be nothing worth" (act 4, scene 4, lines 67–68). Many students are distressed at Ophelia's madness and her death. Even though they didn't predict it, they are not surprised, given the circumstances of her position in a world controlled by the actions of men. We then show act 4, scenes 5 and 7, asking them to focus on Laertes' reaction to his father's murder and his sister's madness and death. Afterwards students write a diary entry as Laertes in which they reflect their understanding of the toll taken on Laertes' integrity by these events; however, remembering Polinus's "few precepts," they are not surprised and chalk it up to his father's influence on him.

We draw students' attention to the corruption inherent in Laertes' decision not only to fight Hamlet with an unbated foil but also to anoint the tip with poison. This leads to a discussion of corruption and the forms it takes in this act. We ask each student group to continue its chart, identifying the aspects of the act that deal with its universal topic (betrayal, corruption, revenge, fear of death, meaning of life), but, again, to leave the Insight column blank until after they have completed reading the play. A group focusing on moral corruption wrote the following in its chart:

Event	Result	Insight
Claudius arranges for the king of England to kill Hamlet.	Rosencrantz and Guildenstern go with Hamlet to England to deliver Claudius's letter to the king.	
Claudius suggests that Laertes fight Hamlet with an unbated foil.	Laertes agrees but will poison his sword so that just a scratch will be enough to kill Hamlet.	

We conclude the study of act 4 by acknowledging the moral poison of Claudius and Laertes and by asking students to consider the behavior of Hamlet.

- What troubles you about Hamlet's behavior?
- Why does he want Claudius to know that he's still alive and is returning to Denmark when Claudius is on to him and had arranged for Hamlet's death?
- What do you predict Hamlet will do next?
- What effect do you think Ophelia's death will have on Hamlet and his subsequent behavior?

Maurice: Hamlet will feel terrible. He'll probably blame himself for her death because he killed her father, and before that he said really mean things to her.

Julie:	No, I don't think he'll be all that upset. I mean, he was really mad at her. He might feel bad about her being dead and all, but he wouldn't blame himself.
Irene:	I agree. He's so caught up in his own problems, such as not killing the king and being mad at his mother and being betrayed by his so-called friends, that he won't slit a vein over Ophelia. Besides, she's a wimp. She never stood by Hamlet.
Maurice:	Come on. She didn't have a choice. She had to do what her father said; that's the way it was in those days.
Fred:	Forget Ophelia. What's he gonna do about Claudius?
Billy:	Nothing, like always. If he wanted to kill Claudius he would have done it a long time ago. I think that he, and everyone else, is going to be killed. That's the way it always happens with Shakespeare.

And so the discussion goes, as students predict Hamlet's behavior in act 5.

Act 5

With their predictions in mind, we show the video of act 5 in its entirety. At the end, students need some time to react to the tragic ending and congratulate themselves on the accuracy of their predictions. However, to get them to consider act 5 as the conclusion to their study of the play as it explores the universal topics of betrayal, revenge, moral corruption, fear of death, and fate, each group is asked to find evidence within the act of events and/or actions that reflect the topic and add them to their chart. Because students have now completed the reading of the play, we ask them to fill in the Insight column not only for act 5 but for the other acts as well. Obviously, this task requires a review of the play. As with previous acts and to get them started, we work together to review the major events in act 5:

- Burial of Ophelia
- Hamlet's conversation with the gravedigger
- Hamlet's revelation of his engineering of the deaths of Rosencrantz and Guildenstern
- Duel with the unbated, poisoned sword between Laertes and Hamlet
- Poisoning of the queen
- Stabbing of the king
- Laertes' indictment of Claudius
- Death of Hamlet
- Naming of Fortinbras as king

The group focusing on revenge created the following chart for act 5:

Event	Result	Insight
Hamlet reveals his engineering of the deaths of Rosencrantz and Guildenstern.	Hamlet takes action to avenge Rosencrantz and Guildenstern's betrayal of their friendship.	Revenge corrupts the avenger.
Hamlet and Laertes duel.	Laertes is killed with the same sword that kills Hamlet.	Revenge destroys the avenger—there is justice in Laertes' death.
Gertrude drinks from the poisoned cup.	Gertrude dies from poison intended for Hamlet.	Revenge, once set in motion, can have unexpected consequences.
Laertes' accuses Claudius.	Hamlet finally avenges the death of his father.	Hamlet acts only on impulse.
Claudius is stabbed.	Old Hamlet is avenged.	Justice has been served.
Hamlet dies.	Cycle of revenge is ended.	Revenge is bitter justice and leaves us wondering if it is worth the price.

Once the work is complete, each group displays its chart. At least one member of each group presents the work and answers any questions or deals with any challenges to the work.

CREATING MODERN COROLLARIES

In preparation for creating their modern versions of *Hamlet*, each group presents its visual review of the universal topics. The ensuing discussion of the fear of death, the role of fate, betrayal, revenge, and moral corruption leads us to ask what comment Shakespeare is making about the meaning of life in this play. At this point, we challenge students to consider these theme topics in modern contexts and to recognize that what the playwright is saying about human nature in 1600 is also true today. These modern corollaries enable students to synthesize their learning. In their groups, they brainstorm for modern scenarios that will allow them to create a story around their theme topic that will include a Hamlet-like character who faces a serious dilemma. To that end we give our students the following assignment:

Hamlet Project

In your groups, you have been working on one of the motifs in Hamlet's search for the meaning of his life: fear of death, the role of fate, betrayal, revenge, or moral corruption.

Your task is to use that motif in a modern story to dramatize your understanding of *Hamlet* through consideration of *one* dilemma related to your motif.

You may choose one of the following dilemmas or make up your own, as long as you focus on at least one motif (they may overlap) and use some metaphorical or symbolic language to trace your idea. For example, Denmark as an "unweeded garden" reflects its moral corruption.

Possible dilemmas:

1. The remarriage of a surviving parent

2. Tragic "chance" or fateful occurrences that threaten to destroy one's sanity

3. Moral corruption of one's society and the temptation to be part of it

4. Betrayal by those closest to you—a friend, lover, or parent

5. Moral responsibility to redress the wrongs

Develop one of the above, or another of your own devising, into a modern *Hamlet.* You need not parallel the play directly, except to use some metaphorical or symbolic imagery to trace your motif and work out your dilemma through a Hamlet-like figure. It need not be a play or in verse; it can be a story with a logical beginning, middle, and end. You certainly are not obligated to end it as Hamlet ends, but your reader should be able to see the connection between what you write and the play that inspired it. (We refer to Jane Smiley's *A Thousand Acres,* based on Shakespeare's *King Lear.*) Your reader should also gain insight into your understanding of Hamlet as a character through your development of his modern counterpart.

You will be asked at the end of your project to write a reflection in which you document the ways that your story has been derived from the original and the use to which you put your diary entries, charts, and visuals [Fig. 7-2]. You will also be asked to show related lines (although, of course, you have modernized them) and related imagery, noting where they appear in the original and in your story.

One group exploring the fear of death decided on the following scenario: "The Hamlet-like character is an honor student who has been involved in a hit-and-run accident. The victim is near death. The student is desperate; he is guilt-ridden but terrified. He considers killing himself."

The students reviewed their idea with us. We applauded their initial thinking but helped them flesh out the scenario so that they would have details enough to create a story. We suggested that they create a family situation that would increase the student's sense of guilt and his fear of detection. Also, his nature has to be such that he dwells on the consequences of death, if he chooses to resolves his dilemma by committing suicide.

A group dealing with revenge considered this minimal situation: "A boy's best friend steals his girlfriend." Obviously, this is an idea with potential, but the

Figure 7-2. Hamlet *Project Reflection*

Reflection _____

_____

_____

Motif _____

_____

Connections between your modern rendition and the original _____

_____

Situation _____

_____

Characterizations _____

_____

Point _____

_____

Related lines _____

_____

Related imagery _____

_____

Key point you wished to make about your theme topic _____

_____

How like or unlike this point was from the original _____

_____

students needed help in developing a direction for the story. We asked: What does the boy do? Does he seek revenge against his friend? Against the girl? Against both? And how? Or does he reject the whole idea of revenge? Before they decide on answers to these questions, we asked them to determine the seriousness of his relationship with the girl and the depth of his commitment to his friend. We also asked them how the friend manages to steal the girl's affections, to determine the context that will allow them to show rather than tell the story and reveal the nature of the characters and the conflicts with which each one, especially the main character, must deal.

A group dealing with betrayal created the following scenario:

> A main character tells her friend in confidence that her father smoked pot when he was a student. When the father becomes a candidate for mayor of the town, the accusation is made in the press that the father was a pothead. The girl confronts her friend, who admits that she betrayed the confidence.

We asked students to decide what prompted the friend to betray the confidence and why the parents went to the local newspaper with this information. Also, students have to explain the consequences of this betrayal for the father, his daughter, and the friend. They will also need to show the emotional effect on the daughter of this situation and consider what she does.

A group focusing on moral corruption devised this scenario:

> A high school student knows that her boyfriend and his buddy have infected the school computer network with a virus that has cost the school district many thousands of dollars. She also knows that her boyfriend's buddy has led the school authorities to believe that an unpopular student who is a computer nerd is the culprit.

We asked this group to decide how the girl knows the truth and how and why her boyfriend and his buddy infected the computers. The group also needed to determine what could happen to the boy who has been accused. However, the major challenge for the group was to depict the conflict for the girl as she agonized over the situation and what action she should take.

The group focusing on the role of fate had some trouble getting started because it was unsure of what role fate actually played in *Hamlet*. We discussed the ways in which fate occurs in the play and determined that Shakespeare sees fate as chance, unexpected events over which we have no control yet which affect our lives dramatically, even tragically. Once students have the definition of fate in this play clarified for them, they have little trouble coming up with a scenario. One group working on the role of fate decided to create a main character whose parents have divorced, remarried, and moved to separate, distant towns. As a result of these new marriages, the student had to decide what to do—live with his mother, his father, or strike out on his own? We asked the group to determine the nature of the character's relationship with his parents before and after the divorce. How was he affected by the divorce? By the remarriages? By the prospect of having to leave town if he lives with either one of them? We reminded them that they must depict the character's dilemma dramatically, and they must create a context within which the character can reveal his problems to the reader.

Once students have an idea to develop, they review their diary entries, charts, and graphs to decide what aspects of Hamlet's character and thoughts to incorporate into their modern stories. We also review with them the elements of a story that they must consider as they develop their scenarios into actual stories. We discuss plot elements, setting and mood, dialogue, character development, and imagery.

We ask each group to outline its idea by filling in the following chart (Fig. 7-3).

Figure 7-3. Hamlet *Project Outline*

Thematic connection

Scenario summary

Setting

Point of view of narration

Characters—description of personalities

Conflict
    Complications
    Climax
    Resolution

ASSESSMENT AND EVALUATION

Assessment is an ongoing process throughout the study of *Hamlet*. Each time we have students complete a diary entry or paraphrase a particular speech from the play, we are assessing their understanding of what they have just experienced with the play. Periodically, we collect these entries and assess them, sometimes as informal quizzes, sometimes just to give us a sense of where we need to go next in our discussion of the play, what we need to help them discover, what we need to emphasize in the next lesson, or what needs to be reviewed. At the end of the study of the play, we have students assemble all their work from the play—diary entries, charts, letters, visuals—into a portfolio that they submit as backup and support for their modern project. This work counts for 40% of the final evaluation of the Hamlet project. In accompanying reflections, students explain how they used this preliminary work to help them create and develop their modern story. They connect the imagery they used in their stories to imagery from the play; they explain the Hamlet-like qualities of their modern protagonist; they clarify for us the connections they made with actual scenes and lines from the play. This reflection counts for 10% of the final grade. The story itself is worth 50% (Fig. 7-4).

Figure 7-4. *Evaluation Summary of* Hamlet *Project*

Diary entries, visuals, charts	40%
Reflection	10%
Modern reenactment	50%

Group presentations are evaluated separately, with 50% of the credit allotted for a group grade and 50% for the individual's contribution to the group effort (Fig. 7-5).

Figure 7-5. *Criteria Sheet for Group Work*

GROUP GRADE (50%)	Excellent	Good	Fair	Poor
Completeness of final product (chart, visual, etc.)				
Quality of interpretation and understanding revealed in product				
Evidence of cooperative effort resulting in final product				
INDIVIDUAL GRADE (50%)				
Extent of acceptance of responsibility				
Completion of significant segment of the task				
Degree of constructive participation in group sessions				
Extent of willingness to compromise and respect opinions of others in the group				
Degree of helpfulness in keeping group on task				
Extent of preparation for each group session				
GRADE FOR GROUP WORK _____				

We circulate during group sessions and evaluate the students and the groups by these criteria. In addition, we provide student groups with an evaluation checklist at the end of the project so that they can reflect both on their own degree of involvement with the final product(s) and comment on the effectiveness of the group as a whole.

As always, we negotiate the criteria for evaluation in discussions with our students; we follow the same procedure when we create the actual rubrics for evaluating key components of our study of *Hamlet*. Whenever possible we involve our students in the process, both as a way of getting them to be invested in the evaluative process and also to help them better understand each assignment. For example, when we discuss the diary entries and the criteria by which they should be assessed, students recognize that the following criteria should form the basis for assessment of diary entries:

1. Accuracy of information from the scene
2. Extent to which the persona adopted for a diary entry accurately reflects the personality of the character
3. Degree to which the persona offers a credible, logical response as that character
4. Completeness of the response
5. Sophistication of interpretation revealed in the response
6. Accuracy of character's voice

Similarly, for the visuals and charts, students agree that accuracy of information, sophistication of interpretation, insight into the motif, evidence of effort, and completeness should be the criteria upon which these elements are assessed. For the reflection, accuracy and completeness are again valued components. Discussion of oral presentations generates lively class sessions and results in the following rubric (Fig. 7-6).

Most of our efforts at building consensus for evaluation are focused on developing a rubric for the final story. We and our students easily agree on the dimensions because we have worked with them so often before: (a) content or meaning, (b) development, (c) organization, (d) language use, and (e) conventions.

However, we need to agree on what we will look for within each of these dimensions. Most of our discussion centers around what we should look for in content; after all, students argue, each story will be unique because each is based on a different motif and reflects a different dilemma. We refer them to the phrasing of the assignment: "Dramatize your understanding of *Hamlet* by developing one motif from the play and recasting a Hamlet-like dilemma into a modern story."

The assignment also instructs them to make use of their diary entries, visuals, and charts as they think about the Hamlet-like figure they create. In addition,

Figure 7-6. *Rubric for Assessment and Evaluation of Oral Presentations*

4	Chooses significant examples from the play to reveal development of motif.
	Makes excellent use of charts, visuals, diary entries to convey significance of motif.
	Presents evidence in well-organized, focused, effective, engaging way.
	Gives smooth, clear presentation with effective pacing, tone, and inflection.
	Uses excellent eye contact and appropriate volume.
3	Chooses examples from the play to reveal development of motif.
	Makes use of charts, visuals, diary entries to convey presence of motif.
	Presents evidence clearly and generally accurately.
	May ramble and digress somewhat.
	May rely too much on written, prepared script.
	Uses generally appropriate verbal and nonverbal delivery tools.
	Pays some attention to audience.
2	Chooses a few examples from the play related to motif but not the most significant ones.
	Makes limited use of charts and/or visuals.
	Has trouble connecting material to motif.
	Presents material with too great reliance on written notes.
	Has some inaccuracy in facts and/or interpretation.
	Tends to digress.
	Hesitates in presentation.
	Pays little or no attention to audience.
1	Presents material largely as summary, failing to make a case for the motif.
	Has incomplete charts and visuals.
	Reveals little understanding of the play or the motif.
	Reveals little preparation and/or speaks directly from notes.
	Has frequent inaccuracies in facts.
	Speaks in a monotone or too fast to be understood.

they are to use imagery from the play to help them develop their modern dilemmas. They have been given possible dilemmas from which to choose and even suggestions of modern situations that might fit the various motifs, but they have been encouraged to use their creativity and ingenuity to develop original dilemmas around their motifs.

To help students get started on their stories, we talk at length about the parameters of the assignment and develop the rubric together. Figure 7-7 is the result of our combined thinking.

On the day that stories are due, students brings two copies to class, one to be graded and the other to be compiled in a class anthology on modern versions of *Hamlet*. They attach the reflection that they have written, in which they have made explicit the connections between the original play and their story. To this reflection they add comments on their self-assessment of their work, using the rubric as their guide. Here they can also discuss the process they went through, the effort they put into their product, the difficulties they may have encountered along the way, and the grade they believe they have earned. Then they meet in their groups to share their stories and select one from their group to read to the class. The stories are fascinating, and each is very different from another. Students love to read what other students have written, both about their own motifs and the others. We collect the stories, evaluate them according to the rubric, and return the graded copy to the students. The other we reproduce and bind as a classroom anthology, being sure to make at least one copy of the entire anthology available in the school library. Students are very proud of their accomplishments and are excited to see their work compiled in a book that will circulate throughout the school as a result of being made available in the school library.

CONCLUSION

Providing our students with a contemporary lens through which to examine *Hamlet* allows them to discover the relevance of the play to their lives and experiences. Like Hamlet, today's teenagers question the meaning of their lives, but usually in implicit ways, such as when they confess their fear of fatal illness, helplessness in the face of "bad luck," despair over the world's injustice, frustration with fickle friends, or confusion over the desire to "get even" with a wrongdoer and the need to forgive him or her. By identifying with Hamlet in persona journals and creating modern corollaries of his dilemmas, students find comfortable contexts in which to explore the meanings of their lives, and at the same time to make meaning of a literary masterpiece.

This meaning comes about as students work collaboratively and individually to understand characterization and character relationships, to predict actions and reactions, to recognize the power of metaphorical language, to discover the validity of their analyses, and to take an active role assessing and evaluating their work. In so doing, they are empowered to take charge of their own learning and to gain

Figure 7-7. *Rubric for Assessment and Evaluation of the* Hamlet *Project*

QUALITY	4 This piece	3 This piece	2 This piece	1 This piece
Meaning: the extent to which the paper exhibits sound understanding, interpretation, and analysis of the task	Reveals in-depth, insightful understanding of one dilemma faced by Hamlet; recasts it creatively in modern terms; effectively uses most suitable imagery, clearly drawn from Hamlet, to develop motif.	Reveals a clear understanding of one dilemma faced by Hamlet; recasts it convincingly in modern terms; adequately uses appropriate imagery, somewhat linked to that of the original play, to develop motif.	Reveals an adequate understanding of one dilemma faced by Hamlet; recasts it in modern terms; attempts to develop motif with some imagery, though not derived from the original play.	Reveals limited understanding of one dilemma faced by Hamlet; modern version has little connection to the original play; little or no attempt to develop motif with imagery.
Development: the extent to which ideas are elaborated creatively and with attention to the task	Makes maximum use of materials from Hamlet log and charts; includes abundant content that relates to the original and reveals a sophisticated understanding of the logic a Hamlet-like figure would bring to the modern dilemma.	Makes use of materials from Hamlet log and charts; has some content that relates to the original and reveals an understanding of how a Hamlet-like character would act in that situation.	Makes minimal use of Hamlet log and charts; presents ideas with some understanding of the way in which a Hamlet-like figure would act.	Makes no use of Hamlet log and charts; presents ideas that are derivative and undeveloped, revealing little understanding of Hamlet and/or the logic of the modern issue.
Organization: the extent to which the piece exhibits logical shape, coherence, and makes use of the genre	Structure is creative and logical; appropriate to express the dilemma and show connection with *Hamlet*, credible ending.	Structured coherently with organization contributing to the Hamlet-like nature of the modern issue and its resolution; clear beginning, middle and end.	Structured logically but with little attention to the connection with Hamlet; begins well, but ending may lack credibility.	Exhibits little or no logical structure and has little obvious connection to *Hamlet*.
Language use: the extent to which the piece exhibits fluency and uses language to create the desired effect	Shows fluency and precision in choice of language; contains credible dialogue designed to develop Hamlet-like character; excellent use of voice; consistent, appropriate point of view of narration.	Shows fluency in choice of language; good use of dialogue; appropriate voice; some attention to point of view.	Chooses generally appropriate language; minimal attention to voice or point of view.	Exhibits inappropriate choices of language that interfere with the effect of the piece.
Conventions: the extent to which the piece exhibits use of standard written English appropriate for point of view and chosen voice	Exhibits spelling, punctuation, grammar, and usage appropriate to the point of view and chosen voice.	Exhibits generally accurate spelling, punctuation, grammar, and usage; errors do not interfere with creating the desired effect.	Exhibits minor errors in spelling, punctuation, usage, and grammar; errors interfere minimally with the desired effect.	Exhibits little or no sense of the proper spelling, punctuation, grammar, and usage for the chosen point of view and voice.

confidence in their abilities to arrive at logical conclusions and some perceptive insights about the nature of humanity and the meaning of life as expressed by Shakespeare. Equally important, students are challenged to reflect on their understandings of *Hamlet*, its literary elements, metaphorical language, and thematic ideas, in story contexts of their own creation. This opportunity to apply learning reveals to them their abilities to internalize their understandings of complex and sophisticated literature. Thus armed with the confidence that only skill and practice can generate, students are more willing and able to examine any text, whether a classic from the traditional canon or a contemporary book from the *New York Times* best-seller list, with some degree of critical and analytical competence. Certainly, this is a valid outcome for any literary study and one, we believe, well worth the time and attention required to study *Hamlet*.

ADDITIONAL TEXTS

Additional texts for which creation of a modern version is effective include the following:

The Pearl by John Steinbeck: The universal elements of racism, greed, pride, and self-concept embedded in this book make it appropriate for transformation into a modern analogue. Even the conflict faced by Kino trying to decide whether to put the welfare of his family above his desire for money resonates with a modern audience. In creating modern versions of this tale, students gain a deeper understanding of the novel and of themselves.

The Odyssey by Homer: This story offers few difficulties to students who translate any of Odysseus's adventures into modern stories. The wealth of detail and symbol provide students with an invitation to connect contemporary situations with those in which Homer's hero finds himself. The creation of modern analogues allows students to see beyond the literal in the epic and in their own lives.

Oedipus by Sophocles: This play presents significant challenges to students trying to make meaning of this complex tale. The writing of a modern analogue affords them the opportunity to explore the issues of right and wrong, of fate and free will, of guilt and innocence, and of actions and their consequences within the context of their own experiences or those of people they know.

Othello by William Shkespeare: This play involves the universal elements of love, jealousy, passion, rage, and revenge. Students have little trouble finding modern corollaries for the core situation in Othello and the action that results. In order to create contemporary versions of Othello's predicament, they must study the original carefully to understand the characters and their complexities and translate these finding into characters and situations that have relevance for them.

Conclusion

We have found the project approach to be very effective in helping students discover the classics in ways that make sense to them and, in some cases, dramatically affect the way they view themselves. Susan, in a final reflection in her senior year, wrote the following:

> As I look back on all the characters in literature that I have met and through whom I have lived, I feel that each one has taught me something about themselves, but more importantly, through them I was able to find parts of myself.

She was referring to her work with such characters as Hester Prynne of *The Scarlet Letter*, Banquo of *Macbeth*, and Hamlet of *Hamlet*.

Jennifer wrote in a similar vein:

> When I read literature, I often find that I am experiencing many of the same things that the characters are experiencing. This is even true of the characters in classic books written so long ago. I can often relate to them and learn from them. I have traveled with Huck Finn in his search for freedom, with Hamlet in his search for what action to take, with Ralph in his frustration at trying to maintain civility in the face of so much savagery, with Darnay as his ideals keep getting him in so much hot water, and with Nick as he tries to make sense of the materialistic society in which he finds himself. Their searches have fueled my own personal search for how to live my life fully and fairly.

Students were especially attracted to the dilemmas faced by Hamlet. Amber wrote the following:

> I swear that everyone who reads *Hamlet* sees themselves in him. I recently had a situation in my own life that is so parallel to Hamlet's that it is frightening, but I made a serious effort to avoid falling into Hamlet's trap. I avoided melancholy by devoting myself to action.

Studying the classics that we have addressed in this book often inspires our students to read other classic texts and has given them the confidence and the tools to read and discover their relevance. Eric, for example, wrote the following:

> At the beginning of the year, I didn't know who I was. I didn't have a clue. It's almost as if I wandered in a fog without direction or purpose. I made my way through this fog, however, with the help of the characters in the literature I read. Besides Hamlet, who helped me wrestle with my concern about the value of my life, I traveled with Prufrock, discovering that I was strong enough to live my life for myself and not for others; with Heathcliff, realizing some of the complexity of life; and with Stephen Dedalus, searching for identity.

Clearly, our students' encounters with the classics of literature have expanded their understandings of themselves and of other people in different times and different circumstances. Perhaps even more important, our students feel competent to tackle more complex books, not only from the classic traditions but also contemporary texts that demand thoughtful, reflective reading. As a result of these experiences with challenging literature, students gain a confidence in themselves as learners that transcends the classroom.

About the Authors

Ruth Townsend holds a B.A. in English Language Arts from UCLA and an M.A. from Columbia University Teacher's College, with additional studies in language, literature, and the teaching of writing. For a number of years she was a teacher at Yorktown High School, where she also served as Coordinator of English. Currently, she teaches at Manhattanville College, is a consultant for Putnam/Northern Westchester BOCES, the Westchester Education Coalition, and the New York State Education Department. She is a Fellow of the New York State English Council and Region I Director for the National Council of Teachers of English.

Marcia Lubell holds a B.A. in English from Radcliffe College, Harvard University, and an M.A. from Columbia University Teacher's College with additional studies in language arts and the teaching of writing. For a number of years, she was coordinator of English at Yorktown High School and a member of the Hudson Valley Leadership Academy Faculty; currently she is a consultant for the Putnam/Northern Westchester BOCES and the New York State Education Department and served as a lead teacher in the New Standards Portfolio Project.

Listed in *Who's Who in the East,* both instructors are experienced classroom teachers and curriculum specialists who have designed and taught many innovative language arts programs and are consultants for Learner Centered Initiatives. Both have contributed to the creation of the New York State Learning Standards for English Language Arts and to the new state assessments. They are frequent contributors to professional journals and have created four computer-assisted programs for writing and reading published by Queue as well as CD-ROMs for four classic literary works—*The Adventures of Huckleberry Finn, Tow Sawyer, The Scarlet Letter,* and *The Old Man and the Sea*—published by Southern Star Interactive They are also the authors of *Language Works* and *English for the Disenchanted,* published by South-Western.

Index